Florida A&M University, Tallahassee
Florida Atlantic University, Boca Raton
Florida Gulf Coast University, Ft. Myers
Florida International University, Miami
Florida State University, Tallahassee
University of Central Florida, Orlando
University of Florida, Gainesville
University of North Florida, Jacksonville
University of South Florida, Tampa
University of West Florida, Pensacola

Dr. Henry Nehrling at Cornell University, ca. 1926.

Nehrling's
Early Florida Gardens

Abridged and Edited by Robert W. Read

University Press of Florida

Gainesville · Tallahassee · Tampa · Boca Raton
Pensacola · Orlando · Miami · Jacksonville · Ft. Myers

Copyright 2001 by Robert W. Read
Printed in the United States of America on acid-free paper
All rights reserved

06 05 04 03 02 01 6 5 4 3 2 1

Library of Congress cataloging-in-publication data are available.
ISBN 0-8130-2425-0

The University Press of Florida is the scholarly publishing agency
for the State University System of Florida, comprising Florida A&M
University, Florida Atlantic University, Florida Gulf Coast University,
Florida International University, Florida State University, University of
Central Florida, University of Florida, University of North Florida,
University of South Florida, and University of West Florida.

University Press of Florida
15 Northwest 15th Street
Gainesville, FL 32611–2079
http://www.upf.com

This book represents selected portions of Dr. Henry Nehrling's *My
Garden in Florida and Miscellaneous Horticultural Notes,* originally
published as a two-volume work in 1944 and 1946 by Guiding Star
Publishing House, as taken from the writings of Dr. Nehrling published
in the *American Eagle,* Estero, Florida.

A companion volume, *Nehrling's Plants, People, and Places in Early
Florida,* is also published by the University Press of Florida.

Show me your garden, provided it be your own,
and I will tell you what you are like.
Alfred Austin

Contents

Illustrations

13. *Ixora* hybrid, a yellow cultivar
14. *Triplaris americana,* "Long John"
15. *Delonix regia,* Royal Poinciana, Flamboyant
16. *Peltophorum pterocarpum,* Yellow-Poinciana
17. *Delonix regia,* "The real king among them all"

Foreword from the First Edition of
My Garden in Florida

I first met Dr. Nehrling on March 21st, 1917. He was working among his plants at Gotha. It was just after the great freeze of February 3rd and I had gone up from Miami to see how his garden there had come through the catastrophe of that day. This is what I wrote in my diary: "I went over the wonderful place of Dr. Nehrling and I was astonished at the number of things he has tested. He is a perfect mine of information regarding plants. . . . He has now a new place at Naples, south of Fort Myers, consisting of forty [sic] acres. The temperature there this winter did not go below 34°F. He expects to develop this more tropical place with the most tender species he can get and wants us to help him. Although he is now sixty-three years old, he feels able to undertake this big work. He is a real pioneer and student of nature of the old fashioned kind, and I want to have him recognized and propose to make him a collaborator of the office."

This, my first impression of Dr. Nehrling, has remained as a clear picture of him through a quarter of a century. I have not felt like changing it either, for it represents to me a personality the like of which I never met again in my travels. I have known many with a passion for plants. I have met many who were keen to collect and dry their fragments. I have known others who lived to make gardens, but none who quite so fully combined their passion for observation with their skill in the propagation and cultivation of a variety of species, keeping them under their constant attention so that they were able to accumulate through many years' observation clear pictures of their characteristics.

As the years have passed and I have seen more of the tropical plants which have, through one source or another, found their way into South

Florida, I have a growing respect for such series of observations as Dr. Nehrling accumulated. They can only be made by a man who is happy to live surrounded by his plants which he treats as pets. They are not such as one makes with his eye on the clock or his watch in his hand. They are such as a man makes who is out alone at dawn in his garden with not even a dog to distract his attention.

I am very glad that Mr. Andrews has taken the pains to preserve in Dr. Nehrling's own simple, but fascinating language, these stories of a great plantsman, one of the real pioneers in the fascinating field of plant introduction, a field in which my own life has been largely spent.

It is gratifying to think that the so-called "development of Florida" has not been quite synonymous with the destruction of its beautiful flora to make room for highways and cities; that some of the pioneers were busy with the study of the plants from foreign countries which are destined to make beautiful the gardens, parks, roadways and dooryards of those who have come to live in this paradise.

Dr. Nehrling's writings should be available to the young people who are making gardens around their houses, for they not only give the facts regarding a host of interesting plants from which they may choose, but they tell in narrative form how one who learns to recognize plants can explore for a lifetime the unlimited variety of beautiful forms which compose the plant kingdom. Dr. Nehrling got away from human troubles by putting his hand on the graceful spathe of a Butia Palm, or by walking through his beds of hybrid Caladiums or counting the Bromeliads on some Oak in the hammock near his home.

David Fairchild
The Kampong, Coconut Grove, Florida (1944)

Preface and Acknowledgments

This abridged edition has been excerpted, reorganized, and edited from 1944 and 1946 volumes that were compiled and edited by A. H. Andrews, editor of the *American Eagle* and editor of Nehrling's *My Garden in Florida*. As Andrews observed of the 1933 Nehrling work *The Plant World in Florida*, edited by the Kays, it did not include the personal narrative of Dr. Nehrling's experience, although "Dr. Nehrling wrote with enthusiasm and a charm that held the attention of the reader from start to finish." (References to "Horticultural notebook(s)" are taken from personal notebooks that Dr. Nehrling kept on his daily rounds, and which no doubt were the basis of the articles published in the *American Eagle*. Andrews made good use of these notebooks in filling space in the printing of Nehrling's *My Garden in Florida*.) Though many of the "notes" that Andrews reproduced in the 1940s from Nehrling's "Horticultural notebook" have here been omitted, the essence of the body of Nehrling's published works remains intact in the present edition; his personal narrative is preserved, including his inconsistencies of punctuation and style. I hope the effort may help to bring about a renaissance in the culture of some of the little-used or long-forgotten but beautiful and useful ornamental plants Nehrling so lovingly described.

Dr. David Fairchild clearly understood the true Henry Nehrling when he wrote that Nehrling combined a "passion for observation" with "skill in the propagation and cultivation of a variety of species." Henry Nehrling was a great plantsman, mostly overlooked as a pioneer in the introduction and cultivation of plants in Florida. On his own and with considerable experimentation, this sage of turn-of-the-century Florida horticulture discovered, for example, why the fruits of exotic figs do not set good seed. Sadly, the pollinators he so wished for are slowly but surely arriving to create problems.

His original writings in the *American Eagle* and in the first edition of *My Garden in Florida* provide insight into the historical reports of the weather from 1894 to 1929, the people active or interested in Florida horticulture, and his sources of plant materials from around the world, and he supplies a record of the use of ornamental and native plants of central and south Florida. This is a personal narrative of his experiences with plants and worldwide correspondents.

Herein lies the colorful tale of a pioneer, a diary of historical horticulture in Florida's subtropical and tropical climes. Dr. Nehrling's horticultural practices and recommendations are as applicable today as they were a hundred years ago, but this is much more than merely a book on gardens. The impact of his life and writings cannot be emphasized enough. He introduced into cultivation and popularized many plant species that have become an important part of our lives. Many of the plants he grew and promoted are today commonly grown for the multimillion-dollar Florida, Georgia, and Gulf states' nursery industry. Nehrling warned us of potentially invasive plants he grew (such as prickly ash and Chickasaw plum) but also promoted for their beauty others that have become a multimillion-dollar problem, such as Brazilian-Pepper, Melaleuca and Old World Climbing Fern. He was part of the brotherhood of botanists and plant enthusiasts who left their mark on Florida, such as J. K. Small, David Fairchild, C. T. Simpson, the Reasoner brothers, John Gifford, Theodore Mead, Charles Deering, and Thomas A. Edison, to name but a few.

Henry Nehrling was a dreamer, visionary, teacher, researcher, writer, philosopher, and poet. But most of all he was a historian, writing of the environment, plants, and people active in horticulture, many of whom assisted him in his quest for gathering exciting plants for his garden, so that his passionate love for growing, seeing, and studying plants could be shared with others. Dr. Nehrling named his Gotha garden Palm Cottage Gardens and called the one at Naples his Garden of Solitude or his Tropical Garden and Arboretum at Naples-by-the-Gulf. Although he waxed poetic at times in his enthusiasm for the beauty of Florida and plants, he was a keen observer, had a prodigious memory, and was a passionate note taker, accurate to minute details. Dr. Witmer Stone of the Academy of Natural Sciences in Philadelphia described him as "A typical German professor of the old school, of courtly manner and enthusiastically absorbed in his work, he made a host of warm friends and was pleased as a child when visitors admired his garden."

This abridged edition has the nomenclature of the plants brought into line with modern botanical rules and concepts. It is what Dr. Nehrling would have done were he conducting the work himself.

His identifications and knowledge of nomenclature were excellent, but as time and research progressed, in some cases the names he used have been superseded by older names found to take precedence as a result of new taxonomic work. In such cases, names accepted today are given in square brackets [ ], and any editorial comment upon names is likewise presented in brackets. The names used by Nehrling can be found in the index. Nehrling's research and spelling of scientific names are impressive, considering the conditions at that time.

Technical manuals consulted during the preparation of the present work are cited in the selected references. There has always been some misunderstanding regarding the treatment of cultivars: they may be indicated by the abbreviation cv. or enclosed in single quotation marks. Hybrids are indicated by an X next to the first letter of the name, which is capitalized and not underlined or italicized.

The two volumes of *My Garden in Florida* edited by A. H. Andrews (1944, 1946) contained over 750 pages of text, much of which had to be deleted due to size constraints in the present edition. I have tried to edit by deletion to avoid changing Nehrling's intent. By leaving out quotations, material about cultivars and varieties that probably are no longer available, repetition, and references to gardens outside Florida, I aim to present in Nehrling's own words his passion and love for plants in Florida. I have used my best judgment in determining if cultural practices or advice are applicable or possibly inadvisable.

As A. H. Andrews reported (1950:126):

Dr. Nehrling was absolutely devoid of business sense. Like a child, he trusted any and everybody and . . . this eventually was his undoing. In 1926 a man representing himself as a wealthy citizen and ornamental nurseryman of Sebring, Florida, contacted Dr. Nehrling at Naples. He admired the Doctor's rare plants; told him what a wonderful nursery he had at Sebring and suggested that they form a business partnership, offering him the presidency of the company at $200 a month and free use of a house which he claimed was worth $15,000.

Dr. Nehrling went to Sebring to view the proposition; was pleased with what he saw and verbally agreed to the transaction. Shortly thereafter a truck appeared at Naples and carried off a load of the Doctor's rare plants. The operation was repeated until some twenty-six loads had been removed, leaving but little of value in the Naples garden. Some of his friends became suspicious and went up to Sebring to investigate. But few of his plants were seen in the Sebring nursery, having presumably been sold. The loss of his rare plant treasures worried Dr. Nehrling up to the day of his death and there is now [minimal plant material remaining] at either garden.

We have lost much beauty through not having preserved the gardens Nehrling describes. Botanical gardens are important for preserving species brought into cultivation because it is more and more difficult to import them, and many are being lost to cultivation, as with the plants Nehrling had in his collections. Many of the plants at Palm Cottage Gardens and the Naples garden are gone due to ignorance, carelessness, and theft.

Curiously, in 1924, Dr. Nehrling wrote to J. K. Small of the New York Botanical Gardens that he was "looking for . . . a hammock. One with a strip of black soil and . . . with marl—I come to you for advice. I simply have to run away from here [Naples], as nothing will grow. The soil is full of stagnant water all through the rainy season, as there is no proper drainage anywhere. My son in law, Louis F. Felipe, will finance my moving to the lower east coast and will start me in business. I would be very much obliged to you for the kindness of pointing out a good tropical hammock in the Perrine region to me. . . . I need about 40 acres. Less will do if the land is too expensive."

That apparently did not work out, for when he became ill he removed himself to Gotha, where his second wife had to give him his medicine four times during the night: "She has taken such care of me, and so patiently that I would not live now if I had not had her care and nursing," he said in a letter of October 1929 to Mr. Codwise. Henry continued: "I intend to sell this place as I have not the money to keep it up, trying to find a smaller and more adaptable place near Orlando. I have a hard time to get enough money for our immediate necessities, and Mr. Andrews has refused absolutely to allow me a fair amount for my many years work. I expected at least $3.00 per week and intended to be satisfied with groceries from the Koreshan Store. Jacke, as well as Mr. Hunt, agree that I should have a moderate compensation." A note by Mr. Codwise on his copy of the letter stated that "Dr. Nehrling died Friday morning early Nov., 22, '29."

As of April 2001, Nehrling's Palm Cottage Gardens house and remaining grounds are being considered for preservation at Gotha near Orlando. Nehrling's Tropical Garden of Solitude is the site of Caribbean Gardens in Naples on the Gulf and is being restored as much as possible as a botanical garden and zoo.

Reading Nehrling expands our knowledge of gardening and renews a feeling for the beauty of plants. This is a historically and horticulturally important treatise by a passionate lover of the state of Florida, of its natural beauty and history, and especially of subtropical and tropical plants. (A companion volume published by the University Press of Florida, *Nehrling's Plants, People, and Places in Early Florida*, contains information on oriental trees, cacti, palms, cycads, Nehrling's friends, and his favorite gardens.)

Acknowledgments

Great appreciation is extended to my colleagues Drs. Dan H. Nicolson and Dieter C. Wasshausen of the Department of Botany in the Natural History Museum of the Smithsonian Institution in Washington, D.C., for assistance with names of plants within their areas of specialty; and to Juan Chahinian, authority on the genus *Sansevieria,* whose collection in Naples, Florida, is one of the finest.

Appreciation is also extended to Richard Nehrling, great-grandson to Henry Nehrling, who has worked so hard to bring about a new edition of his great-grandfather's writings and the restoration of Palm Cottage Gardens at Gotha. Richard has kindly contributed the black and white photographs in the present edition.

Very special appreciation is extended to my wife, Betsy (Elizabeth M. Read), for financial support for the pages of color photographs, adding so much to the book, for proofreading the final draft, and for her encouragement and patience during preparation of the manuscript.

Thanks go also to Dr. Richard P. Wunderlin, Roger Hammer, Jan Roby, and Jean McCullough for reading and making constructive and significant suggestions for improvement of the text.

Robert W. Read
Naples, Florida (2001)

Editor's Note from
Original 1944 Edition of Volume 1

As a novice who makes no pretense to botanical training it is with some trepidation that I place before botanists and plant specialists the published writings of the late Dr. Henry Nehrling, noted plant breeder and botanist, knowing full well the difficulty of compiling and editing voluminous manuscripts, replete with botanical terms, so thoroughly as to turn out a product that is letter perfect.

Dr. Nehrling's handwriting was much of it legible, but he had a peculiar habit of now and then ending a word with a wavelike flourish that was often undecipherable, leaving the reader to guess at its meaning, and if it happened to be a botanical term it was confusing indeed. Many of the plants described were also very rare and not found listed in reference books at hand. Something of the stupendous task involved in editing and publishing these voluminous manuscripts will thus be realized.

The two volumes now being published under the title of "My Garden in Florida" are a reprint from the original publication which appeared in a series of weekly installments in the *American Eagle* of Estero, Florida, covering a period from late 1922 to 1929. When these manuscripts were first offered me for publication I was appalled at the magnitude of the task. Though with some years of actual contact and experience with tropical plants, I had no technical training, and naturally the original publication contained numerous errors. In this revised publication great care has been exercised to correct many of the previous errors, though it seems inevitable that some will slip through in spite of all vigilance.

Several years ago, under the title of "The Plant World in Florida," a volume was issued by the Macmillan Company,—edited by Col. and Mrs. Alfred Kay,—embodying the botanical data compiled from the original publication in the *American Eagle*. In this greatly condensed volume the personal narrative of Dr. Nehrling's experience with plants was necessarily omitted. Dr. Nehrling wrote with enthusiasm and a charm that held attention of the reader from start to finish. It is this interesting personal narrative that is being preserved in "My Garden in Florida."

The horticultural writings of Dr. Henry Nehrling cover a period dating from the early 1890's to shortly before his final illness and death in 1929. The manuscripts were originally submitted to us in hit-and-miss form. Sometimes it would appear that we had finished with a given subject and would begin on another when in would come more copy on the original theme. Ficus species were originally listed under "Shade Trees for South Florida," and while they are undoubtedly wonderful shade trees, it seemed more appropriate to list them in the revised edition under the general heading of Ficus. Thus a great deal of rearranging and compiling has been necessary.

Many plants which Dr. Nehrling referred to as exceedingly rare are now listed by some of the leading nurseries. His Naples and Gotha gardens are no more, but his horticultural articles, though written many years ago, are still full of charm and he ranks today as one of the outstanding authorities on tropical plant lore.

A. H. Andrews
Estero, Lee County, Florida (1944)

Biographical Sketch

Dr. Henry Nehrling, Plant Specialist
and Botanist (1853–1929)

(In republishing the voluminous horticultural writings of the late Dr. Henry Nehrling it is fitting that it should begin with a biographical sketch of this noted botanist and plant specialist. The following life history by Prof. E. L. Lord appeared in *Fruits and Flowers* Magazine in 1925, being republished in the *American Eagle* of Sept. 17th in the same year. It is the most authentic biographical data available.—Editor's Note [A. H. Andrews, 1944].)

Dr. Henry Nehrling, ornithologist, botanist and plant breeder, was born in Sheboygan County, Wis., May 9, 1853, of German-American parentage. He received his early education in the public schools of Wisconsin, later attending the Teachers' Seminary at Addison, Ill., from which he graduated in 1873. The following year he married Miss Sophia Schoff of Oak Park, Ill. While his vocation for many years was that of a teacher, it was only an instrument by means of which he could study nature. In order to study the birds of the United States he taught school in several states, particularly in Illinois, Missouri and Texas. He spent five years in Texas teaching and studying native birds (1879–1884). In 1884 he became interested in Florida and bought a tract of land at Gotha, near Orlando. This tract of land he visited for the first time in 1886. In 1887 he was made deputy collector and inspector of customs at the Port of Milwaukee. He resigned this position in 1890 to become secretary and custodian of the Public Museum of Milwaukee.

During all this period he contributed generously to various periodicals,—German, English and American. Most of his articles were on ornithological subjects. His first book, "Die Nordamericanishe Vogelwelt," was published in 1891, and was followed by a later work, "Our Native Birds of Song and Beauty" (2 vols.). This work was published in 1893, a second edition was brought out in 1896.

During the period from 1884 onward his mind was fixed on Florida as his future permanent home. With this idea in mind he built a greenhouse in Milwaukee and collected seeds and other plant material from various correspondents in the tropics. His series of articles describing the plants in his Gotha garden give, in interesting detail, the source from which many of these plants were obtained. He corresponded actively with many collectors and breeders of rare plants, and was enabled to obtain many plants that had never been before brought to the notice of horticulturists.

In 1893 Dr. Nehrling spent much time visiting the Columbian Exposition at Chicago. While many tropical plants, particularly palms and ornamentals, were of interest to him, nothing attracted his time and attention more than the exhibit of fancy leaved Caladiums in the Brazilian section of the exposition. These were largely the product of the breeding work of Adolf Leitze of Rio de Janeiro. By combining the characteristics of five or six species of this genus Mr. Leitze had produced a wonderful addition to the ornamentals characterized by colored foliage. The richness of color, brilliancy and delicacy of these plants made an impression upon Dr. Nehrling which he never forgot. While Mr. Leitze later produced many more varieties, this exhibit outshone all other flower and foliage plants at the exposition. Since that time many other varieties of fancy leaved Caladiums have been produced so that there is nothing that rivals this glorious product of the plant breeder. Much of the breeding and popularization of this plant has been the work of Dr. Nehrling.

Soon after the exposition Dr. Nehrling resigned his post in the museum at Milwaukee, and bringing his family and plant collection with him, settled at Gotha on the tract of land that he had bought ten years before. He still continued to receive many plants and seeds from all over the world. He was made a collaborator of the Office of Foreign Seed and Plant Introduction of the Bureau of Plant Industry. From this office he received many plants, but also furnished them with plant material obtained from other sources. His collection of Palms, Bamboos and other tropical plants made his garden the Mecca of horticulturists who came to Florida, as well as a perpetual source of wonder to the plantsmen of Florida who were lucky enough to visit it.

Due to his enthusiasm and industry he was able to gather together full collections of the various plants in which he was especially interested. In consequence his studies of tropical plants are the result of active association with the living plant rather than the type of description and study based on herbarium material. Many plants do not lend themselves to herbarium study, either due to the size and weight of the distinguishing parts or to their delicacy. This is particularly true of certain tropical families, such as Palms and Bamboos. These plants, so characteristic of tropical landscapes, have been much neglected by American botanists. It is a fact more thorough study and a wider and more thoughtful use of such exotics is of especial value to Florida, whose development depends much on emphasizing the more tropical aspects of her landscapes and home plantings.

Dr. Nehrling's great interest in the Amaryllidaceae resulted in "Die Amaryllis" (1908). His interest in this group was not confined alone to the taxonomy and morphology, but he has done much breeding, having had an active part in the production of the modern forms of this plant. His studies of the palms of Florida, published serially in the *American Eagle*, are a valuable contribution to the literature on the palm, and are very valuable to those who are interested in the behavior of these plants when grown in Florida. The transference of his activities from Gotha was due to his interest in fancy leaved Caladiums. Due to the fact that the soil and climate of Gotha were not well adapted to the growing and breeding of these plants, he bought some land at Naples, Fla. in 1917 and transferred his Caladiums there. Not only is the soil better for Caladiums at Naples, but the added protection from injurious temperatures has enabled Dr. Nehrling to grow many other species of tropical plants, especially Palms and Ficus. In 1922 Dr. Nehrling moved to Naples, where all his breeding work was being carried on.

While Dr. Nehrling has produced many new and wonderful varieties of plants, it is in the new varieties of Caladiums that the work of this plant breeder is the most noteworthy. To those who are only familiar with the commoner kinds, a bed of a variety such as 'Mrs. Haldeman' is a revelation of delicacy and brilliancy of color. The combination of rose and white, with a small proportion of green, gives a fairy-like effect which it is impossible to duplicate. 'Mrs. Sophie Nehrling,' with its leaves of snowy white veined with rose, margined with a narrow band of green, is a very beautiful variety, although it is at its best only in partial shade. This is true of all of this group, as excessive sunlight tends to change and fade the colors. 'Mrs. Marian McAdow' is a dwarf variety. The major central portion of the leaf is a deep rose, while the margin is of a vivid green. And so one can go on indefinitely trying to give word pictures of these wonderful plants; but if you really wish to know how they look visit Naples and Dr. Nehrling's garden.

The people of the United States should be blamed for the fact that they take wonderful new plants as a matter of course, without any realization of the patience, industry and thought which goes into the breeding of plants. While nurseries and greenhouses help to disseminate new plants, it is practically impossible to collect royalties on them from commercial firms, and the average plant breeder, unless he is subsidized by public or private agencies, obtains only a small income from his creations. It is largely a philanthropic proposition, this breeding of plants, where the people as a whole are benefited by the industry and enthusiasm of the small body of men who make it their life work. We, as a people, should see to it that the rewards are more commensurate with the contribution of pleasurable living, so that a man who creates a wonderful new plant may get at least a reward equal to that of a man who invents a machine gun or a new flavor in chewing gum.

E. L. Lord (1925)

Dr. Nehrling Describes Himself

Recently a friend said to me: "What are you doing here in this wilderness, without neighbors or amusements? This hermit's life would be intolerable to me." I answered him, that a lover of nature is sufficient to himself wherever he may be, and for a plant enthusiast this is not a dull existence, but Paradise. Fortunately the minds of men show even greater dissimilarity than do the soils and climates of their gardens, and whereas my friend craves the bustle of cities, I ask nothing better than life offers in my Florida garden.

Beginning in 1879 when I first experimented with tropical and subtropical plants at Houston, Texas, my enthusiasm for this field of horticulture grew from year to year. It was therefore the fulfillment of a long cherished dream when I purchased some land at Gotha, Florida, in the rolling pine region of Orange County and in 1886 made my first trip to inspect my property and study the possibilities of this land of sunshine and flowers. Imagine my happiness at the thought of a home where I could grow my new plant friends!

When I reached Gotha I first had to clear a few acres for a house and orange grove, and for several years my means did not allow me to indulge my inclinations for an ornamental garden. I had set aside ten acres for this purpose, but it was 1890 before I could clear and plow the highest, driest half of it. In so doing I carefully preserved the few tall pines remaining from a once magnificent pine forest, and some small Live Oaks which are now dense, broad specimens fifty feet high. At first I could spend only a month or two in Florida each year, but a kind neighbor cared for my place while I continued in my position as custodian of the Public Museum in Milwaukee.

As soon as the land was cleared, I searched the hammock woods, five miles away, for plant material. My kind neighbor and I repeatedly walked the ten miles, shouldering the heavy plants on the return journey. We collected small specimens of Magnolia, American Olive, Loblolly Bay, Wax Myrtle, American Laurel, Sweet Bay, and many other treasures. The Magnolias are now large, stately trees, the pride of the garden. They must be at least fifty feet tall. The Loblolly Bays have also grown into big trees although not in their usual proximity to water, and the American Olives are now dense, broad specimens.

The Prickly-Ash which we planted spread over all the adjoining territory and had to be removed. Also the Chickasaw Plum (*Prunus angustifolia*) formed dense thickets by its underground runners, and was almost impossible to keep within bounds. I soon learned that this tree should never be planted where space is limited.

Plant collecting in a dense hammock has its unpleasant features, and this first planting of mine was done under considerable hardships. The November sun was hot, and trails through the woods were practically nonexistent. Indeed many of the thickets were almost impenetrable and in places the dense Saw Palmettos were so tall that I often lost my way. Worst of all, carrying each plant the five miles home became a Herculean task. However, bad as they were, my adventures in the hammocks and swamps seemed great fun when I finally reached home, and I was always ready to make the excursion again, even though it meant a repetition of the hardships.

As my "Palm Cottage Gardens" at Gotha grew and developed from year to year, the results far surpassed any expectations or efforts involved. Kind folk sent me more and more tropical plant material, and I soon found myself surrounded with many rare and valuable palms, trees, ferns, shrubs,— in fact every type of growing plant. Imagine my suffering when a cold wave threatened the district! As the thermometer fell, I would work frantically protecting as much of the garden as possible, but, with thousands of plants to care for, I could do but little.

Finally, in 1917, we had a particularly severe and heart-breaking freeze which killed many of my most valuable plants. Rather than risk another such catastrophe, I decided to move as many of my tender specimens as possible farther south, to a new place which I secured at Naples, on the lower West Coast.

Thus, in my sixty-sixth year, I again became a pioneer in the wilderness. The hardships that I had to overcome and the disappointments that I met were legion. The soil had appeared to be good, but I found that during the rainy season a very high water-table made it impossible for deep-rooting plants to do well. Also in the beginning nothing could be done, even for the shallow-rooted plants, until the soil had been well worked and thoroughly aerated. In my garden at Gotha everything had been different. Although the land there was high, dry pineland, almost all the plants started into vigorous growth as soon as they were planted. There my only troubles had been the occasional heavy freezes, but in this new land there were many days of such disappointment and discouragement that I longed for Gotha again, freezes and all!

However, that is all of the past now, and I have learned to love and understand this more southern garden just as I loved Palm Cottage Gardens. I call this place my "Tropical Garden" and derive much happiness from the great variety of truly tropical species that I can grow here. As I look out of my window at the orchid-laden trees, I wonder what more life could offer anywhere.

In the following pages I am going to describe some of my adventures and discoveries in these two Florida gardens of mine. I wish it were possible to add colored photographs of each one of my plant friends. As with all forms of nature, their beauty must be seen to be appreciated. Then too, no words of mine can picture the brilliant Florida sunshine or the glorious blue sky which forms a background of all this loveliness. In both the cultivation, and enjoyment of gardens, is peace, rest and contentment. Pleasure is not a luxury of life, but one of its necessities, and ornamental horticulture is one of the truest and most stimulating pleasures in life, and may be enjoyed by him who possesses only a window-box, as well as the favored mortal with acres in abundance.

About fifteen years ago an English nobleman visited Palm Cottage Gardens. I had known him for years, by reputation, as a great lover of plants. He was very enthusiastic and repeatedly exclaimed: "How beautiful!" When he left he said: "Yes, your garden is like fairyland, very beautiful and interesting but—untidy," pointing at the fallen leaves underneath the trees which I left there as a mulch and a natural fertilizer. The ground underneath is littered with fallen leaves and the place sometimes looks shockingly untidy, but it is so beautiful that I am quite willing to forgive its disorder.

Dr. Nehrling Describes Florida,
Climate and Soils

When I first came to Florida in April, 1886, I had the impression of being in a dreamland. The salubrity of the climate acted like a charm. The beauty of the almost untouched evergreen woodlands and the many hundreds of small and large lakes, glittering like mirrors in the bright sunshine, impressed me deeply. The diversity of exotic garden flora inspired me with ever increasing enthusiasm. Masses of orange Amaryllis almost dazzled my eyes. Hundreds of strictly tropical plants, such as I had never before seen in the open air, grew here in a wealth and luxuriance that defied description. Here I saw for the first time how nature plants and embellishes her wild tropical woodland gardens—gardens in which the Palm is the main object.

The masses of beautiful tall Cabbage Palmettos on the banks of the St. Johns were a revelation to me. Here they stood in close proximity to each other with scarcely any undergrowth on the forest floor, save some elegant ferns, chaste, pure white, fragrant Crinums and Spider Lilies. Underneath the crowns of many of the Palms I noticed a wreath of charming ferns (*Phlebodium aureum*). The air was filled with the delicious perfume of Magnolia blossoms. Innumerable were the bright-colored and quite often dainty blossoms of the flatwoods. The gardens and outskirts of the woodlands resounded with the song of the mocking-bird and the lively and sprightly chants of the cardinal, and in the evening glow the characteristic call-notes of the chuck-will's-widow were heard from all sides.

I had resided in the primeval forests and on the prairies of Texas and had traveled through a number of the southern states, but nowhere had I felt this subtropical charm. And years of residence in the state have revealed the fact that this irresistible charm, this indescribable happiness grows as one grows older. It is an indisputable fact that the true nature lover, who has enjoyed this delightful climate, the cool ocean breezes, the enchanting moonlight nights and all the charms that nature has spread out with a lavish hand for all those who really seek to understand her, cannot stay away from Florida for a long period without becoming homesick.

Florida is a great silent poem of color and light, of bird song and plant beauty. The glossy foliage of *Magnolia grandiflora* and other evergreens glitters in the bright sunshine, and the placid waters of the lakes sparkle like mirrors. The tourists and winter residents who come and go like the robin and the bluebird do not know Florida as it really is. They come late in the year and leave with the birds. They do not know our summer, the most delightful season of the year.

Florida is unlike any other part of our country. Its characteristics are so many, are so pronounced, that it is impossible for anyone who has not made the state his home for a number of years to understand them. There are no high mountains, no rushing waterfalls, no babbling brooks, but there are thousands of clear, beautiful lakes and many charming springs. The river scenery is another very important feature. The forest-clad banks of the St. Johns, the Oklawaha, the Withlacoochee and Manatee have a worldwide fame. Water in the landscape is a most important asset, not only from an economical point of view, but more so from an aesthetic standpoint.

Along the banks of our picturesque rivers and around the borders of our numerous lakes the most beautiful semi-tropical garden paradises can easily be created. And in addition to all this we have a climate that for equability has few if any equals and no superior.

Temperature Varies Little Throughout Year

Continued observations in various parts of the state show that the temperature is not excessive in either direction during the entire year, the range between winter and summer being about 20°F. The annual mean is about 70°F, and that of spring 71°F, summer 80°F, autumn 71°F and winter 60°F. This may be accepted as applicable for central Florida and approximately for the entire orange belt. There are, however, extremes. When the northwestern blizzards sweep over the state, as is occasionally the case, the entire orange crop may be destroyed and even the trees may be killed to the ground. Early in February, 1895, the temperature at Gotha fell to 18°F. This occurred after an exceptionally warm January while the sap was rising in all subtropical and tropical vegetation. The damage done was immense. At Jacksonville the mercury sank even as low as 14°F.

A similar freeze came Feb. 3, 1917. At Gotha the thermometer fell to 20°F. As almost all the orange and pomelo trees were dormant the damage done was not disastrous. But it wiped out almost all strictly tropical vegetation. I had enjoyed three crops of Mangoes and Rose Apples previous to this freeze. My specimens of *Cecropia palmata* were 35 feet high and a sight to see. I had a clump of *Bambusa tulda* that was 65 feet high, very dense and a picture of beauty. My Australian Tree Ferns (*Alsophila australis*) had attained a height of 12 feet, and my Thorny Bamboo (*Bambusa arundinacea*), the Solid Bamboo (*B. nutans*) and the fine *Dendrocalamus strictus,* exceedingly luxuriant, and from 30 to 50 feet high, were all killed to the ground. Hippeastrums (*Amaryllis*), Crinums, Hymenocallis, *Eucharis* (Amazon Lilies), Gloriosas, Alpinias, Heliconias, Curcumas, Zingiber, Alocasias and Colocasias, Xanthosomas and Amorphophallus were scarcely hurt at all, though all lost their foliage. Fancy-leaved Caladiums, coming, as they do, originally from the forest regions of the Amazon, usually rot in the ground if such a cold spell is accompanied by cold rains.

There is no frost-line in Florida. Slight white frosts may occur all over the state. Naturally the northern part of Florida is much colder than the central peninsula, and the southern or tropical part is almost immune from killing freezes.

The second climatic area is found south of the above mentioned line and extends to the south as far as Punta Gorda on the West Coast and to Indian River Inlet on the East Coast. This is Central Florida,—the orange belt. The orange and pomelo (grapefruit) industry is here the main occupation of the people. In this part of the state the writer has made his home. The gardens are replete with Palms, Bamboos and hundreds, and even thousands of different exotic plants, many of them of a strictly tropical nature. The mercury here very rarely falls as low as 25°F. Were it not for these occasional freezes this part of Florida would be a veritable paradise of tropical plant growth. The landscape here is the most beautiful of the state on account of the numerous small and large lakes abounding everywhere.

Only Southern Florida Is Tropical

The third part of Florida has been termed the tropical region. It lies south of the above mentioned line. Punta Gorda and Fort Myers, Palm Beach and Miami, the Royal Palm State Park and all the keys are found in this area. Here the Pineapple flourishes in the open air. Mangoes and Sapodillas, Avocados and Papayas, Bananas and other tropical fruits thrive here to perfection. Coconut Palms and Royal Palms, the Traveler's Tree of Madagascar, the Royal Poinciana and the Queen's Crape Myrtle [*Lagerstroemia speciosa*], Rubber Trees and Screw-Pines, Crotons and Ixoras, and thousands of other tropical plants, native and exotic, combine to imbue the gardens and parks of this region with a charm not known in any other part of our great country. The temperature here seldom falls as low as 40°F although there have been frosts at times.

It will be seen from the foregoing that the East Coast of peninsular Florida is somewhat warmer than places under the same latitude on the West Coast. This is due to the warming influence of the Gulf Stream,—an immense factor in the climatic conditions of central and Southern Florida. Its immediate influence is most pronounced along the East Coast, but it reaches quite a distance inland. Coming directly from the Cuban waters through the Straits of Florida, pressed close to the shore along Dade County by the Bahama Banks, it flows northward,—this vast body of deep blue water, a thousand times the volume of the Mississippi, 30 miles wide and 2,000 feet deep, with the velocity of fully five miles an hour, the year round. The temperature of this ocean river is about 85°F all the time, creating a constant stratum of warm air which is carried westward by the trade winds,—at least nine-tenths of the time,—summer and winter.

The climate of Florida has been called a humid one. This is true and it is not true. At least it is quite often not as humid as the horticulturist wishes. From November to March it is moderately moist and rainfalls are not infrequent. From March to June the dry season is the ruling factor. Rains are very rare now. The air is exceedingly dry. The dews at this time of the year are very heavy. All the plants are dripping in the morning. These heavy dews are quite sufficient to refresh the trees and shrubs in their dormant condition. The much dreaded forest fires are now of frequent occurrence. No planting can be done during this period, except after a shower. All trees and shrubs set out now are usually lost if not constantly watered.

Summer Constitutes the Rainy Season

In the rainy season the humidity reaches its climax. This period generally begins by the middle of June and lasts until October. Those who do not know the rainy season do not know Florida. Dawn is short in these latitudes. Each sunrise is now a morning of supernal beauty, the sky a fairy tale, the landscape and gardens a love poem. No cloud is to be seen in the blue azure. Up to about 8 or 9 o'clock in the forenoon there is scarcely a breeze, and it often becomes oppressively hot. But suddenly there comes a cool whiff of wind,—another and another,—then a mighty breath begins to blow,—the breath of the ocean. There is no indication of rain. The sky is clear. The breezes blow constantly. But all of a sudden we see a few low hanging clouds moving rapidly onward.

There is no possibility of marking the beginnings and endings of weather at this time of the year. The barometer almost becomes useless. The best weather prophet is at his wits' end. The clouds over us and around us increase in size and deep color until in a very short time the entire sky is shrouded in a dark veil. The thunder rolls and the whole air seems to be saturated with electricity. In the east we see a great white mass moving slowly onward. Like an immense wall it comes nearer and nearer,—a cataract of water.

The character of such a rain is totally different from that of a rain farther north. It pours. No umbrella will protect us. The drops are enormous. And the shower roars so that people cannot understand each other without shouting. When such a rain, as it is occasionally the case, is accompanied by high winds, only the best built houses seem able to shut out the cataract. Others leak in all directions and the rain seems to fall from all sides. Objects only a short distance away become invisible behind the heavy curtain of falling water. In an hour the rain is usually over. The sun shines again and the air is cool and aromatic. Before the rainy season really sets in it often threatens for days. The clouds hang very low, even in fair weather, but the much desired rain does not come. Day after day we wait in vain. The heat becomes somewhat oppressive and our entire nervous system suffers. But finally the clouds seem to burst and the whole air looks like a waterfall.

During the dry season almost all plants seem to be at a standstill. Though there are blossoms everywhere and abundant foliage the real tropical plants only manage to keep alive. But what a change after the first rains have fallen!

Almost all plants start into growth as if touched by magic. Caladiums and Alocasias, Colocasias and Xanthosomas, Marantas and ferns in a very short time grow into exquisite specimens. The weeds also grow and keep us busy from morn to night.

Most Plants from Arid Regions Ill Adapted

There are some plants from the dry regions of Australia and South Africa and from Chile that dislike this humidity. Many *Eucalyptus* species and Australian Acacias are a failure here. *Amaryllis belladonna,* one of the most exquisite and most deliciously perfumed flowers in existence, grows well here, but it never blooms. The white Calla Lily [*Zantedeschia aethiopica*] and the Golden Calla Lily [*Zantedeschia elliottiana*] grow well and flower profusely during the winter months, but they immediately begin to rot when the rainy season begins. They have to be taken up as soon as the foliage begins to die down, and the tubers have to be stored in dry sand and kept in a completely dry place until they have to be planted again in October or November. A few of the most interesting and elegant palms which form such an ornament of the gardens of California, the Guadeloupe Palm (*Erythea edulis*) and the Blue Palm (*E. armata)* and the Chilean *Jubaea spectabilis* cannot be coaxed to grow in Florida. The Erytheas are natives of southern and lower California, and, strange to say, the Washingtonia Palms from the same region thrive all over Florida with a vigor and luxuriance that is phenomenal.

Severe cold spells are rare, but come almost as suddenly as the downpours in summer. Just before a freeze the weather is usually extremely warm and rainy. The mercury may show 80°F and more. The garden swarms with northern birds, mostly palm warblers and myrtle warblers, which arrived during the night,—a sure sign of the coming of a cold wave. Quite suddenly the wind changes to the west and then to the northwest. The thermometer sinks to the freezing point and even lower. We can save most of our choicest plants by banking them a foot or more with dry sand. When dormant the plants can bear a few degrees of frost without harm. The worst freezes are those coming late,—in February and March,—when many of the tender plants, particularly after a warm January, have started into growth. Then our loss may prove disastrous.

Florida Soil Is Largely Sandy

Another peculiarity of Florida is the soil. With the exception of the large areas of muck land, the clay soils of the Tallahassee region and rocky surface of extreme southeastern Florida, the soil is very sandy. The general verdict of the sojourner from the North is that the soil is worthless. The tall pines, the picturesquely beautiful old Live Oaks and the grasses and flowers on the forest floor, however, tell a different story.

It is true, our high pinelands cannot be compared with the rich prairie lands and the loamy soils of the North. The almost pure white sand covering the surface is not very promising. The constant forest fires during the dry seasons have deprived our soils of almost every particle of humus. When properly treated, however, this sandy land of Florida is well adapted for the cultivation of an almost unlimited number of plants. All that is necessary is humus, plant-food. As everywhere else, our soils differ a great deal. There are rich and poor, dry and moist soils. The land is usually classified as high pineland, flatwoods, high and low hammock, cypress swamps and muck land.

For horticultural purposes and for winter homes the high pinelands are well adapted. Numerous fresh water lakes are scattered all over this region, adding greatly to its attractiveness. Oranges and grapefruit grow here to perfection. Originally the soil was covered with a magnificent growth of Long-leaved Pines (*Pinus palustris*) interspersed with numerous picturesque Live Oaks and a few Black Jack Oaks. After the pines have been cut down a very dense and bushy growth of Willow Oaks (*Quercus phellos*) has sprung up, with neat little bushes of huckleberries and blueberries on the forest floor. Pawpaws (*Asimina pygmaea* and *A. reticulata*), the Gopher-root [*Licania michauxii*], wild Persimmons, Sumach and the Briar-root *Smilax* [*S. auriculata*] form the underwood. Coarse grasses, particularly the Wire-grass, cover the ground everywhere. Numerous species of Compositae, such as *Coreopsis, Liatris*, [*Dalea*], *Aster, Rudbeckia, Helenium, Eupatorium* and *Solidago,* form a most delightful ornament to these woodlands. Every day in the year we may cull some wild flower here.

Whenever this white sandy soil is cultivated for any length of time it assumes a grayish and even a dark brown color. Usually this rolling and even hilly land is underlain at a depth of from 2 to 10 feet from the surface with clay. The nearer the clay is found to the surface the better the land is adapted for horticultural purposes. Manure and water are the most important factors. With irrigation and sufficient plant food almost all subtropical plants will grow well here.

The time will come when all these high pinelands around our numerous lakes will be dotted with villas and bungalows and beautiful subtropical gardens,—the winter homes of northern people, who seek to flee from the rigor of the northern winters. There is only one Florida, and there is no healthier region anywhere in the world than these high pinelands.

Flatwoods Sometimes Inundated in Rainy Season

The flatwoods, as the name implies, have a flat, level surface. Usually they are low,—so low in many instances that during the rainy season the surface is very moist, often even covered with water. The soil, though sandy, is black and rich in humus and at a depth of a few feet a thick layer of hard-pan or marl is found. Pines are here also the predominating trees. Representatives of the Heath family are very common, especially Huckle and Blueberries, the beautiful white *Befaria racemosa* and the pink [*Lyonia lucida*]. Buttonbushes, Gallberries (*Ilex glabra*), dwarf Wax Myrtles, and along the edges of the lakes a dense growth of sweet Bays *Magnolia virginiana*, Black Gums *Nyssa* [*sylvatica*], Loblolly Bays (*Gordonia lasianthus*), and many fine specimens of Azaleas [*Rhododendron viscosum*], *Itea virginica,* Dahoon (*Ilex cassine*), dense growing [*Lyonia ferruginea*] with masses of dainty white flower bells, the fragrant *Styrax pulverulentum,* and many others, all interlaced with the red-berried *Smilax walteri,* attract the attention of the nature lover.

The Laurel-leaved Briar, *Smilax laurifolia,* and the very ornamental *Decumaria barbara* with faintly fragrant white flower panicles climb high up in the trees. Large clumps of Royal Ferns, Cinnamon Ferns, Swamp Ferns (*Blechnum serrulatum*) and sheets of yellow Coreopsis, particularly in winter, and now and then a rare and extremely showy red and tall Orchid [*Sacoila lanceolatus*], combine to imbue these woodland scenes with a charm entirely their own, and the many other dainty and often gorgeous woodland flowers, too numerous to mention, add their share of beauty to the picture. Large clumps of Cabbage Palms are also quite often found near the lakes of the flatwoods, while the Saw Palmetto (*Serenoa repens*) is ever present, forming sometimes almost impenetrable thickets.

Flatwoods Most Prolific in Flowers

The flatwoods are the natural flower gardens of the state. During the latter part of February and in March the whole ground in some places is often covered with the beautiful Amaryllis-like Zephyr-flower [*Zephyranthes ata-masco*], the large white blossoms of which perfume the air with a delicate wild-wood fragrance. Here we also find Pitcher-plants (*Sarracenia flava*) in big patches. The ground, densely covered with various grasses, is bespangled with bright colored terrestrial orchids, yellow and blue Pinguiculas (*Pinguicula lutea, P. pumila,* [*P. caerulea*]), with colonies of Polygalas (*Polygala setacea, P. lutea, P. cymosa,* etc.).

At times masses of various *Coreopsis* and other composites light up these woods by their yellow color in a most enchanting way. The Tonka-like perfume of the so called Vanilla Plant [*Carphephorus odoratissima*] is strongly in evidence in these woodlands during late summer and fall, and in September the flatwoods are ablaze with thousands upon thousands of Catesby's Lilies (*Lilium catesbaei*). This is excellent land for farming purposes, Velvet Beans, Sweet Potatoes, Yams, Yautias, Taros, Cassava and all kinds of vegetables yield good crops. The higher portions are well adapted for Orange and Grapefruit culture.

Near by the flatwoods we often have the scrub lands, consisting entirely of pure white sand and running in long lines through high pineland and the lowlands. They are usually only a half mile or a mile wide, but run, like a stream, over a vast territory. The predominating tree is the Scrub Pine or Christmas-tree (*Pinus clausa*). The broad-leaved American Olive (*Osmanthus americana*), dwarf Hickories, and a few stunted Oaks form the arboreal flora, while dense thickets of the fragrant [*Lyonia ferruginea*], dwarf Oaks, Saw Palmettos, and masses of the Florida Heather (*Ceratiola ericoides*), constitute the underwood. The ground is often covered with a soft mat of grayish green lichens.

Beautiful and often very gorgeous flowers abound here throughout the year. Two fine perennial Lupines open in February the procession of floral brilliancy, *Lupinus diffusus* with fine silky white foliage and large spikes of fragrant blue flowers, and *L. villosus* with pale reddish blossoms. Then there is a large and showy morning glory with azure-blue flowers twining over the low shrubs. This procession ends in November when a most beautiful and conspicuous shrub-like composite [*Garberia heterophylla*] with huge trusses of lavender-colored flowers adds a most unique charm to these scrub lands. For horticultural and agricultural purposes this land is useless, although farther south and along the lower East Coast it is largely utilized for Pineapple plantations.

The high hammock lands consist originally of a dense growth of hardwood trees and gigantic lianas. *Magnolia grandiflora,* the most beautiful evergreen tree of the sub-tropics; and Holly (*Ilex opaca*), Live and Laurel-Oaks, the Red Maple, Hickories, Sweet Gum and many other evergreen and deciduous forest trees abound here in single specimens, groups or dense masses of tall Cabbage Palms. The immense growth of the various climbers is surprising. *Smilax* (*S. laurifolia, S. glauca*), the Virginia Creeper, the Trumpet Vine [*Campsis radicans*], the Supple Jack [*Berchemia scandens*], the Cross Vine (*Bignonia capreolata*), the Carolina Jessamine (*Gelsemium sempervirens*), and huge grape vines [*Vitis vulpina*] and *V. aestivalis* clamber high up into the monarchs of the forest.

The low hammocks are similar, but flatter and moister. Here the Moon-flower [*Ipomoea alba*] clambers luxuriantly over the trees. The Climbing Aster (*Aster carolinianus*) crawls over low trees and shrubs, while underneath it the chaste, pure-white and deliciously perfumed flowers of *Crinum americanum* open. Many species of the Mallow family, such as *Hibiscus grandiflorus, H. coccineus, Kosteletzkya virginica* and others, often with brilliant flowers, add a very gay character to these low moist hammocks. In some places we may come across colonies of the very distinct, handsome Needle-Palm (*Rhapidophyllum hystrix*).

Epiphytes Abound in Low Hammocks

The many epiphytes occurring in these humid forests add another charm to the landscape. They cover the trunks and large limbs of the trees and hang in long festoons from most of the trees. This epiphytic growth proclaims more than anything else, that we are in a subtropical clime. It consists, aside from mosses and lichens, mainly of bromeliads, orchids and ferns. The various air plants or Tillandsias are most conspicuous not only by their numbers, but also by their often very large size. [*Tillandsia simulata*] and [*T. bartramii*] are rather small, but they make up in numbers what they lack in size. Quite often the moss-covered trunks and limbs of large trees are completely covered with them. In April the gorgeous bracts, brilliant red in color, of

Tillandsia fasciculata are a most fascinating ornament to all the lowland woods. Imposing clumps and masses of the large *Tillandsia utriculata* decorate many of the trees, particularly Oaks and Cypresses. These air plants are often collected by the lover of the beautiful and fastened to trees and posts around the house.

Spanish-Moss [*Tillandsia usneoides*] festoons almost all the trees in Florida, even in the high pinelands, and in its company we often find the soft gray *Tillandsia recurvata*. Farther south we find many more of the members of Bromeliaceae; some of them extremely beautiful. Orchids are well represented in these low hammocks woods by *Epidendrum conopseum* and [*Encyclia tampensis*]. In South Florida other species, larger and more brilliant cover the branches and trunks of the trees. Near Naples I found [*Encyclia cochleata*], *Epidendrum nocturnum, E. rigidum, E. anceps,* [*E. difforme*], [*Polystachya concreta*], [*Polyrrhiza* or *Polyradicion lindenii*], *Cyrtopodium punctatum* (the Bee Swarm Orchid), [*Oncidium undulatum*], [*O. ensatum*] in the moist woodlands.

Among the ferns growing upon trees the most common is the Resurrection Fern [*Pleopeltis polypodioides*], better known under its old name (*Polypodium incanum*). This dainty little species covers the bark among orchids and bromeliads or alone like an emerald green carpet. In dry weather it shrivels up, but after a rain it always expands again and resumes its brilliant green color. The Grass Fern (*Vittaria lineata*) hangs down in graceful clusters from the trunks of the Palms, and underneath the crown of leaves of these palms very attractive wreaths of the Golden Polypody (*Phlebodium aureum*) are a great ornament. Now and then we may find in this region also the Strap-Fern (*Campyloneurum phyllitidis*) in the humus gather in crotches of old Live Oaks, and the rare trailing *Polypodium swartzii* [?]. All these epiphytes derive their sustenance from the air and partly from the humus that gathers around them. Formerly immense wild orange groves were found in these hammocks.

Swamps Mainly Forested with Cypress

Florida has been called the land of swamps, although real swamps, consisting of bottomless morasses are few and far between. The most common form is the Cypress swamp, covered with the Bald Cypress (*Taxodium distichum*) and the Pond Cypress [*T. ascendens*]. Here we find many of the plants again that we meet in the low hammocks. Ferns are exceedingly abundant and so are Swamp Honey-Suckles (Azaleas), Andromedas, Smilax and other moisture loving plants. The old Cypresses harbor most exquisite clumps of Air Plants (*Tillandsia*). The ground is frequently covered with Sphagnum moss and among it we often find the Partridge Berry (*Mitchelia repens*) and a small interesting fern [*Woodwardia areolata*]. Here I also found a number of other elegant ferns especially *Dryopteris normalis* of J. K. Small [probably *Thelypteris kunthii*].

3

My Garden in Florida

In the spring of 1883 I purchased a piece of land in the high rolling pine region of west Orange County. I usually spent a month each year, or every other year, in Florida. At such times I laid out and planted my garden or I rambled around in the woods. I always returned to my northern home and to my occupation with new interest and new thoughts. It was mostly the month of November that found me here in my garden, and the planting was mostly done in this month. The impressions I received were deep and lasting and I felt convinced that wherever situated, and whatever difficulties nature places in one's way, she also provides ample compensation for all who endeavor to investigate and understand her ever varying, never ending works. [From Horticultural notebook.]

Palm Cottage Gardens at Gotha

There is no place in this world that I love so much as I love my garden. There is nothing like it in Florida. It has characteristics entirely its own,—features not found anywhere else. Garden and plant lovers from all parts of the country are charmed with it. Thousands come and go each year and enjoy with me its many attractions. Though I had pictures of tropical beauty in my mind when I planted it I never followed strictly the rules of the landscape designer. There are no lawns and broad open spaces. Single groups and dense masses of trees, shrubs, palms and bamboos are the main features of Palm Cottage Gardens. There are wild portions with narrow paths leading from one place to the other. Native trees and shrubs form the foundation of the garden, Japanese and Chinese evergreens, hardy bamboos and palms closely follow in their wake.

The assemblage of plants is a most refined one, beautiful alike in foliage, form and flowers. All the real aristocrats of our native flora, as well as those of the far Orient, have found a place in my collection, where they grow side by side with plants from Australia, South Africa, Brazil and Argentina. Hundreds of strictly tropical species were interspersed, but almost all of them succumbed to the killing freezes in the course of time. My losses were quite disastrous at times, but a larger number of the very best and most ornamental species came out of the struggle for existence without much harm.

This is high pineland soil, and it contained originally not even a particle of humus. It had the appearance of pure white sand. In its highest parts the clay stratum lies from 12 to 15 feet below the surface. During the dry season all the moisture was rapidly absorbed and the soil became as dry as dust. Forest fires frequently raged over the place, not only consuming every leaf and grass blade, but also injuring and killing the plants that had been set out. Sometimes the water in the adjoining little lake rose two or more feet during the rainy season and killed all the plants along its borders. Cattle and hogs breaking through the fences were a constant menace for many years. Lack of means handicapped me from the very beginning, and only by great personal sacrifices was it possible to reach my goal. Great and many were the obstacles placed in my way, but I never lost confidence in the final success.

Early in the winter of 1883, a friend of mine, the late Francis von Siller, a kindred spirit, went to Florida to investigate and study the climate and soil of the state. He made excursions all over central Florida and finally found a place in the high rolling pineland, ten miles west of Orlando, which appeared to him a perfectly ideal locality,—healthful, picturesque, dotted with numerous lakes, and well adapted for orange culture and winter homes. Mr. H. A. Hempel from Buffalo, N.Y., had settled here several years before, and had named the place Gotha, after his place of birth in Thuringia. Mr. von Siller wrote me about his discovery, and I requested him to select for me a good tract of forty acres. This land is situated only a half mile north of the village.

Arrival in Florida

In April, 1886, I made my first trip to the land of sunshine and flowers to inspect my property and to study its possibilities. I was very much pleased with the results. After having closely examined the many tropical plants in the various gardens, my enthusiasm was aroused and it grew more intense from year to year, though I realized the nature of the poor soil and the many obstacles in the way before me. My first start was to have five acres cleared and to plant an orange grove. The ornamental part was vividly in my mind, but my means did not allow me to follow my inclinations immediately. Not until November, 1890, was I able to start my garden. Ten acres were set aside for this purpose, and five acres in the highest and driest part were cleared and plowed. The last remnants of a once magnificent pine forest,—about a dozen tall trees,—were also preserved. Some of these trees, particularly the Live Oaks, are now dense broad specimens about 50 feet high.

Fortunately I found here another kindred spirit, a man well educated and an ardent lover of nature, Mr. Franz Barthels, who had settled near my place. He understood me and was willing to carry out my ideas and care for my plants, while I was following my occupation as custodian of the Public Museum in Milwaukee. The very first step I took was to search the hammock woods, five miles away, for plant material. Mr. Barthels and I walked this distance repeatedly and carried the plants home on our shoulders. They consisted of small specimens of *Magnolia grandiflora*, *Osmanthus americana* (American-Olive), Loblolly Bay, Wax Myrtle, Lancewood [*Ocotea coriacea*], Red Bay (*Persea borbonia*), Laurel-Smilax (*Smilax laurifolia*), Sweet Bay [*Magnolia virginiana*], [*Lyonia lucida*], *Zenobia pulverulenta*, *Leucothoe racemosa* and several others.

The Magnolias are now large and stately trees, the pride of the garden, at least 50 feet tall; the Loblolly Bay, though always found near water, have assumed a good size, being about 30 feet high, and the American Olives are dense and broad specimens. The Wax Myrtles have formed round and dense clusters of bright green, and the Smilax clambers up into the trees. We also collected little plants of the Carolina Jessamine, one of our most beautiful and refined native plants. It covers at present quite a number of trees in my grounds, and when in bloom, the bright yellow flower-bells exhale a most delicious perfume which pervades the air of the entire garden. I also planted several Hollies (*Ilex opaca*), the Dahoon (*Ilex cassine*), Wild Plum trees, the Prickly-Ash [*Zanthoxylum clava-herculis*] and a dense growing Hawthorn (*Crataegus*) with pendant branches.

Hollies and Dahoons are at present a feature in the garden, but the Prickly-Ash became a nuisance by spreading over territory not belonging to it and it had to be removed. The common Wild Plum (*Prunus umbellata*) forms a very dense, reclining, broad and shapely tree, while the Chickasaw Plum (*P. angustifolia*) has formed dense thickets by underground runners. It is almost impossible to keep it in bounds, and it should never be planted where space is limited. Deciduous trees and shrubs form only a very small and inconspicuous part in my garden. They should not be planted unless they are exceptionally beautiful. Such a small tree, one of the very best of leaf-shedding natives, is the Fringe Tree (*Chionanthus virginica*), common in many of our hammocks. Its leaves are large and leathery and almost ever-green, and when in bloom in early March it is a most lovely object, the pure white fringe-like flowers covering it like a sheet. This tree or tall shrub was also collected and carried to the garden.

Planting Begun under Hardships

This first planting was done under considerable hardships. The November sun was still quite hot and the road and the trails through the woods often invisible. Plant collecting in a dense hammock has its unpleasant features. Many of the thickets were almost impenetrable, and the extremely dense masses of Saw Palmettos in places were so tall that I at one time lost my way. This particular hammock had the reputation of being alive with huge diamond rattlesnakes. And there were ticks and red bugs, all with the wild desire to get into your flesh. Such things annoy one at times, and carrying home the collected plants seemed like a huge burden. But all my various adventures in the Florida hammocks and swamps were a source of pleasure after I had come home, and I always felt a strong desire of making these excursions again, even if I should have to undergo similar or worse hardships.

In Milwaukee I at once began to build a greenhouse, partly to imbue my sons with a love for tropical plants and to train them in their cultivation; partly for my own pleasure, but mostly for the purpose of growing the plants necessary for my Florida garden. Good friends helped along whenever they could. Mr. Henry Pfister, for many years head gardener of the White House, in Washington, sent me many plants which he thought could be grown successfully in Florida. I received seeds from many sources, particularly from Blumenau, Brazil, and from Buenos Aires, from La Mortola, Italy, and from Hong Kong and Darjeeling. The late Mr. C. Wercklé (of Ocean Springs, Miss.), and his enthusiastic son, Carlos Wercklé in San José,

Costa Rica, presented me with many most beautiful shrubs and bulbs. Carl Springer, at that time near Naples, Italy, one of the most enthusiastic and learned gardeners of our times, enriched my collection with all the various Crinums he had brought together, and with all the varieties of *Amaryllis belladonna* he grew in his own garden in southern Italy. Mr. Erich Wittkugel of San Pedro Sula, Honduras, made excursions into the mountains, forests and tropical lowlands and collected for me many bulbs, but especially bromeliads, orchids and epiphytic ferns, which he consigned to me in large dry goods boxes.

I opened with much anticipation and intense interest the packages of plants and seeds that came by parcel post from Trinidad, Jamaica, Caracas (Venezuela), Mexico, Honduras, Costa Rica, Barbados and Australia. The late Mr. James Douglas, one of the best-known English gardeners of his time and a frequent contributor to the *Gardener's Chronicle* and the *Garden*, enriched my collection with the finest new Hippeastrums (*Amaryllis*) from his own glass houses. Dr. E. Bonavia sent me a number of his finest hybrids of *Hippeastrum pardinum,* among them the singularly beautiful "Queen of Spots" and "Spotted Orfeo," and Mr. James O'Brien added several tubers of the then new and magnificent *Gloriosa rothschildiana,* which has since proved such a great success in Palm Cottage Gardens. This climbing Lily, one of the most gorgeous of bulbous plants, is one of the glories of my garden, flowering more or less profusely all the year round. I have raised a number of fine hybrids from this species and *G. superba* and vice versa.

I have two fine specimens of the rare *Talauma hodgsonii* in my garden. When reading in the Himalayan Journals about this tree and its grand foliage and purplish-red flowers I was very anxious to obtain seeds of it. I wrote to Mr. Kennedy, Superintendent of the Botanical Station at Darjeeling, Sikkim, India, and at the same time to Sir Joseph D. Hooker, for many years director of the far-famed Kew Gardens, and one of the noblest and most amiable men it ever has been my good fortune to correspond with. The seeds came and I planted them at once. Several germinated and I was in possession of a few fine small seedlings when Sir Joseph D. Hooker's answer came,—quite a lengthy letter and very friendly. He told me that the seeds of *Talauma hodgsonii* as well as those of other species of the Magnoliaceae, soon lose their germinating power, and that so far it had been impossible to raise this species from seeds in Europe. The best way would be to obtain young plants from the Himalayas in Wardian cases. Only one specimen of

Talauma hodgsonii lived. As I was afraid I would lose it I sent it to my friend, Dr. William Trelease, of the Missouri Botanical Garden, where Mr. August Koch, one of the head gardeners, succeeded in raising a second plant by layering. This is the one now in my possession.

Impressions of Chicago World's Fair

The year 1893 may be properly called a red letter year of my life. It was the year of the World's Columbian Exposition in Chicago. Many a day I spent in the White City. It appeared to be like fairy-land, and the whole is now in my memory like a dream. The impressions of the combined exhibits of rare tropical plants and of the many large single specimens of palms and foliage plants will never fade from my memory. Here I saw, for the first time in my life, masses of new Fancy-leaved Caladiums. They came from the largest hybridizer of these brilliant foliage plants, Adolph Lietze in Rio de Janeiro. When I admired the richness, brilliancy, delicacy of these often translucent colors, I was reminded of art, not of nature. In this, as many other cases, nature simply surpasses art.

Mr. Lietze has raised in succeeding years much finer, much more varied, much more brilliant hybrids, but at that time even connoisseurs, like Dr. L. Wittmack, the editor of *Die Gartenflora*, and others were of the opinion that the climax had been reached. Today those on exhibition and most all of Lietze's later hybrids are in my collection, and the display in my Caladium lath houses, where hundreds and thousands are grown in dense masses, cannot be compared with anything else, be it flowers or foliage plants. There is nothing like it. They stand incomparable above all other plants in lasting beauty, variety and brilliancy. The thousands of visitors who come and go when the Caladiums are at their best, from June to October, have only an eye for the brilliancy of these foliage masses. They entirely overlook the orchids, bromeliads, Marantas, ferns and palms. The latest hybrids of Mr. Richard Hoffmann of London and some of my own even outrival in gorgeous color the Brazilian kinds. For years the Caladiums have been the greatest attraction of my garden.

There were many other plants on exhibition that strongly appealed to me,—Palms, Cycads, Gesneriads, Marantas, Ferns, and stately tropical foliage plants. In front of the Arizona building stood four handsome specimens of *Dasylirion longissimum* [= *Nolina longifolia*?]. All four grow now in my garden, but they scarcely made any headway in their size, though perfectly healthy. A fine large plant of *Dasylirion acrotriche* is one of the features of the garden, being admired even by those who do not care much for plants.

Early Mistakes and Failures

Many mistakes were made by me; many plants were lost, and two Australian Torch Lilies were among them. They need a rather moist soil and some shade here. The Japanese had many rare and highly ornamental plants on exhibition, though their dwarfed trees struck me as an abomination. Among palms a dense specimen of the Bamboo-Palm (*Rhapis humilis*), about three feet high and a picture of elegance was particularly admired. It finally found a home in my lath house. Having reached a height of about ten feet by eight feet in diameter it is at present more striking than ever before. Scarcely any other plant in the Japanese exhibit attracted so much attention as the Sacred-Bamboo (*Nandina domestica*). Its elegant airy foliage and its dense growth commanded admiration. An additional charm are its bunches of rich scarlet berries in late autumn. This plant belongs to the family Berberidaceae, and its common name is misleading, as it is not even distantly related to the Bamboos.

Many other plants were added to my collection after the exposition closed. I remember some fine specimens of [*Araucaria angustifolia*], *Damara robusta* [?], Dracaenas and Cordylines and many others. None of them could be coaxed into a vigorous growth on the high and dry pineland soil. Even the New Zealand Flax (*Phormium tenax*), of which I succeeded in later years in growing fine tufts in the moist rich soil of my plant-shed, refused to start. I was unable to spend my vacation in Florida the World's Fair year, but early in November, 1894, I again enjoyed the balmy breezes of the ideal sunny autumn days in my wildwood garden. Many new plants were added and more land was cleared. A lath house was built near the border of the lake for moisture and shade loving plants.

Among the many branches of study which nature affords for man's pleasure, it is difficult to find one which is at once so full of marvel and beauty, and at the same time so open to the enjoyment of all as that of ornamental horticulture. The pleasures never cease. There is always something new and beautiful to admire. Every new plant that is added is an object of delight and hope.

The Forest Flora of Japan

In 1893 Prof. C. S. Sargent published his "Notes on the Forest Flora of Japan" in *Garden and Forest*. These articles were a revelation to me. They outlined a new and most important direction in my horticultural work. Side by side with our native evergreens those from Japan form today a most conspicuous feature in my garden. When I came home from Florida, and after I had again read and re-read these "notes" I sent an order for all the plants that were obtainable to Japan, and in May, 1895, I received a large consignment of bamboos, Camellias and other Japanese evergreens. In November I forwarded all of them to Florida and planted them in the positions which they now occupy. I have scarcely lost a single plant except a few specimens of *Michelia compressa, Damnacanthus indicus* and *Podocarpus nagi*. From early in October to Christmas *Camellia sasanqua* is in full bloom. Some of the specimens are at present ten to twelve feet high and very dense. Their flowers are large, in form like a single rose and of a fine rosy-red color. The double white form of this species is more spreading in growth and not so tall. This is a gem. Nothing can out vie it in purity and beauty. *Camellia japonica* was represented in many forms, among them a number of semi-double varieties, the largest and most elegant flowers imaginable. Though Camellias are slow growers some of the bushes have attained a height of eight and nine feet. They begin to bloom early in December. There are early and late varieties.

Professor Sargent found the Broadleaved Holly (*Ilex latifolia*) particularly striking, and he says that it is perhaps the most beautiful of the Japanese evergreen trees, not only on account of its brilliant red abundant fruit, but also on account of its large fine leaves. It bears its dense bunches of vivid red berries for the first time this year. *Ilex integra* is also a very beautiful and distinct species, being like the former, often cultivated in temple gardens. Its brilliant red berries are very ornamental. My particular favorite among the evergreens of Japan, however, is the fine, tall, dense and somewhat columnar [*Ternstroemia gymnanthera*], invaluable as a single specimen and in groups, and indispensable in Florida landscape gardening. I have never seen it outside of my own garden. Its flowers appear in June in drooping short racemes, exhaling a very pleasant, though not strong perfume. The berries ripen in September bursting open and displaying their mealy flesh and brilliant red seeds.

Among the plants forming at present very conspicuous objects either as single specimens or in groups, the Star Anise [*Illicium anisatum*] is very prominent. It is also one of the sacred plants of Japan, with fine, large and very aromatic leaves. It never forms a tree here, but grows in bush form, being very broad near the ground and pointed near the top. Coniferous trees were only represented in two species, both Podocarpi. My two specimens of *Podocarpus japonica* [?] have made a splendid growth, being dense and upright with narrow myrtle-like leaves, deep glossy green above and silvery-white beneath. The much more beautiful *P. nagi* did not thrive so well. Only one specimen among a dozen is alive. It grows in dense shade underneath Magnolias and Oaks. Rich moist soil is what it requires.

Judgment Should Be Exercised in Planting Bamboos

No one should plant species of Bamboo with running rhizomes for ornament in Florida. Arundinarias and all the members of the genus *Phyllostachys* soon become nuisances and are extremely difficult to eradicate. Only those growing in tufts or clumps should find a place in the garden. A fine large clump of the hardy tufted species is the embodiment of every grace, elegance and beauty imaginable. There were about twenty-five different Bamboos in this collection, which all came under Japanese names. For quite a while I was unable to identify my plants until Mr. A. B. Freeman-Mitford (Lord Redesdale) sent me a complimentary copy of his classic book *The Bamboo Garden*, early in 1897. One of them, labeled Taisan-chiku, appealed to me at once as a strong-growing, distinct species. I have now three very large and beautiful clumps of it. It grows over 50 feet tall with thick blackish culms. This proved to be [*Bambusa oldhamii*], and is the only hardy large-growing Bamboo. Its native home is Formosa. A fine little specimen, labeled Sui-chiku, was identified as the most elegant [*Bambusa glaucescens*], while the Taiho-chiku proved to be the silver-variegated [*Arundinaria viridistriata*], and the Oroshima-chiku, the small growing gem *B. gracilis* [?]. I found all the three in large and stately specimens in the gardens of Orlando. Mr. Theodore L. Mead of Lake Charm imported all of them directly from Japan ten years before I had received mine. They have been grown in the Mikado's empire since times immemorial for ornament, but they seem to have been brought there from India. The hardy [*Bambusa oldhamii*] was not represented in the gardens of Florida before I introduced it.

The members of the Cycas family have always been special favorites of mine. In glasshouses, though of great importance, they neither attain the size, nor the density of growth, nor the luxuriance and beauty they assume when planted out in the open in Florida. *Cycas revoluta* is a common ornament of our gardens. As it is an extremely slow grower I decided to order a number of stems in their dry state, ten to forty pounds in weight, directly from Japan. They came with the above mentioned plants and I sent them immediately to Florida. The largest specimens are now huge plants, pictures of health and beauty, with trunks four to five feet high and with magnificent leaf-crowns. As there are male and female plants in the collection, I am able to gather seeds by the bushel every year.

In the meantime most of the palm seeds I had received from South Brazil, Argentina and from Haage & Schmidt (Erfurt, Germany) had sprouted and I had hundreds of nice little plants. [See companion volume, chapters 4 and 5.]

Magnolias and Live Oaks Are Favorites

Although palms and bamboos form the main characteristics of my garden, there are many beautiful native Magnolias scattered all over the grounds. Among all the broad-leaved subtropical trees, *Magnolia grandiflora* and the picturesque Live Oak are my special favorites. There is no nobler, no more refined tree in the world than a well-grown specimen of this Magnolia. It is my ideal of a tree,—the queen of beauty, the poet's dream,—beautiful alike in growth, form, foliage, flowers and fruit. It was the dream of my boyhood days to spend my old age in a garden replete with Magnolias and Live Oaks, and to listen to the song of the mocking-bird and cardinal. All this has been realized and much more. I have succeeded in creating a real Eden, and the Magnolias belong to its most precious jewels. It was the first tree I planted, and as I have said before I carried it for miles through the almost pathless woods on my shoulders. Although the tops were removed and only the bare stumps planted, several of the specimens are at present 50 feet high and provided with branches from the ground to the top. In order to show its incomparable beauty and stateliness, it requires room for its development.

I made the mistake to plant all my specimens too close together. They ought to be planted 50, or still better, 70 feet apart. As a rule the Magnolia is a most difficult tree to transplant from the woods. Only the mere stumps should be set out. All the beautiful leaves and branches, the entire stem must be sacrificed. The best time to plant these stumps is the month of November. In the spring vigorous sprouts will shoot up. I usually remove them all except one,—the most sturdy. The easiest and most successful way is to plant pot grown small specimens. Set out in the cool autumn days, without breaking the ball of soil, they are almost sure to live. Isolated specimens allowed to grow naturally, always are the most symmetrical and perfect. In the course of time a most stately conical, half-round or pyramidal tree is formed,—a delight to everyone who is near to nature's heart. As it grows exceedingly well on high pineland, it should be one of the most generally planted trees in all gardens, large or small. As an avenue tree it has no rival, except our picturesque Live Oak. For park planting, there is no more effective tree.

Clusters of glaucous-leaved Coconut [probably refers to *Butia*] are by way of contrast particularly adapted to be placed in the foreground of large Magnolia groups. The large deep green, glossy foliage glistening like a thousand mirrors in the bright sunshine, the large pure milky-white, deliciously fragrant flowers, and the dense and noble growth combine to create a most delightful effect. And even the seeds are very ornamental. As soon as the cones open their seed receptacles, the brilliant red, oily, highly aromatic seeds are displayed. Before dropping they are suspended on web-like silky threads. Mockingbirds, cardinal redbirds, brown thrashers, woodpeckers, blue jays and other birds swarm among the trees, finding a richly set table for their sole use. Many seedlings come up in the woods all around my garden from seed dropped by the birds.

Not being satisfied with the Magnolias from our forests, I collected seeds wherever I had the opportunity to find particularly fine varieties. A few of the very finest specimens in the garden were raised from seeds collected by me on the banks of the Mississippi near New Orleans. Nurserymen have done nothing to propagate especially fine varieties and to offer them in their catalogues. But there is one exception,—the late Samuel B. Parsons of Flushing, N.Y., a man of high ideals and an unlimited enthusiasm. He had, at one time, a most beautiful subtropical nursery on an island in the St. Johns in Florida, a branch of his famous Flushing nursery. He collected all the different varieties of Magnolia and propagated them, and from him I obtained the entire set, consisting of about fifteen forms, in 1893.

There is one variety with foliage showing a fine rusty-brown tomentum on the underside, which by way of contrast exhibits a most beautiful sight when the wind moves the leaves. Another variety has small laurel-like leaves, and a third one has almost round foliage. In one variety the seed cones are brilliant red. All these forms flower profusely when only a few feet high. They were planted out here in the fall of 1894 and some of them are now from 30 to 38 feet high. Their growth is much more open and not so symmetrical as in our best "Florida" forms. Most all of my Oaks, *Grevillea robusta, Cunninghamia [lanceolata]*, and even the pines are covered with the long gray streamers and festoons of Spanish-Moss [*Tillandsia usneoides*], but it never settles on the Magnolia permanently.

Fragrance has been called the song of the flowers, but the language in which this song is made known to the world, like other tongues, is best learned in youth, and happy are those whose childhood days have been spent in the country and who have thus insensibly absorbed the essence of Nature's poetry. A friend of mine, who traveled in many countries, compared the fragrance of *Magnolia grandiflora* with the mocking-bird's song, being typical and purely American, while the dreamy, delicate sweet perfume of [*Magnolia virginiana*] was compared with the nightingale's love song. And, indeed, there is nothing like this enchanting scent. It always carries me back to Buffalo Bayou near Houston, Texas, where I inhaled this perfume for the first time, forty years ago.

The Sweet Bay, Swamp Magnolia or White Bay [*Magnolia virginica*] is one of our most abundant native evergreen trees, being found either interspersed with other moisture loving species or quite often growing in solid groups by itself in our bayheads and swamps. The pretty foliage is bright green above and silvery white underneath. When a strong breeze displays the white underside the impression of a solid bank of pure white flowers is suggested. The rather small cup-like, pure white flowers are abundantly produced from April to the latter part of August. The air is literally filled with the strongly delicious perfume where it grows, and after each rain, when the breezes are cool and soft, this extremely sweet and strong fragrance, exhaled by innumerable white flower chalices, is wafted over wide areas. This noble tree is rarely found in our gardens, although it grows well in rich moist soil.

Every Tree and Shrub Has an Individuality

Every species of tree and shrub has its special attractions, an individuality of its own in leaf, flower and growth. It helps to add variety to its surroundings. How wearisome becomes the sameness of large stretches of ground only covered with one or a few species of trees or shrubs! We soon become tired and our eyes look for relief. In order to avoid sameness in our gardens, we must introduce as many forms as possible, and nature has, with a lavish hand, spread out a most beautiful variety of fine evergreens, and it is only necessary to make use of them.

Our picturesque native Live Oak (*Quercus virginiana*) is an aristocrat compared with the plebeian Water Oak (*Quercus nigra*) [possibly the Water Oak intended is *Q. laurifolia,* commonly planted in the Orlando-Tampa area]. Always fantastic in form, never symmetrical, always picturesque and beautiful, it even has found favor with the new settler, who always preserves the fine, old, time-honored specimens in the woods when clearing land. The trunks usually lean over to one side, or huge branches, not far from the ground, grow in a certain direction. The bark is rough and light gray, the leaves dense, deep green, the crown immense, and the whole top always festooned with streamers and garlands of Spanish-Moss. There is a fine old specimen in my grounds, so immense and so beautifully picturesque that only the brush of the artist could do it justice. I never have seen a finer specimen. Under its shade the writer hopes to find his final resting place. It grows extremely well in high pineland, and with a little care in regard to pruning, it is well adapted for avenue planting.

How different is the color of the foliage in the various species! *Magnolia grandiflora* exhibits very dark green glossy leaves; in [*M. virginiana*] they have a much lighter color, while its silvery white underside is almost always in view. The Cabbage Palmetto is bluish-green, the American Olive, Laurel-Cherry, Loblolly Bay, Holly and Dahoon, all show different tints of green. The most striking green, however, very different from all others, is seen in the Wax Myrtle (*Myrica cerifera*), in its green color. In landscape work this splendid although rather short-lived tree is indispensable, being one of the most characteristic in form. Indeed I know no other tree, native or exotic, that grows in the same effective way. The dense evergreen serrated foliage exhales a very pleasant spicy odor when we touch the branches in passing by. This aromatic scent is quite strong after every rain in early spring and during summer. For this perfume alone I would not miss the Bayberry, as it is called in Florida. The seeds are bluish, small, covered with a waxy coating and are relished by many birds, particularly Myrtle warblers.

There are many other fine native ornamental evergreens, such as the Laurel Cherry (*Prunus caroliniana*), which forms beautiful dense evergreen specimens, fine for avenue planting, but our notice of all of them must necessarily be brief, and can only serve to call the attention of the plant lover and amateur horticulturist to the wealth of floral beauty which is within his reach.

While in St. Augustine in the fall of 1895 I collected a lot of berries of the Florida Cedar or Juniper *Juniperus silicicola* and also drupes of the Swamp Red Bay [*Persea palustris*]. I succeeded in raising hundreds of fine young plants. The Cedars are at present a feature in the garden, provided with branches to the ground and very dense. Some of them are 25 feet high and near the ground almost as broad. Seedlings of the Florida Cedar come up all around my place, and in some instances several miles away. The birds disseminate the seeds.

In the autumn of 1896 I set out a small pot-plant of *Grevillea robusta,* and the next year several more followed. The largest one is at present over 60 feet tall and, in March, when in flower, it looks from the distance like a huge flame. The peculiar bunches of blossoms are unlike anything else we grow in our gardens, and each blossom is so full of honey that the bees should be kept busy as long as they last, but for some reason I have never seen many of them among the flowers. This honey is very sweet to the taste. The Grevillea forms a large and rather dense tree with fine, much-divided, fern-like foliage. Seedlings come up by the thousands under my specimens. People call it Australian Oak and Silk Oak,—misnomers, because it belongs to the family Proteaceae, which is not even distantly related to the oaks. It should be called *Grevillea.* All the species are natives of Australia.

For over half a century the late Mr. P. J. Berckmans of Augusta, Ga., was the leading spirit of horticulture in the South Atlantic States, particularly Georgia. The plants he recommended to me and added to my collection form today a most important part of my garden. Almost all were of Japanese and Chinese origin. I have already referred to the Camellias, invariably called the "Japonica" in the South. Mr. Berckmans sent me, among others, *C.* 'Donckelaardii,' *C.* 'Chandleri Elegans' and other semi-double hybrids, the most elegant and the largest of their class. All Camellias thrive well on high pineland, although slow in growth. They are, however, so beautiful and so refined and noble that no good garden is complete without them. Camellia flowers must never be cut with stems, as this injures the blooming of the next year very seriously. Never cut any. Leave them and enjoy them where they grow. Camellias need a mulch of good old stable manure each year. They should only be hoed very lightly to keep down the weeds. In addition to *Camellia japonica* I received several plants of *C. thea*, the Tea shrub, a perfect success here and flowering profusely every year in November.

Magnolia fuscata or, rather, [*Michelia figo*], the Banana-Magnolia or Ba-nana-Shrub, one of the most popular and highly prized of all exotic ever-greens, was represented in a dozen fine small specimens. They are all alive, and most of them are strong, dense, bushy plants 10 to 15 feet high. Like all the plants from this source they were set out in November, 1897. It grows best in an isolated, rich and somewhat shady position, but it also looks well in small groups, particularly on the north side of other large evergreen shrubs.

The Banana-Magnolia is a jewel among evergreen exotic shrubs. It has always occupied a high rank among my special favorites, since I inhaled for the first time its fragrance in the gardens of New Orleans, over forty years ago. It is the glory of the Southland gardens all along the South Atlantic and the Gulf of Mexico, being hardy as far north as Tennessee. It was introduced from its native home, southern China, very likely, long before the Civil War. It is close to the heart of every Southerner on account of its dainty, delicately fragrant flowers. A single bud, creamy-white with a purplish hue, hidden among the dense foliage, where it can not readily be seen, is sufficient to pervade the air with its strong, extremely delicious perfume. It has been likened to the odor of ripe bananas, but this conveys only a vague idea of its real character. For weeks and even months my entire garden is pervaded with this fragrance, as the specimens are scattered all over the ornamental grounds. The first flowers exhale their sweetness in the last days of February and the last ones I have noticed early in May. The flowers are not always fragrant. On very cool days and in full sunshine they frequently withhold their odor. The flowers are small, star-like, pure creamy-white and each petal is slightly edged with purple. The growth of the Banana-Shrub is dense and very symmetrical, rather globose, being provided with branches to the ground. The leaves are of medium size, elliptic-oblong and rather smooth, dark-green. At this time when everybody in Florida searches for plants that are hardy and flowering in winter this fine exotic, together with *Camellia japonica, C. sasanqua,* the Indian Azalea (*Azalea indica*), the Sweet Myrtle (*Myrtus communis*), *Raphiolepis indica* and *Pittosporum tobira* should be found in every garden.

Mr. Berckmans also introduced and disseminated the still more powerfully fragrant *Magnolia pumila* (*M. coco*)[= *Michelia figo*], a rather straggling evergreen shrub with fine large leaves and white flowers. These blossoms, which appear here in May, are so intensely, so delightfully and so peculiarly fragrant that I am unable to name any plant that exhales a similar perfume. Sometimes the odor reminded me of [*Vanda tricolor*], at other times of Gardenias, Tuberoses and Garland Flowers, all mixed together. I had only one plant which grew well in my garden and attained a height of five feet within twelve years, though it is stated that it grows about twelve feet high in its native home, southern China. Unfortunately I lost my plant, and I was unable to obtain another one. This is a gem and it should again be introduced. It deserves to find a place in every good garden in the orange section on account of its strong characteristic perfume. In consideration of this unique and delightful fragrance friends of mine called it the "Heavenly Incense Shrub."

Nowhere in Florida have I seen the deciduous Japanese and Chinese Magnolias. They are fine winter-bloomers here, and are still better adapted for northern Florida. I have handsome specimens of [*Magnolia quinquepeta*], *M.* ✕*Soulangiana, M.* ✕*S.* 'Lennei,' [*M. heptapeta*], and I had a fine large plant of *M. stellata,* which was destroyed by a forest fire. All these Magnolias thrive splendidly on high land if well cared for and kept free from scale insects. All grow in bush form and eventually attain a height of 20 to 25 feet and all flower in the winter months. [See also Oriental Trees and Shrubs in the companion volume.]

Japanese and Chinese Evergreens

Mr. Berckmans had brought together a splendid collection of Japanese and Chinese evergreens, and among them he considered the many species and varieties of Silver Shrubs (*Elaeagnus*) of particular value for ornament as well as for utility. The Climbing Silver Shrub [*E. pungens* 'Reflexa'] is most beautiful and most fragrant of all the shrubs I grow. It is excellent for arbors and for pergolas. It is a most vigorous grower, climbing by its reflexed, blunt-pointed hooks high up into the Oaks, Pines and Camphor Trees. The young shoots are very long and of a rusty-brown color. The leaves are oblong, deep green, glossy above and silvery-white underneath, with numerous minute dark-brown dots. The flowers appear late in October and all through November, filling the air of the entire place with a sweet Carnation-like perfume that can be noticed many rods away. The flowers are small, inconspicuous, whitish, freckled with brown and shaped like a Clove. The fragrance is so delightfully pleasant that it often attracts visitors to the gardens who inhale it passing the place in their automobiles. Shortly after New Year's Day the berries ripen in great abundance. They are oblong-ovate, red, covered with minute brown dots and are very juicy, reminding in flavor and substance of the Currant. *E. macrophylla* and [*E. pungens*] are also beautiful dense evergreen shrubs, half climbers, with large foliage and with much larger berries. The flowers are as fragrant as in *E. pungens* 'Reflexa.' An excellent jelly and wine can be made of these fruits, and they are a great treat for our many winter birds, particularly the robins and the brown thrashers.

Elaeagnus pungens 'Simonii' is a particularly fine berry-bearing plant. I have a beautiful yellow-variegated *E. pungens* 'Maculata,' a dense and very effective half-climbing shrub that has been a favorite with the Japanese since times immemorial. I also grow *E. pungens* 'Frederici Variegata,' *E. pungens* 'Tricolor' and a few others. All these climbing and half-climbing Silver Shrubs or Oleasters, forming very effective dense evergreen specimens within a short time, flowering late in autumn and exhaling a delicious perfume and in addition bearing an abundance of Currant-like berries in midwinter, are indispensable as garden ornaments and for landscape work. In several parts of my garden *E. pungens* 'Reflexa,' *E. pungens,* and *E. macrophylla* form almost impenetrable thickets, the living places of cardinal redbirds, brown thrashers and later in the season of numerous winter sojourners. Underneath them and in the equally dense *Pittosporum tobira* the bobwhite breeds and the chuck-will's-widow hides in daytime and hatches its young. All of them grow rampantly on high pineland. With a little care the very important Gumi *E. multiflora* (*E. longipes* [?]) and *E. umbellata,* both bearing large fine fruits in great abundance, grow well here. But they need attention to do their best. I have good specimens of both, and a large tree of *E. angustifolia.*

One of the most cherished shrubs or small dense evergreen trees of the South Atlantic and Gulf regions is *Pittosporum tobira,* a native of China and Japan. In Houston, New Orleans and Mobile I have seen most beautiful dense, and extremely ornamental trees of it fully 15 to 20 feet high. Such specimens can be grown into a tree-like form if only one shoot is allowed to grow. All suckers must be removed. I grow my Pittosporums in dense low specimens, often 10 to 15 feet in diameter and only 6 to 8 feet high. The thick, deep glossy green, leathery leaves are obovate, narrowed to the short petiole. The flowers appear in dense terminal umbels and are of a creamy-white color and very fragrant, reminding strongly of orange blossoms. This species is so beautiful and distinct, it is so easily grown and forms such shapely specimens that it is indispensable for garden decoration. Not long ago I found a most beautiful clump of a bromeliad [*Tillandsia variabilis*] on one of the branches of this Pittosporum, not thicker than my little finger. This Tillandsia is not found in the immediate neighborhood of the garden, and the thistle-like seeds must have been carried by the wind a long way before they found a foothold on this plant. I have also a fine specimen of the silver-variegated form, *P. tobira* 'Variegata.' This is not as vigorous in growth as the type, though a very good and healthy grower. It is very effective in its place.

Another choice tree-like shrub is the fragrant evergreen *Viburnum odoratissimum,* of which I have several fine specimens. In order to display its unique beauty it ought to be grown in isolated spots, where it has space enough to develop its lower branches without interfering with other surrounding trees. Only when this is the case this evergreen snowball forms an ornament of unrivaled beauty, being densely supplied with branches from the ground to the top. Its form is naturally very attractive, growing in a cone-like way and having rather large light-green dense foliage. The flowers appear here in April in terminal clusters. They are milky-white and slightly fragrant. In its native countries, China and Japan, it is one of the most popular garden ornaments. It grows well on high pineland, but prefers richer and moister soil. I was so much struck with the beauty of this species in the parks and gardens of New Orleans and Mobile, where fine dense specimens often 25 feet high occur, that the impression never has faded from memory.

Quite a number of rather distinct evergreen Privets were included in Mr. Berckman's consignment, among them *Ligustrum lucidum* or *L. japonicum,* one of the most ornamental and effective street trees of New Orleans. It is of medium growth, with dense weeping branches and bearing in the fall clusters of bluish-black berries. Unfortunately this finest of all Privets did not succeed. *Ligustrum ibota* [= either *L. obtusifolium* or *L. tschonskii*] and *L.*

lucidum, both with showy white clusters of flowers, have done well and are very ornamental.

Camphor Tree Thrives on High Sandy Land

The Camphor Tree (*Cinnamomum camphora*), in quite a number of large specimens, forms a conspicuous object in my grounds. My first small plants came with the above consignment. No other Japanese tree has been planted so much as the Camphor Tree, and there are large old trees, some perhaps forty years of age, in a few gardens nearby. It thrives well on high sandy lands and grows fast if well fertilized. Young trees, half-globular in form, look very fine and are a great ornament, particularly when the young, very light green leaves appear, forming a strong contrast to the old dark green foliage. It is a ravenous feeder and sends out its feeding rootlets to a great distance, so that nothing in a circumference of forty feet will be able to get established. I had to remove quite a number of rather large specimens in order to save the more ornamental plants growing near them.

Cinnamomum cassia (Cassia-Cinnamon Tree) is a very beautiful orna-mental evergreen tree from southern China. Though thriving best in rich moist land, it grows equally well on higher soil, particularly near residences where it now and then receives applications of fertilizer and water. It is a dense and beautiful tree in its young state and this beauty even increases in older specimens.

[*Cinnamomum burmannii*], from southern Japan, forms a dense and very handsome tree. My specimen had strongly nerved leaves as those of the Camphor Tree. *C. loureirii,* also from southern Japan and China, is a very ornamental small tree. Both species were represented in the grounds of the Sanford House at Sanford, Fla., in fine large specimens many years ago. But, all the rare plants disappeared.

In addition to those mentioned I received the Sweet Olive *Osmanthus fragrans* (*Olea fragrans*), a treasure in every plant collection on account of its delicious fragrance; it thrives well here, but its growth is very slow. My speci-men is only 1½ feet high, but it flowers regularly in winter and perfumes the air with an indescribable sweetness. In order to induce it to a stronger growth it is necessary to bud or graft it on some good species of Privet. The Holly-leaved-Olive (*O. aquifolium* [*heterophyllus*]) is a much stronger grower, forming fine low, but rather broad specimens in the course of time.

The small white flowers are very fragrant. The Indian Hawthorn (*Photinia serrulata*) from China, a most beautiful dense evergreen shrub, assuming in the tenacious soil of southern Georgia and northern Florida a height of 20 feet, grows well on sandy soils if rich compost, mixed with some clay, is used in setting it out. Cultivation and some old cow manure help it along wonderfully, but it never looks so thrifty and ornamental as farther north.

Eriobotrya japonica, the Loquat, is a highly ornamental and a very useful tree from Japan and China. It is so beautiful that it should be found in all good collections. It looks best as an isolated specimen. Crowded with other shrubs and trees, it soon loses its characteristic beauty.

Conifers Prominent in Collection

Mr. Berckmans sent me all the coniferous trees that he thought would do well here. The Cedar of Lebanon (*Cedrus libani*) did not thrive, but the Deodar (*C. deodora*) made an open specimen in the course of time. It needs shade on high pineland. The *Retinisporas* (now *Chamaecyparis*) grew well for a few years, and so did [*Platycladus orientalis*], but then they became scraggy and really ugly. The species of conifers, comprising the real Cypresses, were a success from the beginning. The most beautiful of all the Cypresses is *Cupressus torulosa* from the Himalayas. It only grows on high dry land and it does best in the dry rocky soil in the Miami region. This is the jewel of the genus. I have a specimen about 25 feet high that has lost all its lower branches on account of too close neighbors. Only dense trees of it, provided with branches from the ground, are beautiful. My next best species is [*Cupressus lusitanica* 'Benthamii'] from Mexico, of which I have a very dense tall and broad specimen. [*C. lusitanica* 'Knightiana'] is also fine. [*Chamaecyparis funebris*], a native of China, with pendulous branches and dense growth, formed a feature of the grounds for a number of years. It died after it had reached a height of 35 feet. The picturesque columnar Italian Cypress (*Cupressus sempervirens*), such an ornament of the southern European landscape, grows well in my garden, but it loses all its lower branches in the course of time and with this even its beauty is destroyed. I had over a dozen specimens, but at present I have only one good tree growing among Magnolias and evergreen shrubs, where its tall, overtowering column looks very beautiful.

Paths lead in all directions through my garden, and only in walking among them my plant loving friends as well as I myself can enjoy the many different shrubs and trees, as they always lead by the rarest and most interesting. It is impossible to overlook the most effective, and it is not difficult to notice the most dainty. The other day, when walking along one of these paths with a plant lover, he suddenly burst out with the exclamation: "Oh, an Araucaria! I never have seen this species before. How beautiful and unique!" It was not an *Araucaria*, however, but [*Cunninghamia lanceolata*] which Mr. Berckmans sent me in 1897. I have two fine specimens, one of them about 30 feet high. The form of this fine conifer is rather narrow, somewhat columnar, very dense and the branches are arranged in a verticillate manner, being spreading and pendulous. The leaves are bright glossy green, linear lanceolate, sharply pointed, whitish below, and about 1½ to 2 inches long. Its only fault is that there are many small, dry, brown branches scattered over the lower part of the tree which detract somewhat from the singular beauty of this fine conifer from China. Its lower branches brush the soil. My specimens are covered with Spanish-Moss, which serves to shade the trunk from the sun. It prefers a half-shady position and as a fertilizer a mulch of old cow manure. I have never seen the *Cunninghamia* outside of my own garden.

Seeds Received from Hong Kong

In the same year I received from Mr. C. Ford, Director of the Botanical Garden of Hong Kong, China, seeds of a number of trees and shrubs, which form at present a great attraction when in bloom. The most striking is *Raphiolepis indica*, one of the choicest evergreen shrubs I possess. Its form is quite dense and it never grows taller than about 6 or 8 feet. In March it is always covered with its showy white or pinkish flowers relieved by a red calyx and red stamens. It produces its flowers in dense panicles at the end of each twig, and is as showy and as floriferous as an Azalea. Planted in the foreground of dense dark evergreen Chinese and Japanese shrubs, such as [*Michelia figo*], [*Ternstroemia gymnathera*], *Pittosporum tobira* and others, it produces a beautiful effect when in bloom. The black seeds [fruits?], as large as a pea, ripen in November. All around my place in the woods young plants have been produced by these seeds which were carried off by the birds. This Indian Hawthorn is a native of southern China, where quite a number of fine garden forms exist which have not yet been introduced.

Rhaphiolepis umbellata is a stronger grower, attaining a height of 10 to 12 feet. It is a native of southern Japan, but I received the seed from Hong Kong. The leaves are larger than in the former species, and the flowers are pure white and fragrant. Under the name of [*R. umbellata* forma *ovata*] I received seeds from the same source. This is, in my garden, a low spreading shrub, only a foot in height, but it is very floriferous and healthy; said to be a variety of *R. umbellata*. All the species, as far as I have experimented with them, do exceedingly well on high pineland, needing scarcely any care, but they all appreciate a mulch of old cow manure.

[*Radermachera sinica*] flowers in my garden in July and August very abundantly. It is a night-bloomer and the long flower-trumpets cover the ground every morning. The corolla is pale sulphur-yellow, funnel-shaped, with crimped margin. The blossoms exhale a strong carnation-like perfume. When given space to develop, its abundant large, dark-green, much crimped, bi-pinnate foliage and its luxuriant growth, with the additional charm of its large funnel-shaped upright flowers, combine to make it an object of great beauty. It is a rapid grower and perfectly hardy here. It requires good, rich soil and now and then applications of fertilizer rich in ammonia. It grows easily from cuttings placed in July and August. It grows easily from cuttings placed in sand.

The late John Saul of Washington, D.C., was a lover and grower of many rare and beautiful tropical and subtropical plants. From him many rare things could be obtained, which are not found in any of the catalogues of today. His collection of Gardenias was a splendid one. I still grow not only the common double form of the Cape Jasmine *Gardenia jasminoides* (*G. florida*), but also the large-flowering *G. jasminoides* var. *major,* and var. *majestica,* both very distinct and beautiful and much larger than the common form. From this source I also received a plant under the name of *G. citriodora* (*Mitriostigma axillare*), a gem, of dainty growth and exquisitely fragrant single white flowers. It is a native of South Africa, but it grows well here with proper care, and flowers very profusely in May and June. This one is quite unique in growth as well as in fragrance. It is not as hardy as the common Gardenia. I lost my large plant, 4 feet high and as much in diameter, in the freeze of the early February days of 1917, and have not yet been able to replace it. It went through several freezes, was cut down, and always sprouted again from the roots, but this time it was killed outright.

Some Winter Flowering Shrubs

One of the finest, most distinct and most satisfactory shrubs in my garden is *Brunfelsia hopeana* (*B. uniflora*), a native of Brazil. It is a low shrub, scarcely more than 3 feet high, but it is very dense and in mid-winter it is covered with flowers, which appear in such abundance that the leaves can scarcely be seen. They are deep violet in the morning, lighter colored towards noon and almost white in the evening, exhaling a pleasant odor of violets. It flowers best in half-shady positions. It is perfectly at home on high pineland and has not suffered from cold.

From Mr. Saul I also received [*B. pauciflora* var. *calycina* 'Macrantha'], a much stronger grower with large leaves and larger flowers. This species is also a native of Brazil. Its flowers are violet and change to a lighter color before fading, but they lack fragrance. It is perfectly hardy here. This is one of the showiest and most floriferous evergreen shrubs in my garden, being especially valuable as a winter bloomer.

Another most beautiful species came under the name of *B. calycina* [= *B. pauciflora* var. *calycina*]. It is a large-flowering and also a large-leaved kind. It is of free growth and produces large trusses of bright violet-purple flowers for several months during the winter. [*B. pauciflora* 'Eximia'] is an extremely ornamental shrub when covered with its deep violet-colored flowers. It blooms here from January to May. *Brunfelsia latifolia* is a very distinct winter-flowering species. The flowers are deliciously fragrant, being of a dainty lavender color, changing to a pure white before fading, and the freshly opening flowers show a distinct white eye. All these Brunfelsias are hardy here and very important shrubs for half-shady places. All come from Brazil.

One of the most strikingly beautiful small trees or dense shrubs is the Australian *Pittosporum undulatum,* known as the Victorian Box in California. It is suitable for all positions where a dense foliage effect is desired. Normally a tree, attaining a height of 35 to 40 feet, it can easily be kept low by pruning. It looks best in an isolated spot, where it has room to spread, and where it can develop its lower branches to all sides. The abundant foliage is deep green and undulated. The flowers appear here in March on terminal branches in dense clusters. Their color is white and they exhale a most delicious Jasmine-like perfume, particularly noticeable at night. This fine shrub should be planted in groups and as single specimens near the house where its fragrance will always be appreciated by those who enjoy the perfume of flowers. This odor never becomes objectionable, like that of the Gardenia, the Night-blooming Jasmine and the Tuberose. I had a very beautiful specimen about 25 feet tall, but being very much exposed, it was killed back by a severe freeze. I now grow it in bush form, but quite a number of smaller plants I intend to train in such a way that they will form dense and shapely trees.

Myrtle Family

Mr. John Saul also enriched my collection by quite a number of different Sweet Myrtles or Bridal-Myrtles (*Myrtus communis*) which form very conspicuous objects in my grounds. All thrive best in half-shady spots and in rich soils, soon forming dense and beautiful specimens. All are natives of southern Europe, the Azores, etc., where they have been grown as garden plants since ancient times. Poets have sung their praise. In many countries the bride wears a Myrtle wreath, hence the name Bridal-Myrtle.

There are quite a number of distinct varieties of this handsome strangely scented shrub in cultivation. The type is a strong, upright grower, attaining here a height of 10 to 12 feet. The most floriferous kind is *Myrtus communis* var. *melanocarpa* (*M. montana*), a strong upright grower, very dense and covered early in May with beautiful pure white flowers. The flowers are produced in such abundance that the leaves are scarcely seen. The fruit is black and abundantly produced. This form attains a height of 15 feet and more. *M. communis* var. *latifolia* has large broad leaves. It is a more open grower. I have a specimen that is over 15 feet high and very shapely in form. The most dainty of all the Myrtles is [*M. communis* 'Microphylla']. It is a dense, upright grower, never taller than 5 or 6 feet, with small, dark green, scented leaves. This variety forms beautiful hedges when properly cared for.

The late Sir Thomas Hanbury, whose world-renowned garden at La Mortola, Ventimiglia, Italy, is replete with rare subtropical plants, has for more than a quarter of a century distributed carefully collected and scientifically labeled seeds free of charge to all plant and flower lovers who ask for them. A catalogue is sent out each year in thousands of copies and it is only necessary to give the number and seeds soon follow. After the death of this distinguished benefactor, Lady Hanbury followed the same practice. In my garden are many fine specimens raised from the seeds I received from this garden. I can only mention a few which did especially well and which at present form features in the garden.

Foremost of all are the Bottle-Brushes, particularly *Callistemon rigidus,* a dense shrub, with beautiful bottle-brush shaped flowers, blooming from March to May. These flowers are glowing red. A still finer and much taller species is *C. speciosus,* the most highly colored of all the Callistemons, the golden yellow anthers contrasting beautifully with the deep red filaments. This species grows into a dense shrub, with gracefully drooping branches, and with a little training it eventually becomes a small dense tree, being loaded here in May with its beautiful showy flowers. [*Callistemon citrinus*] is of more open growth. The flowers are very showy bright red. I have also *C. salignus* in my collection with flower-brushes of pale yellow color and a species with beautiful lilac-colored flowers. Several species of *Melaleuca, Leptospermum* and *Metrosideros* were also raised from seeds which I received from La Mortola. Two specimens of *Hakea nitida* [?] have attained a height of 18 feet. All these plants are natives of Australia, and all are perfectly hardy here. Outside of my own garden, I have never met with them anywhere in Florida.

Oleanders

No garden in the orange region is complete without at least one variety of Oleander (*Nerium oleander*), an old-fashioned, but a very beautiful and distinct plant. It grows here almost without any care and my plants have never been troubled with insects. Large specimen plants of the two most common varieties, the fragrant double rosy-red and the pure white single kind, have attained a height of 25 feet and a diameter of 30 feet and more. In order to induce them to flower most abundantly, it is necessary to prune them annually. This should be performed after the flowering season. Neglected plants do not show their full beauty. All of them appreciate now and then a top-dressing of good stable manure. Treated in this way, the Oleander soon becomes an object of great beauty, and when in bloom belongs to our most showy shrubs. It usually begins to flower early in March, and flower-trusses of the fragrant double-rose-colored and the deep crimson varieties can be seen as late as October and November.

I have the following varieties in my collection: *Nerium oleander* var. *roseum* with beautiful bunches of double rosy-red and deliciously fragrant flowers. *N. oleander* 'Album,' single and double forms; pure white, scentless; extremely showy; very vigorous. *N. oleander* 'Atropurpureum,' single and double form; glowing red and very fragrant. All these forms soon grow into very beautiful specimens, flowering abundantly. Reasoner Bros., Oneco, Fla., have not only distributed all the above forms over the state, but many of the beautiful new varieties and hybrids. It is a pleasure to study the catalogues of this firm. It would require a long separate article to describe all the ornamental plants introduced by the Royal Palm Nurseries of Oneco, Fla.

During the summer months, from June to September, no other tree or shrub displays such a brilliance in color and blooms so abundantly as the Crape-Myrtle (*Lagerstroemia indica*). Though a deciduous species and without fragrance, it is found in all gardens, forming the background of groups of Bridal-Myrtles and dense specimens of [*Michelia figo*]. It is an indescribably beautiful object in my garden from late in May to October. Its huge trusses of brilliant rose-colored flowers contrast charmingly with the dark foliage of the evergreens. There are purple, lilac and white forms. All are beautiful, but the rose-colored variety is the most exquisite. Though widely cultivated in India, the Crape Myrtle is probably a native of China.

Cycads Always Attract Attention

Near my house are two plants which always attract the attention of visitors. They are both extremely ornamental, and both belong to the Cycad family. One of them is *Dioon edule* from Mexico. Its leaves are hard and spiny, reminding almost of metal, and when its long male cone, covered with a white wooly substance, is in flower, usually in September and October, the rather unpleasant musty odor pervades the air for a great distance. My specimen has a very thick, short, massive trunk, which is completely covered with the Resurrection Fern [*Polypodium polypodioides*]. The specimen is a picture of health and beauty and is probably over a hundred years old. It was bought by the late Alexander Mitchell of Milwaukee in Edinburgh, Scotland, in 1871. After his death it came into my possession, and I sent it to Florida in 1897, where it since has grown. It was quite a large specimen when purchased in Europe.

The other plant is *Cycas circinalis,* a native of India. This specimen came from Horticultural Hall, Fairmount Park, Philadelphia. There is nothing in my garden that can compare with it in dense growth, grace and refined beauty. It is about 6 feet tall, and each leaf measures 6 feet in length and 18 inches in width. Each summer two sets of leaves are produced, 25 to 26 in each set, and one looking just like the other. I do not know of a more elegant and symmetrical plant. The young leaves show a most beautiful light glaucous color, becoming dark glossy-green towards winter. Unfortunately this species is very tender. The trunk has, however, never been injured, and young leaves appear again after the weather has become warm, usually in April. This Cycad is extremely rare in our gardens, as it is not in the trade, and when a specimen is offered the price is usually a very high one. I have planted *Zamia floridana,* our native Coontie, and the more robust but very tender *Z. furfuracea* near it. The latter was a present from my friend, Mr. Walter N. Pike, for a number of years the able and enthusiastic editor of the ornamental department of the *Florida Agriculturist.*

I also have a most exquisite specimen of *Cycas pectinata,* a native of Nepal, Assam, Martaban, where it grows in pine forests at 2,000 feet elevation. It is hardier than the former, the leaves are longer (7 to 8 feet), and they have longer stems. The central leaves are more upright, but elegantly recurved. It is not quite so dense as *Cycas circinalis,* though equally beautiful and stately. The specimens are female plants. I have never succeeded in adding a male plant to my collection. A fine small plant of *Cycas siamensis,* which I have raised from seeds received from the Hong Kong Botanical Garden, and which proved to be perfectly hardy, was unfortunately lost by carelessness. Of *Cycas media,* an Australian species, I have a fine young plant, added to my collection by Dr. George T. Moore of the Missouri Botanical Garden, while my large specimen plant of *C. pectinata* came from Dr. John Macfarlane, from the Botanical Garden of the University of Pennsylvania. From Horticultural Hall, Fairmount Park, Philadelphia, I also received two fine specimens of the beautiful *Ceratozamia mexicana,* a very elegant Cycad, the young leaves of which show a beautiful rosy-bronze hue.

From Dr. George T. Moore came *Dioon spinulosum,* much more graceful than *D. edule,* and *Encephalartos caffer,* a very dense and stately South African species. The small *Bowenia spectabilis* from Queensland and *Macrozamia spiralis,* also from Australia, are perfectly hardy here, both requiring shade. There are several old specimens of the latter species in the garden of the late E. H. Hart at Federal Point. Though I have made many attempts to add new material to my Cycad collection, I have been only successful in gathering about a dozen species in the course of thirty years, a small fraction of the total number. Of our native *Zamia floridana* I collected about three hundred fine specimens, about eight miles north of Ormond, in the deep shade of moist hammock woods. [See also Propagation of Cycads from Cuttings in the companion volume.]

In the foregoing I have only attempted to give a rough outline of my garden. I have not even mentioned the strictly tropical plants, such as *Hibiscus rosa-sinensis, Tecoma stans, Tabernaemontana coronaria,* the Allamanda and Bauhinias and others which add an indescribable charm to the grounds when in bloom. The hardy climbers, like [*Macfadyena unguis-cati*], *Trachelospermum jasminoides,* and the tender liana-like [*Pyrostegia venusta*], flowering in midwinter, the blue *Solanum azureum* and the vigorous *Solanum wendlandii,* the fragrant *Quisqualis indica,* the very beautiful *Petrea volubilis* and *Bougainvillea glabra* 'Sanderiana' can only be mentioned. The collection of Hippeastrums (Amaryllis), which I have grown and cross-bred since 1879, is one of the grand sights when in bloom, in March and April.

The thousands of tourists and winter sojourners who arrive at Palm Cottage Gardens in winter get only a faint impression of the real beauty of the distinct foliage plants under the half shade of my lath house. In summer, during the rainy season, and in September and October, the whole place is like a veritable dreamland. At this time about all the tropical plants are in full bloom. The Fancy-leaved Caladiums, however, are the main attraction from June to November. I usually plant 250,000 Caladiums every year. My collection consists at present of about 1,500 named varieties. The beds are 200 feet long and 10 feet wide.

No pen and no pencil can give an idea of the indescribable beauty of these color masses when at their best. The color ranges from the purest white to the deepest red, and from the most delicate transparent bluish and pinkish-white to the deepest translucent claret, scarlet and purple. Some of the colors sparkle and scintillate like precious stones or like the plumage of the humming birds. There is nothing in the whole floral kingdom that can compare with this brilliancy and beauty. All my flower and plant loving friends, even those indifferent to the beauties of nature, are carried away when they come upon the Caladium masses. They only have an eye for these color effects, and seem to have lost all interest in the rest of my plant treasures.

My garden, more natural than artistic, is my paradise. No words can express the delights and pleasures, the enthusiasm and inspiration it affords. The dreams of my younger days have been realized. Here I find rest and tranquility in this time of hate and unrest. Here I find peace and happiness. While writing these lines (September 5) I hear the belated call-notes of the chuck-will's-widow, and during the day the young mocking-birds sing on all sides their soft, sweet notes, very different from the loud and exhilarating spring song. Numerous cardinal redbirds flit through the dense growth of the Oleasters. During the night the various sounds in the Giant Bamboo [*Bambusa oldhamii*] near my bedroom window appeal to me as a message Nature has to deliver,—a message of hope and love. The rustling in the large fan-shaped leaves of the Sabals and the sighing in the pines sound like a consolation. And in the morning when I awake my eyes fall on a beautiful specimen of *Butia* [probably *B. bonnetii*] with its lovely crown of leaves and its trunk embellished with a dense growth of foliage of the Golden Polypody (*Phlebodium aureum*).

When at my desk in my study, I enjoy on one side the beauty of a large Magnolia, the elegance of large tufts of Bamboos and Palms and on the other side a vista through the foliage displays the rippling waters of the lake, while still another view shows a large group of various West Indian Cabbage Palms. Wherever I may occupy a position on the verandah beautiful views of rare and handsome plants delight the eye. But after all, flowers and plants, and even Palms and Bamboos and Cycads, are comparatively worthless unless we talk about them, read about them, dream about them and bring them at times into the very midst of our intellectual being. The interest in each plant is infinitely increased if we know something about its history. [For more about palms and cycads please see companion volume.]

How many of those who ramble through a fine Florida garden pause to ask where the different plants come from, what their natural habitats are like, and who discovered, collected and introduced them into cultivation. To him its scientific name sounds like a poem. The Cannon-ball Tree, the Tamarind, the Royal Poinciana, the Fiddle-wood Tree, the banjo-leaved Fig and a host of others always bring these points vividly before my mind. The names of celebrated naturalist travelers, such as Wallis and Roezl, Fortune and Maries, Hartweg and Wendland, Linden and André, Wilson and Popenoe constantly accompany me when I have an opportunity to study a large collection of tropical plants. The hardships encountered by these men of science, their enthusiasm and love for the beautiful, their often untimely death in the solitude of tropical mountain fastness or in the hot jungles, or in crossing a rapid stream always make the plants particularly interesting, and often fill the same with sadness. These names are to me of much more importance than those of great statesmen or warriors.

My late friend, Dr. E. Bonavia, for many years surgeon in the English army in India, wrote me: "I made a trip to Jaypore. One thing I saw was charming, viz., a Neem Tree [*Azadarachta indica*] one side covered with the rare purple sprays of *Antigonon leptopus*. It was so fine that it is a wonder this fine climber is not oftener sent up a Neem or any other tree. The contrast between the deep rose flowers and the dark green feathery foliage of the Neem was perfect." Some years ago a most vigorous specimen of the Antigonon (also called Rosa de Montana, and Love's Chain) was running along a wire from the Rosalind Club house to the center of Orange Avenue at Orlando. In graceful garlands a sheet of vivid rosy-red was displayed for four or five months during the summer, and the sight was a most impressive picture. Unfortunately the Antigonon is only a summer bloomer, and our tourists see nothing of this glory.

"In gardening there are griefs as well as joys, and in the hours when plants long cherished, sacred or old friends, are torn to pieces by a storm, killed to the ground by a frost, eaten to the core by a worm, their buds half devoured by a lubber grasshopper, or struck to death by the burning sun, we wonder if the joy and pleasure outweighs the pain. We know it does when joy returns, but till then the heart is troubled by its doubting—that mist which dims nature's dearest silvered mirror." [From Horticultural notebook.]

4

Florida Air Gardens and Bromeliads

In my rambles through the woodlands and primeval forests of Florida scarcely anything has been to me so attractive, such a constant source of pleasure and delight as the often dainty, sometimes gorgeous Bromeliads growing on the moss-covered trunks and branches of trees. Nothing shows more plainly that we live in a humid, subtropical climate. There are few species in north Florida; they become more abundant farther south, and form a conspicuous feature of the landscape in southern Florida. Orchids are found in their company and sometimes epiphytic Ferns.

Many people call the orchids bromeliads, or air-plants, and ferns parasites. This is wrong. They are epiphytes. The mistletoe is a true parasite, grafting itself in the woody substance of its host, and finally killing it. It only subsists on the life-sap of its unfortunate victim, making use of it for its own advancement, and represents, not inaptly, a certain human class. On the other hand, the epiphytes use the forest tree only as a means to fasten their roots on its bark, and never derive any subsistence from their host. A little humus from fallen leaves accumulates around them as time goes on and this is sufficient to supply all their wants.

All epiphytes are inhabitants of trees. The tree supplies them with a home, gives them a chance to live and to multiply, and protects them against the ravages of browsing animals. The small, fluffy seeds are easily carried great distances by the wind. They find a foothold on the rough bark of trunks and limbs, particularly of Live Oaks, where they germinate. Often large patches of the bark are densely covered with small seedlings, and even the smallest branches are encircled by dense masses. Evidently they derive all their nourishment from the air. For this reason they are popularly known as Air Plants. They never injure their host plant like parasites.

Epiphytes, particularly Bromeliads, form a charming ornament to the trees of the forest. They are not found on all trees, however. Our noble *Magnolia grandiflora* is rarely selected as a host plant. Live Oak is their favorite. These monarchs of the forest, with broad crowns and thick, horizontal limbs are so densely covered with orchids and bromeliads, that they exhibit beautiful air gardens. Such a forest giant in extreme south Florida forms one of the most wonderful pictures in the landscape. The botanist and plant lover always views them with interest and intense pleasure.

Even the rather stunted Live Oaks on the scrub lands of the southwestern coast regions are covered with countless number of different bromeliads. I have counted seven species on one tree. As dwarf Oaks do not afford much shade the leaves vary from reddish-brown to deep maroon-purple. Bald Cypress (*Taxodium distichum*) is another tree often with tufts of *Tillandsia* despite its rather dry, fibrous bark. When the brilliant red flower-spikes of *Tillandsia fasciculata* are at their best, in March, April and May, the cypress swamps of south Florida are imbued with an indescribable charm.

The old wild Custard-Apple Trees (*Annona glabra*), often hanging over creeks and ponds, are always covered with many epiphytes, especially bromeliads. On such trees near my home at Naples-on-the-Gulf, I have collected the following species: Ferns—*Asplenium serratum* (Bird's-nest Fern), *Phlebodium aureum* (Golden Polypody), *Campyloneurom phyllitidis*, *Vittaria lineata* (Grass-Fern), *Nephrolepis exaltata* (Boston-Fern), and *N. biserrata*. Orchids—[*Encyclia tampensis*], [*E. cochleata*], *Epidendrum nocturnum, E. difforme, E. anceps*, [*Polyrrhiza* or *Polyradicion lindenii*], *Cyrtopodium punctatum*, [*Polystachya flavescens*], *Bletia purpurea*, [*Oncidium undulatum*], and [*O. floridanum* or *ensatum*]. Bromeliads—*Tillandsia bartramii, T. fasciculata, T. balbisianna*, [*T. paucifolia*], *T. recurvata*, [*T. setacea*], [*T. flexuosa*] and [*T. variabilis*]. A few sprays of *Tillandsia usneoides* were also present.

Bromeliads are found rarely in the high pine woods; more commonly in high hammocks, and most abundantly in low forest lands and in Cypress swamps. They seem to grow most luxuriantly where the vapor rises [i.e., where dew forms] during the night, supplying the plants with the necessary moisture.

I have always admired Spanish-Moss (*Tillandsia usneoides*), though there are some who fail to appreciate its distinct beauty and great ornamental value. It is the most abundant of all our bromeliads. It forms an ideal feature in the landscape and is extremely graceful, its long, soft, gray festoons and streamers hanging from many a forest tree. It does not seem to find the conditions favorable on the branches of *Magnolia grandiflora*. On the other hand, it covers my Australian Silk-Oak. Growing too thickly, it may now and then smother a few small branches, but it never commits serious harm. In orange groves, however, it cannot be tolerated, as it interferes considerably with the development of the fruit.

I have always admired the old picturesque Live Oaks covered with the dense and long streamers,—often 6 to 8 feet long,—of the Spanish Moss. In early March the flowers appear in considerable numbers. They are three-petaled, glossy yellowish-green and slightly fragrant. Through multiplying by its hairy light seeds, it has a much more effective way of getting established on favorable trees. The wind frequently detaches small branches and even entire festoons and carries them from one tree to the other, where they become established.

Tillandsia recurvata, Ball-moss: Wherever Spanish-Moss is found in abundance, particularly on high pineland, this representative of the Pineapple family is a common plant, growing in small, soft, grayish tufts, among the Spanish Moss or by itself on the branches of trees. We immediately notice the relationship between the two species, though its growth is entirely different. The flowers are violet blue. In my place at Gotha, Ball-moss is common. It has settled even on the shingles of the roof, on the posts in my lath house and covers the telephone wires. Here at Naples, 225 miles farther south, for one reason or another, Spanish-Moss is rarely seen.

Tillandsia bartramii, T. tenuifolia [by the description, both seem to mean *T. setacea*]: This dainty little gem is a common plant from Georgia southward, being abundantly found in all the hammocks of Florida. At Naples, on the Gulf Coast, it is one of the most conspicuous ornaments of all the Live Oaks, and is found always in company of at least five other Tillandsias. The other day I found a large specimen of our largest species, *T. utriculata,* and underneath it a large tuft of this species, measuring 14 inches in diameter by 12 inches in height. The leaves were blood-red, crimson-maroon and glossy, needle-like in shape, very dense and erect. In deep shade the leaves are more or less green, but in full sun they are always beautifully red. The pretty blue flowers appear on long slender spikes.

[*Tillandsia variabilis*]: This most elegant, beautiful and very rare species is of medium growth. It established itself in Palm Cottage Gardens, though it naturally occurs in cypress swamps many miles distant. In the spring of 1919 I found three fine clumps of it in the garden, one in the top of a [*Cupressus lusitanica* 'Knightiana'], a second one on the horizontal branch of a Live Oak, and a third one on a branch of *Pittosporum tobira*, only a few feet above the ground. The limb on which it settled is scarcely half an inch in diameter. The winds must have carried the seeds from a great distance. The thin leaves are about 12 inches or more long, glaucous green, suffused with deep crimson and growing in a dense and most elegant rosette, recurving to all sides. The flower-scape is very slender, about 15 to 18 inches long, rosy-scarlet, overlaid with a thin mealy substance, with conspicuous flower-bracts of the same color. The flowers are violet-blue, contrasting beautifully with the brilliancy of the stem and bracts. Flowering late in June, the red of the scape is observed early in May, the flower-bracts are still striking two months after the flowers have faded. I took one of the clumps with me to my new garden at Naples, fastening it with other species to the trunk of a Red Maple.

Tillandsia balbisiana: This is a pretty and very interesting little species, common in south Florida, particularly on Live Oaks and in cypress swamps. It flowers early in April and is usually at its best at Easter time. The growth is bulb-like, rather slender, with a rosette of long, narrow, whitish lepidote [scaly], often twisted leaves. The flower-stem is slender, about 8–10 inches long and provided with long narrow bract-leaves, standing quite a distance from each other. The stem, as well as the bract-leaves, is rosy-red, overlaid with a white scurfy substance that gives them a beautiful pink color. The petals are lilac. The blossoms, though quite showy, are only of short duration, but the red flower-stem and the red bracts keep their color for months. The plant grows in small clusters, but never in such intricate masses as [*T. paucifolia*], which often occurs with it on the same branch. It is a very lovely and distinct species and thrives well under cultivation, growing best if fastened to the branch of a tree or palm.

[*Tillandsia paucifolia*]: This small growing species grows in dense, intricate masses, especially on dwarf Live Oaks and scrub pines, often in company of *T. utriculata, T. flexuosa, T. bartramii, T. fasciculata* and *T. balbisiana*. There are often twenty and more rosettes of leaves in one large clump. Another peculiarity is displayed in the extremely lax foothold of such a clump. Only a few small rootlets appear to support it, as it is easily removed from its place of growth. In its appearance it reminds one somewhat of *T. balbisiana*, but its leaves are thicker, much shorter, recurved, somewhat twisted, densely lepidote, and are arranged in a bulb-like rosette. The flower-stem is thick and short, only four or five inches long. The bracts on the flower-stem are thick and only a little shorter than ordinary leaves. After the flower-stem has reached its normal size it changes to a beautiful deep rosy-red color, and the bracts assume the same tint, the entire spike being overlaid with a wooly white substance imparting to it a light rosy-red or pink hue. When in bloom this little *Tillandsia* is very attractive and remains so for a long time in full beauty. It is very common in south Florida.

[*Tillandsia flexuosa*], Corkscrew-bromeliad: This is one of the most lovely and interesting of all our native Bromeliads. Only about a hundred yards from my little bungalow, here at Naples, a narrow strip of scrub land stretches from north to south. There are many dwarf Live Oaks, numerous scrub pines and patches of Ceratiolas (known to the natives only by the name Rosemary). In places these Ceratiolas form dense, almost impenetrable masses. The ground everywhere is covered by a soft fine carpet of light silvery-green, much branched lichen, only a few inches high. The branches of the trees are covered with various Tillandsias almost to the breaking point. The most conspicuous of all, the giant of the genus *T. utriculata*, with leaves often 3 feet long, is found in countless numbers and underneath it grow dense clusters of beautifully red-foliaged [*T. setacea*]. *Tillandsia balbisiana* is extremely common and [*T. paucifolia*] is also very abundant. The large *T. utriculata* is here often found growing on the ground amidst the masses of Ceratiolas. The vivid red color of the flower-bracts of *T. fasciculata* (the Cardinal Air Plant) changes every tree and shrub into brilliant air gardens of indescribable beauty.

Here among these masses of bromeliads we find a species,—new to us,— the lovely [*T. flexuosa*]. It is not as abundant as any of the former, and it is not brilliant when in bloom. It escaped my attention when I previously searched for it. In this scrub, however, it is quite abundant and very distinct from all its congeners by its corkscrew-like twisted leaf-rosette, about 6–12 inches high. The leaves are beautifully banded horizontally with deep green, chocolate-brown and whitish. The inside of the twisted leaf-rosette is deep orange-red. This Corkscrew Air Plant, as it is called by some of the natives, is indeed a most lovely and highly interesting medium-sized bromeliad and an acquisition for any collection. I have it planted in pots in a compost of osmunda fiber and sand, as well as in boxes of mulch, charcoal and sand,

and it always has started into a healthy and fine growth. The flowers are inconspicuous and there is no vivid color in the bracts. The beauty of the plant rests in its peculiar twisted form and in the banded leaves.

Tillandsia fasciculata, the Cardinal Air Plant: Florida is a most wonderful and mysterious state. The mysteries in air and sky, the setting of the sun, the bright moonlight, the roaring of the waves, the deep dense Cypress swamps and hammocks, the evidently monotonous Pine barrens, are endless and form a lifelong study to those who find pleasure in the love of nature. There is always something new and beautiful to enjoy. The lure of the woodlands bordering streams and lakes is irresistible. Especially the winter season in Florida is full of enchantments, full of ideal charms.

During the past few years we had a class of people in the state who could talk only about land sales and subdivisions. Their sole ideal of life was the chase after the dollar. Fortunately this time has passed. Never before have I met so many nature lovers, so many enthusiasts and dreamers,—people of an excellent education, high culture and refinement. Never before has the beauty of our distinctly tropical and subtropical gardens, of our palm hammocks and groups of old Live Oaks and magnolias, of our rivers and lakes and beaches been so keenly and so enthusiastically appreciated. Constantly I am approached by winter sojourners, carrying bunches of branches, leaves and flowers, either cultivated or wild, who are anxious to obtain all the information they can about them. Numerous are the letters containing long descriptions of certain plants that have been seen in their rambles and automobile trips. Many of these tourists travel over the state with a poet's eye and with loving appreciation and interest.

Almost every winter visitor, and even our Florida natives, are usually interested in our epiphytic growth,—in our Air Gardens. Not long ago I had a letter from such a winter sojourner describing in glowing terms a vivid red "orchid,"—masses of them, that had been observed in many thousands of specimens on the branches and trunks of forest trees in south Florida. It was claimed that this beauty alone was worth the trouble to come to Florida and enjoy it.

Of course I knew at once that the plant in question was no orchid, but a bromeliad, the most lovely and brilliant of all our native air plants,— *Tillandsia fasciculata.* It is particularly abundant in cypress swamps, and the tall trees are frequently decorated with big clumps of them. Late in March, and in April, the glowing red flower-scapes, which are very conspicuous and can be seen from quite a distance, form a most brilliant ornament to the localities where it is common. It looks as if numbers of cardinal redbirds hover in their nests.

The rather long leaves, narrowed gradually to a sharp point from the base, are arranged in a very symmetrical rosette. Their color is glaucous-green, but they assume a deep silvery purplish hue during the flowering period. The flower-scape is scarcely more than 8–10 inches long, brilliant cardinal-red, and the large flower-bracts, closely set together, forming a compact, shortly branched truss, are also of a most brilliant glossy red color. I have many tropical bromeliads in my collection, but there is none so charmingly beautiful. Plant lovers often gather it and fasten it with wire firmly to their shade trees. They invariably call it the "Red Orchid." Red Air Pine is another name.

Late in March, 1919, I made, in company of two kindred spirits, an automobile trip from Gotha to Naples, a distance of about 225 miles. The glory of nature was keenly felt, but it was indescribable. Everywhere in the woods and Cypress swamps, and along brooks and rivers, trees and shrubs were in full bloom and bromeliads were everywhere in evidence, often in immense clumps, nestling between the crotches of large limbs, on horizontal branches and on the straight upright trunks of cypresses. There were all the Tillandsias I have mentioned in the foregoing, but *Tillandsia fasciculata* was the one usually seen in masses on the cypress trees. There were few when we started, between Orlando and Kissimmee, but they gradually became more abundant till they formed a feature in the landscape from Punta Gorda southward.

From Naples to Fort Myers all the cypress swamps were aglow with the dense masses of this species in full bloom. I scarcely ever before had seen such charmingly vivid and delightful wildwood pictures. The delicious fragrance of the white flowers of [*Styrax americanum* var. *pulverulentum*] filled the air, and the milky white trusses of the climbing *Decumaria barbara* were suspended from the tall cypresses. Dense masses of flowering *Itea virginica* were seen in every direction in the rich mucky soil, while the innumerable white balls on dense bushes of [*Lyonia ligustrina*] were edging the swamps and watercourses. The scenery was so varied and beautiful, the air so soft and balmy, all nature in such a joyful mood, that Nicholas Pike's beautiful paragraphs in his book, *Subtropical Rambles,* came vividly into my mind: "Every sense was absorbed in the surroundings. I was feasting on the scene and feeling, as I ever do when out in the wild, that this is truly a joy-giving world in which we live. Miserable mortals that we are, grabbing everlastingly after the 'almighty dollar,' and neglecting everything great and good, passing on and off this busy stage without enjoying, scarcely conscious of the beauty created expressly to give delight to man and to elevate and prepare him for a still brighter sphere."

April 20, 1925, I made the following entry in my Horticultural notebook:

It is Easter, and I am alone in the wilderness of South Florida. In the evening I hear the surf, the Gulf of Mexico being only about a mile to the west. The loud calls of the whippoorwills near my little bungalow imbue every night with a delight that can be only felt, but not described, while during the daytime the joyous notes of the mocking-bird make the air ring with sweet music. The enticing perfume of the Sweet Bay filling the air far and near, the long trusses of the Bee-Swarm Orchid (*Cyrtopodium punctatum*) and of [*Oncidium floridanum* or *O. ensatum*], the brilliant red flower bushes of the oriental *Renanthera coccinea,* and of striking *Cattleya* hybrids, attached to the trunks of Cabbage Palms, combine to let me forget the hard and tedious daily pioneer work.

The air is remarkably soft, cool and breezy. At present I particularly enjoy the hundreds of brilliant red spikes of *Tillandsia fasciculata.* It lights up all the trees in my cypress hammock, growing everywhere in big clumps. One plant, forming a large clump, shows eight vivid flowerstems. Each stem grows from the center of the leaf-rosette. All the leaves are gracefully arching to all sides. The flower-stem is always bright deep rosy red, and the bracts of the flowers are brilliant scarlet. The flowers, violet-blue in color, are not fully opening and they are only of short duration. The beauty of the plant lies in its brilliant stem and bracts.

I went into the woods nearby and cut down a number of small cypresses which had big clusters of plants around their crowns. I set them like posts in the soil among my other bromeliads, after I had lopped off the tops of the branches. They form now a great ornament to my bromeliad collection, increasing the flowering profusely.

When the seeds ripen the entire stem assumes a chocolate-brown color. Late in summer, or early in fall, the seed capsules burst open, showing a glossy brown in the inside. The fine fluffy seeds are carried easily by the wind. Wherever they settle on the rough bark of trees and shrubs, they immediately begin to germinate. I have seen small branches entirely encircled by the dense growth of small plants, and the bark of trees, particularly of

Live Oaks, appears as being sown with some kind of lawn grass, so dense is the stand of the tiny seedlings.

The destruction of many thousands of acres of forest, caused by fires, and ruin due to the nefarious activity of land agents and "subdividers," has also destroyed our most beautiful air gardens. Dr. J. K. Small, the celebrated botanist, writes:

> Again returning to the mainland, we continued our journey southward, but only as far as Palm Beach. En route we encountered more dead gardens. The beautiful cypress heads, 8–9 miles north of Palm Beach, had been swept by fire. These terrestrial and aerial gardens, with their underbrush gone, were made very conspicuous by the black poles of the pond cypresses. Trees bore myriads of black knots attached high and low— the charred remains of the dense clusters of air plants, generations old, which only the season before were gay in their highly colored inflorescences—a sight to make one weep! (*Journal New York Botanical Garden*, Vol. 24, p. 209.)

All the Tillandsias are easily grown and kept in good health on verandas and in glasshouses. Heavy soil they do not want. A mixture of peat, leaf mold, lumps of charcoal, and good drainage in the pot is all they require. In warm weather the rosette of leaves should always be kept full of water. I always succeeded with them in pots much better than I did with Cacti. They are easily kept clean. Their wants are few and easily supplied, and they always attract the attention of all flower lovers.

To the real nature lover, particularly to the plant lover, the charms and enchantments Florida has to offer are endless. To look for these fascinations and to study and enjoy them should be the main object of every intellectual and cultured man and woman who comes to Florida. The true plant enthusiast is so much absorbed in this beautiful world of ours that he finds no time for sordid and valueless pleasures and for morbid dissipations. Nothing ennobles the human soul more, elevates it more, electrifies it more, than to be surrounded by and associated with nature's beauties. This is really one of the greatest pleasures life can offer to mankind,—a pleasure irresistible to all cultured people. I often think of this truth when I enjoy the beauty of our air gardens on the large horizontal limbs of the various forest trees. Through this additional decoration which nature provides, our old moss-covered, picturesque Live Oaks are imbued with a most lovely and poetical aspect.

Even those persons with little love and interest for the beautiful in nature cannot pass this beauty without expressions of delight and wonder.

Tillandsia utriculata: The subject of the present sketch is the giant among all our native bromeliads. It is one of the most striking and perhaps the most symmetrical of all our foliage plants. Large specimens, saddled on large limbs of our trees, are always surprisingly impressive. The leaves are very broad and clasping at their base, tapering gradually in a narrow point. They are to three feet long and recurve elegantly to all sides. There is a restful green with a conspicuous silvery hue. Exposed to the full sun, they always assume a most lovely deep purplish tint, and the stems and bracts also are more or less tinged with the same color. The flower-scape is stout, tall (3–4 ft.) and much branched. Though the inconspicuous whitish flowers are quite abundant, they are not showy. The beauty of the plant rests in its perfect symmetrical rosette of leaves and in its large size. As in all the epiphytic bromeliads, the flower-stem issues from the center of the leaf-rosette, which is always full of water.

The plant forms no offsets as all our other Tillandsias do, and is entirely reproduced from its fluffy seeds which are carried in vast numbers by the wind to other trees, where they adhere to the bark and soon germinate. Some of the small Live Oaks in the scrub, even their smallest twigs, are often covered to the breaking point with masses of tiny leaf-rosettes. These seedlings are so small that several can find room in a thimble. Though found also on cypresses, Red Maples, Pop Ashes, and various other trees and shrubs, they prefer the rough bark of the Live Oak to grow upon. Roving cattle are very fond of the leaves and for this reason we usually find these Tillandsias far out of the reach of these animals. I quite often have found large specimens in the center of *Ceratiola* bushes growing in the sandy ground and not attached to the stems or branches.

These large Tillandsias or air plants are at present mostly confined to south Florida, being found most abundantly from Arcadia and Fort Pierce southward. Before the big freeze in February, 1895, they were quite common as far north as Lake Apopka, and even in the hammocks near Sanford I have seen them, and I have been informed that they are now regaining their old territory. They are particularly abundant on all the Live Oaks in and near Fort Myers and Miami, forming a conspicuous feature of the landscape, often associated with the red-flowering *Tillandsia fasciculata* and other species.

These plants strongly remind one of the pineapple. (They are, as all bromeliads, really members of the Pineapple family, and are usually called Air Pines.) Another common name is Air Plant, and some people even confuse them with orchids and call them by that inappropriate name.

I shall never forget my first introduction to this large *Tillandsia*. I became acquainted with it in the following manner: Before the big freeze in 1895, many Live Oaks near my home place at Gotha were decorated with numerous large specimens. While roaming around in the woods in November, 1891, I was much attracted by the large leaf-rosettes and I decided to collect a number, not only for my nearby garden, but also for my glasshouse at Milwaukee. These Live Oaks were not very tall, but they were very broad and quite dense. I climbed one of the most picturesque ones until I could get a firm foothold on one of the large horizontal limbs, from where I could reach the largest specimen just above my head. It was firmly saddled on its perch. After I had carefully loosened its roots from the bark, I found that it was quite heavy. It tipped over and a stream of cold water came over my head and shoulders. This specimen—a large one—must have held considerably more than a pint of water in its leaf-rosette. Later I found that all these large bromeliads held water in their urn-shaped bunches of leaves. During the warm months I keep my cultivated bromeliads filled with water.

Along the highway between Arcadia and Punta Gorda we find many beautiful groups of Live Oaks. I have passed them time and again on my way from Gotha to Naples. They harbor immense numbers of exceptionally large and fine specimens. As I have already pointed out, the beauty of these plants is striking, and as they grow equally well on shade trees and posts, they are eagerly collected by tourists and plant lovers. Many of them are even carried far north in the tourists' automobiles. In a certain group of broad Live Oaks, between Fort Ogden and Nocatee, every tree formed a dense air garden of great beauty. Some of the plants were small, but the largest specimens could scarcely find room in a wagon box. My wife and I collected in 1919 many dozens for my garden at Gotha. They seeded abundantly and spread over some tall Italian and other cypresses, Florida Cedars and other trees. A few days ago, Easter 1927, I passed this certain group of Live Oaks again but, alas! Most of the interesting and beautiful air gardens had disappeared. Only a few small specimens could be detected. Tourists and other motor-car travelers had carried them all away.

In Florida this and other native bromeliads ought to be fastened tightly to the trunks and branches of such shade trees as Oaks, Cypresses (evergreen), Magnolias, or on palm trunks, *Grevillea robusta* and others. Mr. John Hackmeister has adorned the small oaks in his garden at Naples beautifully with various species in his accurate and systematic way. They form a very distinguished and impressive sight. I have also seen them fastened to fine large Florida Ficus or Rubber Trees (*Ficus aurea*), where they form objects of great beauty, though they are rarely found on the wild examples of this tree. Many of the still larger and most beautiful exotic species could be used in the same way.

For pot culture I know scarcely any other plants that are accommodated so easily and grow so well as the various native and exotic bromeliads. Well-drained pots and a light sandy soil mixed with charcoal and, if obtainable, with granulated peat, must be used. No fertilizer in any form must ever be applied. In winter too much water must be avoided and in the warm summer days an almost daily sprinkling overhead is beneficial.

Catopsis "nutans" [possibly a mixed description of two distinct species?]: This very distinct and beautiful bromeliad, growing often in tufts on trees and shrubs, is quite common in south Florida, particularly in the hammocks of Dade and Monroe Counties and southward. It is much more tender than all the previously described species of Tillandsias. Though neither its flowers nor its bracts are showy, the plant itself is bluish in color, being covered with a fine white mealy substance. The old leaves are plain green. Six to twelve leaves form a very symmetrical vase-like rosette. They are 10–12 inches long, quite thin and leathery, and are lorate [strap-shaped] in form.

Our south Florida plants undoubtedly have come originally from Cuba where this bromeliad is very abundant. Very likely the winds have carried the fluffy seeds to our shores, or they came in the plumage of the migrating birds. They are spread over all the West Indies, Guiana, the Amazon Valley, Colombia, the Andes of Peru, etc. The plant lover who penetrates the dense and tropical hammocks of extreme south Florida never fails to rave over the beauty of the dense tufts of these Catopsis specimens.

As is the case with many of our bromeliads, this one varies a good deal in size and form, some specimens being large, while others are smaller, more compact and denser. All the *Catopsis* species,—about fifteen in number,— are rarely seen in collections outside of botanical gardens. I saw my first specimens in Royal Palm State Park (formerly Paradise Key)—the most exquisitely tropical spot in Florida. Some were seen in big clumps high up in the trees, while in a few instances some fine specimens grew at a height of only six to ten feet from the ground.

Catopsis "berteroniana" [the description fits *C. floribunda* more closely]: This *Catopsis* appears to be much more abundant in extreme south Florida than the former. Large clumps are found on many trees, particularly in moist hammocks. Its leaves are narrower and more pointed than in the preceding species, about an inch broad in the middle, 8–12 inches long and plain green. There are from ten to twelve leaves in the funnel-shaped rosette. The plants usually grow in dense tufts on the larger branches of forest trees in dense shady hammocks. The flowers appear on long scattered branches. They are quite interesting, but not showy, being a dull whitish color.

I have been able to add only the above two native species to my collection, while the much more showy kinds are still on my list of desired ones. [It should be stressed that collecting wild plants in designated parks is illegal and that most native species are now rare and do not thrive under cultivation.] The most interesting appear to be the following:

Guzmania monostachia (*G. tricolor*): This is the most beautiful of all our bromeliads when in flower. Before the advance of the settlers who have no eye for any of the beautiful tropical plants, and whose interest is only concentrated in such money crops as tomatoes, this species was quite common in the hammocks of lower Dade County, and it is still quite abundant in some spots in Monroe County. In many places the trees were loaded with these Guzmanias to the breaking point,—consisting of beautiful, large, dense tufts, often showing a dozen of their bright colored spikes of bracts and flowers at the same time. I saw large Live Oaks, completely covered with large elegant clumps of Guzmanias, often associated with *Catopsis "berteroniana"* [probably *C. floribunda*], *Tillandsia fasciculata*, *T. utriculata* and several species of the smaller growing kinds. Unfortunately, I have never seen them in full bloom in their native wilds, but judging from the several that flowered in my collection, the large masses in these aerial gardens must be a most enchanting sight when in bloom. The flower-spikes over-tower the dense rosette of rather thin bright green leaves,—much lighter green than those of the other bromeliads growing with them on the same trees. I have always been much elated when the flower spikes, at first green as the leaves, appeared in the center of the funnel. Several weeks before flowering the green shows red lines, and finally the vivid red bracts of the torch-like flower-spikes are a sight to be remembered. The flowers are white and quite fugacious, but the brilliant color of the bracts lasts for about six weeks or more.

Evidently this species varies a good deal in its native habitat. Forms with white bracts and some with red bracts striped or blotched with white have been described from Jamaica, and in our extreme south Florida hammocks a fine and distinct variety,—[*Guzmania monostachia*] var. *variegata*, with leaves striped with white,—has been found. It is very interesting on account of its color combination,—green, red and white. So far, I have not been able to obtain a specimen of this rare Guzmania.

Last Christmas I received a package of most exquisite water-color paintings as a Christmas gift from my friend, Mr. Richard F. Deckert, of Buena Vista (Miami). It contained, among others, a wonderful watercolor painting of [*Guzmania monostachia*]. Mr. Deckert is a kindred spirit,—a lover of nature and particularly of plants,—but he is at the same time an artist of first rank and an acknowledged authority in herpetology. No one in Florida knows (and paints) snakes, lizards, etc., as well as he does. Many of his colored illustrations appear in scientific journals and periodicals of the country.

Bromeliads are all confined to America. The great majority are tropical plants. Many of them are terrestrial,—the largest among them, but the majority are strictly epiphytic, growing usually only on the trees of the forest. I have described our native Florida species. With the exception of one species which is found in Texas, all occur in Florida and one also in southern Georgia. Mexico is full of them, also the West Indies and South and Central America. The most beautiful species occur, according to Wercklé, in the mountain forests of Costa Rica and in the Andes. My collection consists at present of over 100 species, almost all of them strictly tropical.

The collecting and cultivation of bromeliads, under glass up north as well as in the open air in extreme south Florida, belong to the greatest and most intensely absorbing pleasures the lover of nature can find. If we exclude the almost always formidably armored terrestrial species, those of an epiphytic nature, all inhabitants of tropical American forests, are the most desirable for special plant cultivators. They show such a variation in their size, as well as in their flowers and in the coloration of their leaves, that the surprises are constant and lasting. There is always something new and interesting turning up in a collection of select bromeliads. All of them have a more or less dense rosette of foliage,—formal, to be sure, but charmingly diversified in the various species; often beautifully colored with red or purple, or marked with vivid red spots or streaks, or being transversely cross-barred, while in many the flowers, and particularly their brilliantly colored and long-lasting bracts form the main attraction. In bygone days I have grown under glass the most exquisite of orchids, but I find my collections of epiphytic bromeliads here in extreme south Florida much more fascinating and interesting; much more absorbing.

Guzmania musaica (*Caraguata musaica*) [*Guzmania musaica* is accepted today]: This is my special favorite,—a gem of the first water. I love it for its wonderful individuality, its rare color combinations, its vigorous growth and for its discoverer, the late Gustav Wallis, an idealist, a passionate plant lover, an excellent botanical collector and a highly educated man who sacrificed his life for science in the wilds of Colombia.

This is one of the finest foliage plants ever introduced, being a plant of distinct habit, and when well grown, either as a specimen, or in clumps, assumes noble proportions. It has but few equals. The broad, strap-shaped leaves, 15 to 20 in a sessile rosette, are from 1½ to 2 feet long, 2–3 inches broad, somewhat horny in texture and beautifully mosaic in appearance on account of their marking. Their color is bright green transversely banded very irregularly with deep green and brown and purple.

In its native habitat, in the mountains of Colombia (or New Granada), it is found growing in moist, shady situations from 3,000 to 5,000 feet above sea level. It grows evidently equally as well on the trunks of trees as on the ground covered with rich leaf-mould. The plants appear to be exceedingly difficult to import alive, and seed is not easily obtained, owing to its becoming ripe at the commencement of the rainy season. I received my first plant from the Buffalo Botanical Garden through the kindness of Mr. Henry Elbers. It thrives well either on trees or in pots and boxes here in extreme south Florida. It soon forms beautiful little colonies especially in rather large boxes filled with leaf-soil, osmunda fiber, charcoal and peat. Its stout flower-scapes appear usually in May or June. They are clothed with ample yellow and red-striped bracts topped with green, and the wax-like flowers are clustered at the top, nestling in the broad vermilion bracts. The lower part of the flower is orange; the upper white.

The introduction of this noble bromeliad created a sensation among the illustrious plant lovers of Europe. Wallis thought he had discovered a *Tillandsia* and called it *Tillandsia musaica* while the specialist, Prof. E. Morren, named it *Massangea musaica*. Ed. André called it *Caraguata musaica* and Dr. Mez, the latest bromeliad specialist, calls it *Guzmania musaica*. This exquisite bromeliad is a native of the mountain forests of Colombia, Province of Ocana, at an elevation of over 3,000 feet. Its discoverer, the late Gustav Wallis, has the following to say about this gem among epiphytes:

> I discovered *Tillandsia musaica* during December, 1867, and sent it to Mr. Linden in 1868. I paid it another visit in 1873, and saw it bearing many seeds. The plant grows at 3000 feet elevations in a certain very dense forest next to Teorama, at a small distance from Ocana, in the Magdalena territory. It is not strictly an epiphyte, since it very often grows on the soil and only sometimes ascends trees. Very often I found a profusion of young seedlings. The capsules were not ripe in December nor in January. The inflorescences stand on stalks of 1½ to 2 feet in length.
>
> The broad bracts of the younger inflorescences were very showy. I believe the bracts were scarlet, the flowers white and waxy. There are two other species which I observed, closely allied to it. The one was found in fertile woods of the Murri stream, a tributary of the Atrato, at a long distance from the locality of the first. This species or variety may now be well developed in the nursery of Messrs. Veitch. The other one is *ne plus ultra* of the highest effect. It would be a grand thing for winning first prizes at exhibitions and gaining honors for the sacrificial health of the collector. It has never been introduced alive into Europe. It grows at elevations of 5000 feet, and excels the two named plants in its strong texture, beautiful color and high growth. (*Gardener's Chronicle*, Vol. II, 1874, p. 657.)

Gustav Wallis mentions in the foregoing two species or varieties as distinct from his type as discovered by him near Ocana, but evidently one of them is only a local form growing in a different locality and at a much higher altitude. Among the plants I have seen there is a great variation, not only in their smaller or larger growth, but also in the more vivid or more inconspicuous coloring. There are many surprises and much interest in store for the true plant lover, not only in obtaining these two new forms mentioned by Wallis, but to add to one's collection as many specimens of the type as possible from the various localities where these glorious plants grow in abundance.

Another celebrated collector, the late Albert Bruckmueller, gives the following most important supplementary account of this jewel among bromeliads in the *Gardener's Chronicle* of January 23, 1875, p. 115:

This handsome plant is as yet very rare in Europe. Wallis and Roezl both sent over some boxes filled with these plants, but very few of them arrived alive. In 1873 I brought a few boxes over with me. Some of the plants traveled well, but many died after unpacking. It is, no doubt, one of the prettiest of epiphytes, particularly as regards the variegation on the leaves, which is of all known colors. I promised to send Mr. Bull some dried flowers, for none had been seen in Europe, and he was doubtful whether it was a true *Tillandsia*. After my return I collected some flowers, and forwarded them with a sketch, and it has now been ascertained to be a species of *Caraguata*. This plant flowers in January and February, when it throws up a spike, and flowers but once, after which the plant does not produce any more leaves, but keeps its color as before. When the flower is gone it produces below the stem a stolon 10–12 inches high, of a flesh-color, changing to a brilliant scarlet as it reaches maturity. The flowers are close together, white and thick like wax, from an inch to an inch and a half long, about 20 to 25 flowers forming a bullet-shaped inflorescence, which stands upright on a spike.

In places where this plant grows moisture is abundant during the whole year, but I observed they grow more vigorously where well ventilated than in the thick forests. It is only found in one small district at an elevation of about 5000 feet, and as it is a scrambling plant, the trees and palms are covered with it from bottom to top. Some of the plants, when not within reach of a tree to climb upon, have five or six shoots or branches, forming quite a clump, and I notice that they do quite as well this way growing in a kind of leaf-mould to an enormous size, the leaves being 4 inches broad and from 18–24 inches long. When I cut some off, I found a year later that the trunks or stems had produced a lot of young ones, forming large tufts of beautiful specimens. Very large plants can be formed in this way for decorative purposes, covering walls, rock-work or tree ferns, and where moisture can be conserved, would make a beautiful display. I have some plants in my garden (here at Ocana) growing among rocks, fully exposed to the sun. They do well and keep their beautiful colors. Seed is very difficult to obtain, and the season when it is thoroughly ripe must be carefully watched, as it sometimes damps off by the excessive wet.

Almost all the plants that have been sent to Europe as yet have perished, very few having arrived in good condition, but I think a stock of it might be obtained by means of seed. There are several varieties amongst them, some being light green, variegated with dark green, others of a brownish color. Some have long; some short leaves. There is no doubt that it is one of the most elegant decorative plants ever introduced. The charming and remarkable variegation of the leaves, like illegible writing, will soon cause it to gain much attention for decorative purposes.

(Bruckmueller, whose fine sketches of tropical plant life appeared in the *Gardener's Chronicle*, was murdered by a fanatic Frenchman at Ocana soon after the above article appeared in print.)

[*Guzmania musaica*] belongs to the high and very distinguished aristocracy among bromeliads. In this country it is only found in comparatively few choice collections, though it grows vigorously where Cattleyas and similar orchids are grown. It is a veritable gem. Large specimens, consisting of six or more leaf-rosettes, are particularly effective and very showy. It is a moisture loving species like most of its congeners. In central Florida it grows luxuriantly in lath houses. It dislikes our hot sun and thrives well only in cool, moist shady places. During cold weather it needs some protection. Even a very slight frost will hurt it beyond recovery. In this respect it is quite as tender as [*Guzmania zahnii*] from Chiriqui.

Though my experiments here at Naples are by no means complete, nevertheless I have arrived at the conclusion that this species, as well as hundreds of others, is perfectly hardy here and thrives with a luxuriance that was and still is a surprise to me. Large specimen plants growing in clumps, whether on tree trunks or on the ground, are charmingly beautiful. There is nothing like it. Being always exceedingly valuable as a foliage plant, its beauty is much enhanced when in flower. Indeed it is one of the finest foliage and flowering plants ever introduced. A group of the three most exquisite [Guzmanias], consisting of *G. musaica*, *G. zahnii* and *G. sanguinea*, is one of the loveliest, one of the richest and most refined, as well as one of the most enchanting pictures that can be imagined. It is a dream. But this dream comes true in south Florida.

[*Guzmania sanguinea*], André's Red Bromeliad: This beautiful red bromeliad from the Andes of Colombia is extremely rare in American glasshouses. In fact, I have seen it only once under cultivation. Mr. Henry Pfister, for about thirty years head gardener of the White House Conservatories, had it in a few large and perfect specimens in his orchid collection. With equally large and fine specimens of *Guzmania musaica* and *G. zahnii*, it formed a trio as impressive and elegant as it was refined and unique. I have not been able to obtain it in this country, and the few specimens I have had came from the firm of Chantrier in France. Under cultivation in south Florida it grows equally as well as *Tillandsia lindenii,* and it requires the same treatment. Its beauty consists in the color of its fine leaf-rosette, a striking vermilion or blood-red. It is a gem among its congeners, and forms a most exquisite object among aroids and ferns, and is of special importance among orchids.

Edouard André, its discoverer, gives the following account of this species in the *Revue Horticole*:

> I gathered the first specimens of this new bromeliad in May, 1876, in the western Cordilleras of the Andes of New Granada, between Tuguerres and Barbocoas, at a place called Los Astrojos. It was growing here and there in epiphytic fashion on large trees which it lighted up with its fine bold-red foliage. The colors were so vivid that the Indian cargueros who frequented this route, called the 'terrible road,' often gathered living plants of it in order to plant them as a votive offering on a cross formed of two trunks of tree ferns (*Alsophila*), and which had on this account received the name of '*Cruz de las bicundos*' Bicundo or *Vicundo* being the name of bromeliads in this district of New Granada, [*Guzmania sanguinea*] being named *Bicundo colorado* on account of its red color. I collected a considerable number of specimens which were dispatched with the first plants of *Anthurium andreanum,* when I discovered this beautiful aroid, but the bromeliad perished before reaching Europe. In 1880, in a new exploration organized by some amateurs of the south of France, I succeeded in introducing good seeds of this Caraguata. These produced the plants from which the description and figures were taken, which are now published for the first time.

The accompanying illustration from a pen and ink drawing by Mr. Stuart Anderson, the artist, so well depicted the habit and general aspect of the plant as to render a description well nigh superfluous, but naturally it does not afford any idea of the wonderfully rich color of the foliage which André describes as being of a "tender green tinted with red, gradually becoming in the earlier stages of growth spotted with violet-red, which changing later on to blood-red, increases in intensity as the flowering time approaches. The coloration varies in individual plants to the extent that some are entirely purple, while others are more or less spotted."

This description, while giving a fair idea of the merits of the plant, scarcely is doing it justice, and it is doubtful if word painting could ever fully picture its beauty. The contrast between the rich clear green of the base of the leaves and the blood-red hue of the foliage generally is very striking. I am aware that this bromeliad is one of the most distinct and effective of the whole family. Its grace and brilliancy entitle it to a foremost place among the finest foliage plants. Its decorative value is as striking as it is unique. It must be added that it is of moderate growth, rarely exceeding 15 inches in height by about 18 inches in diameter. The flowers are not showy, being of a pale straw color. They form a crowded spike which barely issues from the crown.

The first specimen I ever saw was extremely striking. It haunted me like a beautiful dream. It was almost uniformly red,—very bright red,—not a deep red, but of a tone suggested by the leaf-tips of another bromeliad—*Nidularium spectabile*. At the base of the leaves the color always passes into green. Many other specimens I have seen since, all seedlings, exhibited a variation in red shades that was really surprising. Some were glowing red almost entirely, others showed a sheen of purple. In still others it had a more mottled appearance, and in a few it was almost blood-red. Young specimens show only partly red leaves, the green color predominating. With the approach of the flowering period the brilliant red of the leaves increases, practically covering the entire leaf. From these remarks it is easy to imagine the brilliant character of the [*Guzmania*] of the western Andes.

The culture does not differ from that of other similar bromeliads. In its native home it grows in rather cool mountain forests saddled on horizontal limbs of large trees or on their trunks. It is a true epiphyte, but under cultivation it does well in pots or boxes or in pans, in peat, fern fiber and sphagnum moss. In former years I grew all my bromeliads in such compost, treating them in the same way as I treated my orchids. In Florida I began to get more careless regarding the potting material, and I usually took what was most handy,—rough leaf-mould, charcoal and sand. Now and then I added a mixture of sphagnum moss and musk, and for the strong-growing kinds I even used a little old dry cow manure, such as is found everywhere in the woodlands of Florida. Placed in a half-shady, moist situation they always started into vigorous growth when the rainy season set in,—all of them without a single exception, even our native air plants, Marantas and small palms.

I have found in the course of time that most of the Bromeliaceae, though the majority of them being of a decidedly epiphytic character, grow well in almost any kind of soil,—light or heavy, rich or poor,—if not of an adhesive nature. They demand an open compost. All dislike commercial fertilizer, but well rotted cow manure applied in a careful way benefits their growth very much and increases the size and the brilliancy of the inflorescence. This gorgeous *Caraguata* [= *Guzmania*] is no exception from the rule. It grows well in almost any compost of an open nature, but I usually grow it in leaf-mould, fern fiber, charcoal and a little old cow manure in suitable boxes. When in luxuriant and healthy growth, it is so beautiful and conspicuous, even in a large collection, that it has received a common name. People have called it "Flame Crown."

[*Guzmania zahnii*]: This is another jewel among bromeliads and one of my special favorites. Like [*Guzmania musaica*] and [*G. sanguinea*], it is a plant of very brilliant coloring, and as a foliage plant alone occupies a high rank. Even in a large collection of epiphytes it is always conspicuously prominent, as the predominatingly red leaf-rosettes make it always an object of brilliancy and distinction. It is not seen very often in American glass-houses, but whoever happens to possess it in his collection prizes it very highly. Its first introduction created a sensation among ardent plant lovers. It was first collected in that rich field of orchids in the mountains of Chiriqui just north of Panama, about 1870. Its discoverer was the German plant collector Zahn, who sent his plants to James Veitch and Sons of London. A description and a colored plate of it appeared in the *Botanical Magazine*. Its praises in English, German and French garden periodicals sounded through the entire horticultural world. The first consignment appears to have consisted of only a very limited number of plants, and further importations were impossible on account of the untimely death of the collector, Zahn, by drowning. The exact locality where it had been discovered seemed to be lost.

In 1883 Richard Pfau, who had established himself in the plant business in San Jose, Costa Rica,—a passionate lover of plants and an enthusiastic collector, especially of orchids,—regathered Zahn's Caraguata in Chiriqui. While searching for some rare orchids he came unexpectedly upon it in large colonies. The large trees and palms of the moist mountain forest, in rather shady places, were covered with the brilliant red leaf-rosettes of this beautiful species. The sight made him unspeakably happy. It appeared to him as if he had entered fairy-land. Beautiful orchids, dainty Gesneriads, luxuriant Aroids and many epiphytic ferns were its next neighbors, and were often found on the same trees.

Pfau said that the brilliancy of the big clumps outrivaled in beauty anything he had ever seen. All the plants were found either saddled on huge horizontal branches of mostly evergreen forest trees or on the upright trunks of large trees and palms. Some trees were completely covered with this gorgeous "Caraguata." There were thousands of small plants and there were big clumps and large specimens. Other bromeliads, especially Aechmeas and Tillandsias, were also quite often seen on the same trees, but none could compare with *G. zahnii*. He gathered a good supply and transmitted them to Europe, where it soon became a favorite with plant lovers. At present it is found in all good collections, though it is one of the most tender species we have to deal with. It thrives well with Cattleyas and other orchids, and is very successfully grown in the open in extreme south Florida, where it very likely can be naturalized in dense shady hammocks. As my supply as yet is only small, I have not been able to experiment along these lines. The rare beauty of the species charms every lover of plants.

I received my first specimen from my friend, Mr. August Koch, who is in charge of the conservatory—one of the best in this country—at Garfield Park, in Chicago. It thrives equally well in pots and in boxes filled with leaf-mould, charcoal, peat and mulch. In extreme south Florida there is not much danger of losing it by frost, though in cold nights this "Caraguata," as well as its congeners, should be removed to a plant-house or lath shed which can be heated by oil stoves. It has been successfully used by the hybridizer.

[*Guzmania osyana*]: All lovers of epiphytic plants consider this species as a treasure. As it grows well in pots or boxes, soon forming large clumps or masses of brilliant leaf-rosettes, it is particularly desirable where rare and distinguished pot plants are cherished. For propagating purposes it is necessary to take off the young growths as soon as they have attained a fairly large size and to pot them separately. The most exquisite specimen plants of [*Guzmania zahnii*] I have admired in the White House conservatory many years ago, when Mr. Henry Pfister had charge of the collection. They were grown in large pans among orchids and ferns and aroids. Some of the specimens of this species and *G. musaica* had from 8 to 10 finely developed leaf-rosettes and made a grand and unique show among the Cattleyas and Dendrobiums.

Bromeliads must never be crowded together. Each plant must have all the room necessary for developing its beauty. Only then it will show its unique and refined character. This holds particularly true with *G. zahnii*. The beauty of an orchid collection is much enhanced by placing large show specimens of this fine red-headed bromeliad, and the mosaic leafed *G. musaica* among them.

This species resembles a *Tillandsia* in habit. It branches near the base, and ultimately forms a dense tuft. Its leaves, which are about a foot long and upwards of an inch and more wide, are broadly sheathing at the base, where the color is yellowish amber, veined and lined with crimson; the upper part, as it ages, becomes suffused with reddish-crimson, the tips, narrowed gradually to a point, only being green. The flowers which are borne on dense panicles, are golden yellow as are also the short intermediate bracts, those that are lower down on the stem being larger, boat-shaped and lengthened into long points, tipped with scarlet. Below the flowers the stem bears a quantity of large, long, and narrow bracts of a brilliant scarlet hue. There are about 20 to 30 leaves to a rosette. They are always distinguished by a bright red, semi-transparent hue.

Aechmea mariae-reginae, Flora de Santa Maria: Costa Rica is a real gold mine of beautiful and distinct bromeliads. Many entirely new species have been discovered by the well-known botanical collector, Carlos Wercklé, especially in the grand mountain forests near Cartago. In a letter to the author he has the following to say:

> According to some of my correspondents, *A. mariae-reginae* is found rather abundantly in the woods near San Jose, Costa Rica. It was introduced into cultivation by the late Hermann Wendland, the great palm specialist and for many years director of the Royal Gardens, Herrenhausen, Hanover, about 1863. In its native home it is known as the Flora de Santa Maria and is used there extensively in decorating the churches. In Europe it created a sensation when first exhibited in full bloom. I quote the following from the *Gardener's Chronicle* (Vol. 31, 1871, p. 1064):

Under the name of *Aechmea mariae-reginae* has appeared at one of our flower shows during the present summer one of the most beautiful bromeliaceous plants ever introduced to our gardens. It was first exhibited at the Regent's Park early in July by its introducer, Mr. Wendland, and received a first-class certificate, and it was again exhibited a few days later at the Royal Horticultural Society's show at South Kensington, where it also received a first-class certificate, and in addition, a silver medal for its superior excellence and extreme beauty. This handsome *Aechmea* is of somewhat robust habit. The leaves are 18 inches long and of an intensely rich rose-pink. The flowers, which are tipped with blue and change to salmon-color with age, are arranged compactly upon the upper portion of the spike, and materially add to the beauty of this extremely grand plant. The bracts are very persistent, retaining their rich color in full perfection for several months.

When I first saw this noble plant in full bloom in Mr. Henry Pfister's wonderfully arranged orchid collection in the White House conservatories in Washington, D.C., about forty years ago, I could not find words to express my admiration. The specimen grew in a big pan, and there were about five flower-spikes in full splendor. As far as I can remember, the plant had a diameter of about a yard. It was associated with other bromeliads, lovely specimen ferns and numerous orchids in full bloom. The pan around its edges displayed a fine growth of creeping [*Fittonia verschaffeltii* var. *argyroneura* var. *verschaffeltii*], hanging gracefully over the sides.

It is usually found in our botanical gardens and in the conservatories of several parks, but rarely in private collections. It has been offered now and then in the trade. Its price was not high. Its unique beauty ought to have entitled it to universal recognition. In Florida it forms one of the most valuable and conspicuous verandah plants. Here it grows most luxuriantly, and it is only necessary to keep it from frost during the winter. This is easily done by removing it into the house. In south Florida it is perfectly hardy, and plants fastened to rough-barked hammock trees soon form very large and fine specimens. When in full bloom a large plant with half a dozen flower-spikes is a sight never to be forgotten. Every plant lover who sees such a plant in bloom for the first time declares it a gem. There are quite a number of such gems in this family, but this is one of the real, most conspicuous and most valuable jewels we possess. Its main good qualities are found in its beauty and its extraordinary easy growth in pots, pans and boxes, as well as an epiphyte on big old tree trunks.

As in the case of all epiphytic bromeliads this *Aechmea* holds a considerable amount of water in its vase-like leaf-rosette. This serves to collect plant food in the form of particles of fallen leaves, dust and insects, and to keep the plant alive and in good condition during our dry season. Scarcely any watering is required, as our heavy dews seem to supply all that is necessary. Only a half-shady or a shady position is essential. Fastened to the trunks of large Live Oaks or palms, it soon forms most effective clumps that are worth a journey from distant localities to see and admire. With me it usually flowers in April and May. In Costa Rica it is used during the celebrations of Corpus Christi for the decoration of altars.

Everywhere in south Florida and in other tropical humid localities this *Aechmea* should be grown. I have grown it in boxes 4 feet long, 2 feet wide and 8 inches deep, filled with peat, leaf mold, charcoal and osmunda roots. It formed in the course of four or five years specimens 3 to 4 feet in diameter, and when in bloom the picture was an indescribably beautiful one. Even when not in flower, if well grown, single plants in rather small pots make a good table decoration on account of the stiff glossy green leaf-rosette.

5

Orchid Notes

A number of the readers of the *American Eagle* are anxious to know more about the behavior of Orchids in Florida. Though I have had a large number of these beautiful and fashionable plants in my collection for the last thirty-five years, and many since I made Florida my permanent home twenty-five years ago, I never made a specialty of their culture. I added only such species that I could obtain for a liberal price and which I thought would do well in Florida with a minimum of care. I also gathered all the native epiphytic species and fastened them with copper wires to the trunks of my big trees in the cypress hammock.

I can sum up my experience thus: orchids do exceedingly well in Florida, particularly in pots, planted in a mixture of osmunda fiber, charcoal and potsherds. They need, however, careful attention, and must never get so dry in our dry season—their season of rest—that the pseudo-bulbs shrivel up. Cattleyas, many Laelias, Chysis, Dendrobiums, most of the Vandas and many others do very well, if kept in half-shady places in the open in Florida. The gorgeous Odontoglossums, the Masdevallias and other species from the high mountain regions of the Andes do not flourish in our hot, humid summer climate. Likewise the strictly tropical species, like many of the Malayan Dendrobiums, Aerides, etc., need a warm glasshouse in winter even in Florida.

In cold season most all of the orchids need protection from frost. At Gotha, my former home, I treated most all of them as I treated my bromeliads—with the exception of *Vanda tricolor* and *V. coerulea*. The pots were placed close together, laid sidewise, and were covered with dense cedar branches and dry pine needles. They need, however, frequent inspection, and must not be watered while thus stored away. It would be much more advisable to remove all orchid pots to a frostless house or shed during the winter. If a glasshouse is available, this would be the proper place for them.

Every child almost in this country knows the name of Luther Burbank as a hybridizer, or as the papers put it, as a new plant creator. He always had the publicity of his work close at heart. The public does not know that we have hundreds of great hybridizers, just as important as Burbank, in our country. They are, however, mostly scholars and shun publicity. That we have such a man, only much more accomplished, in Florida is scarcely known. But he exists and has existed here for almost half a century. He never sought publicity; a man of high culture, a scientist, an accurate observer, a scholar; a man controlling several languages—in short, a man of a classical education and a hybridizer of the first rank. The first most beautiful hybrids of the fancy-leaved Caladiums in this country came from him. A number of the most lovely crimson Amaryllis, Gladiolas, etc., were added by him to our garden flora. But his name has been placed with indelible letters in the list of orchid hybridizers.

Orchid hybridizing is the most difficult, the most exact and the most painstaking of all cross-breeding. The organs of orchids are extremely complicated and often so small that the work can only be done in using a powerful microscope. The seed is almost as fine as dust, and the sowing of this seed requires a most accurate scientific training and unlimited patience. Thousands upon thousands of the most exquisite hybrids, especially of the genera *Cattleya* and *Laelia,* have been raised by him and many of them brought to a flowering stage after years of patient waiting. His scientific work is his pleasure. He has never looked for great money results. This man is Mr. Theodore L. Mead of Lake Charm, in Seminole County. I have quite a number of his most brilliant hybrids, some growing as epiphytes on the trunks of trees, others in pots. Many of them flower during the winter. There were times when Mr. Mead's glasshouse was crowded with noble specimens in full bloom. He may, perhaps, be induced to write about what he has accomplished, and how these gems of the plant world must be treated.

Gorgeous flowering species we do not have in a wild state in Florida, at least none that can compare with the Cattleyas and other vivid flowering genera. Our south Florida *Cyrtopodium punctatum,* the "Bee-Swarm Orchid," growing sometimes in immense clumps on the trunks of cypress trees, is an exquisite orchid seen close by, and a "winter bloomer," flowering in March and April, and [*Oncidium undulatum*] has flower-stems often 6 to

8 feet long and hundreds of fine brownish flowers, but it too must be seen at close range to admire it. Both are very tender, and more difficult to manage under cultivation than the brilliant large-flowering Cattleyas, Laelias, Dendrobiums and Phalaenopsis.

One correspondent wants to know whether or not the tropical terrestrial orchids,—i.e. species that grow in the soil and not as epiphytes on trees— could not be planted and used for cut-flower purposes. I have grown the Dove Orchid (*Peristeria elata*) from Panama—a most vigorous and beautiful white-flowered species. It has bulbs as large as swan's eggs, with long narrow leaves. The flower-stems attain a height of from 4–6 feet. Grown in well drained, moist, rich soil it does well and flowers in June. The wonderful tropical Lady-Slippers, the Paphiopedilums, of which there are hundreds of species and hybrids, have only partly succeeded with me. My experience with them is too superficial and scant to warrant definite conclusions.

There are many most brilliant tropical terrestrial orchids that should be introduced and tried. One of them is *Phaius tuberculatus* [possibly *P. tankervilliae?*], one of the most beautiful orchids ever discovered. Florists have relegated it to the list of "iffy" plants on account of its difficult culture in pots under glass. Very likely it will do exceptionally well in south Florida.

I have found that the orchids from extreme southern China all do exceptionally well in south and even central Florida,—[*Phaius tankervilliae*], [*Arundina graminifolia*], and [*Bletilla striata*]. The first one is a winter-bloomer, flowering in March. It requires rich, moist mucky soil. The last one flowered even with much success in the rich leaf-mould and higher land. This spring I have had the very rare, but exceedingly magnificent *Renanthera coccinea* in flower, starting to open its first blossoms late in February and lasting in full beauty to the middle of April. It is one of the most difficult orchids to grow under glass, but here in my Naples garden it has made quite a rampant growth. Although this species is really an epiphyte, my specimen grows in the soil near a Cabbage Palm, its thick, fleshy roots embracing the rough palm trunk very tightly. It gets much sun and has assumed a height of about 8 feet. The flower panicle, flat and horizontal, consisted of hundreds of extremely brilliant cardinal red flowers and could be seen for a long distance.

I have also had the large flowering and most brilliant purple, yellow and white *Vanda teres* [= *Papilionanthe teres*] in bloom—an Indian species— and growing well with me in boxes on osmunda fiber, sphagnum moss, pieces of charcoal and potsherds. The stems attain a height of five to six feet. It must be provided with strong sticks on which the aerial roots find a support. I have also several fine specimens of [*Cymbidium finlaysonianum*] in my collection, an interesting Himalayan terrestrial orchid. One specimen grows vigorously on cypress stumps; the others flourish in boxes, filled with mulch, osmunda fiber and potsherds. The pendant flower-spikes show about 20 flowers each, white and chocolate brown.

Large beds of [*Arundina graminifolia*] are grown in Hong Kong for cut flowers in ordinary garden soil, the supply of flowers continuing for several months. I am disposed to think that most of these semi-hardy Chinese Orchids could be grown extremely well in Florida. They ought to become American cut flower specialties, especially *Phaius grandifolius* [= *P. tankervilliae*]. These Orchids grow side by side with *Lilium longiflorum* and *Chrysanthemum indicum,* and are more floriferous and vigorous than either of the other plants.

> *Renanthera coccinea* is perhaps the most striking of Chinese epiphytes, but importers complain that it is a shy bloomer. This is, no doubt, the case where it has not sufficiently rested and ripened with sunlight in the proper season. Even in China, where it is often seen flourishing on trees surrounding temples and monasteries, the plants grow rampantly, but are always green and succulent if its groves are not too dense. If grown on semi-deciduous trees or pollard stumps, or ordinary blocks exposed to the sun, it will, however, flower luxuriantly. Its brilliant reddish-brown panicles measure from 2 to 3 feet in diameter and dangle around the tree from top to bottom, a blaze of cardinal bloom. After the first dry season the leaves of the young shoots turn to a yellow-green if they are well exposed to the light; this is the sign of well-ripened wood, and they usually flower well. If Orchid growers would keep the syringe away from their plants as much as possible during the resting season, and hang them horizontally well up near the glass, I think they would be more successful with this magnificent Orchid. *Dendrobium aggregatum* is a plant that likes similar treatment, but is not by any means so fastidious. Plants of this species grow well on splits or trunks of Mango wood, Neem [*Azadarachta indica*] and Silk Cotton wood (*Bombax* [*ceiba*]).
>
> Other terrestrial Orchids that can be grown in the same way as the [*Phaius tankervilliae*] are [*Eulophia* sp.?], [*Pecteilus susannae*], *Spathoglottis fortunei* and [*Bletilla striata*]. (A. B. Westland.)

The many letters I receive from everywhere in the state show plainly the tremendous interest in these wonderfully interesting and aristocratic plants among plant lovers. Beautiful collections exist in south Florida. Since Prof. Chas. T. Simpson made it known to the world that many of the finest tropical kinds, such as the gorgeous *Phalaenopsis schilleriana* and others grow well on the tree trunks in his hammock on Biscayne Bay an almost unlimited enthusiasm has overcome the cultured plant lovers of south Florida. Dr. John Seeds has a beautiful collection and Fennell grows thousands of them at Homestead. The late Chas. Deering had a fine and large collection, and many hundreds are found scattered all over south Florida.

I have grown hundreds of Orchids in my home garden at Naples, where some of the *Cattleya* and *Laelia* hybrids, raised by Mr. Theo. L. Mead, have flowered abundantly on the trunks of tall Cabbage Palms. One specimen had, last spring, 17 large trusses of beautiful flowers and many others flowered equally well. A *Renanthera coccinea,* from southern China and Hong Kong, crawled upon a smaller Cabbage Palm, and is now about 12 feet high. It has opened its brilliant red flower trusses every year since it has become established. The Australian *Dendrobium phalaenopsis* blooms profusely every year on the trunk of a red Maple, and so does *Dendrobium nobile* and many of the finer Epidendrums. A number of the large flowering hybrid Cattleyas flower equally well. These specimens were all fastened to the trunks by wire, without even a trace of moss or peat.

It may be of interest to many of my readers to quote an article in the *Garden* by the late Geo. Syme, who has been connected with the Botanic Garden in Jamaica. Mr. Syme writes:

Peregrine remarks in the *Garden*: "It is an open question whether the kind of compost used for potting Orchids is a matter of so much importance as some think. No doubt Orchids must have some kind of rooting material, but what it is they actually subsist upon nobody seems to know. . . . It cannot be right under our dull skies (in England) and artificial conditions to put such plants in a spongy mass of peat and sphagnum, [in] which nine out of every ten Orchids are potted, resulting in ill-ripened and barren bulbs, of which one hears so many complaints. . . . A bulb set upon a bare board, covered by a thin coating of sphagnum moss, seems as much at home as anywhere else, and is much better under command, both at the growing and resting periods."

From somewhat extensive observations on the habits of Orchids in Jamaica, I have reason to believe that much truth is embodied in these quotations, as the bulk of the evidence presented in the following notes will show. It may be well to state at the outset that while Jamaica in a general way is subject to heavy rains, it does not follow that the Orchids, even of the higher mountains, are always saturated with moisture. They are frequently subjected to protracted droughts. The rainy seasons of the year extend through the months of May and October with frequent, but uncertain showers between.

Our species of Orchids, generally speaking, do not like deep shade,— certainly not those that possess large attractive flowers. The exceptions to this rule are probably not worthy a place in an extensive collected selection. They like plenty of diffused light, such as is to be had on the skirts of the forest or on mountain sides and ribs where the trees are seldom so dense and the direct rays of the sun strike them for a longer or shorter time daily. I never find epiphytic Orchids growing naturally where moisture in any great measure can possibly lodge long, or at any rate so long as to affect the plants prejudicially; not even when they become sub-epiphytic in their habits and affect on rocks or banks, for when on the latter there is usually only a sufficiency of soil overlying the subjacent rock bed to cover their horizontally creeping stems and roots. But wherever these epiphytes are growing, whether on the vertical bole, horizontal branches, or in their forkings, there are to be found little stay-points or crevices in the rifted bark, or under mosses, Jungermannias, and lichens where a lodgement is given to particles of decayed vegetable matter that are during rains washed from the higher reaches of the trees. In these crevices the Orchid roots not only find welcome sustenance, but often partial protection from the glare of the sun.

We have here species which seem to covet direct exposure to the sun's rays, while others are obviously happy on a north aspect on the boles of usually much isolated, sparsely branched trees. Other species there are, but confessedly of rather small dimensions, which affect the twigs or smaller branches of trees, and especially luxuriant and numerous are they on decayed twigs, which are held in position by hinges formed of the Orchid roots passing splint-like backward to the live branches, of which until lately the decayed portions formed extensions. Thus bound, these decayed twigs last and dangle there doubtless for years. The Orchids seated on them are for the most part composed of one or two full-grown fertile plants and numerous tiny seedlings, which latter have germinated since decay not only commenced, but when it was well advanced in the tree twigs, so that we have here an instructive lesson to the effect that well decayed vegetable matter, however small in quantity, in all probability contains the essential food of such plants.

In my peregrinations after plants I frequently come across trees that are almost completely covered,—trunks and branches,—by a promiscuous collection of Orchids and Bromeliads, and by way of spreading undergrowth masses, Jungermannias and lichens. Such trees are almost invariably stunted and less vigorous than their fellows, as shown by their short growth and sparse foliage. This starved condition might be attributed to the effects produced by such a motley host of squatters, but I prefer to consider it otherwise and attribute the presence of Orchids, Bromeliads, etc., to finding a suitable nurse-bed and resting-place on trees whose vegetative vigor was, for some time previously, lowered by the effects of hurricanes or the premature giving out of their food supplies. I have also observed that there are very few of our so-called epiphytic Orchids but what frequently find a befitting roothold on rocks, and I am further enabled to state that in a general way such plants are seemingly more "at home" than are affiliated members on the most suitable trees. This is especially true of plants that are established on fossiliferous limestone rocks.

This system of rocks has an extensive range in Jamaica, and where exposed gives to the region a most singular aspect. They are known as honeycombed rocks, from the curious structure of the cells, often of considerable size, composing the mass. They seldom present a smooth surface, but nearly always a series of pockets of variable diameter and depth which not infrequently extend quite through the block. In the interior ranges of the island, at least, the system since its formation has been much disturbed and shattered. Over the irregularities and into these innumerable cells the Orchid roots easily wander and dip where vegetable mold, formed by the decay of leaves from the overhanging trees, is in store for them. Besides this, the probability is great that, assisted by the influences of the elements, the Orchid roots in some measure dissolve and assimilate the fertile limestone as food.

Some such action as this and some such tissue-rearing food supply only can account for the literal acres of unusually large and luxuriant plants of such species as [*Encyclia cochleata*] and *Brassia maculata* as I have seen growing in communities on the rocks. The first of these species (also quite common in South Florida), when growing on trees and ordinary rock (in contradistinction to the limestone), almost invariably develops two leaves to each pseudo-bulb or branch, so that it is a characteristic vegetative condition. But, curiously enough, it is broken through in case of the plants growing on the honey-comb limestone referred to, inasmuch as these generally produce three, and not infrequently four leaves to each branch. Setting aside for the moment influences of a more practical kind, have we not in these limestone-reared plants of [*Encyclia cochleata*], with their branches terminated by three or four leaves instead of two, the initial yet perhaps incipient step toward the creation of a local variety?

There is in plants what may be termed a specific vigor which is embraced in the general part and average dimensions attained by the specific community, and these characteristics are doubtless impressed on the species by the molding power of the succeeding conditions of life. Although several species of Tree Ferns whose trunks are beset with prickles and portions of stipes (leaf-stems) which persist for years, offer what to one's imagination ought to be a good and safe roothold for Orchids, it is nevertheless true that I have seldom seen Orchids of any kind take advantage of it. I think I am not wrong in stating that ninety percent of the Tree Ferns growing here do not harbor Orchids.

Orchids are found in such comparatively small quantities anywhere (In other countries, I am led to believe, as well as in Jamaica.) that it is doubtful if there is even any competition for existence among them such as we see going on among other families of plants. Neither can it be said that there is competition between epiphytic Orchids and the members of other families. They seem to have no vegetable enemies or rivals, unless it be parasitical fungi. Their comparative paucity is probably owing, in the first place, to the fact of only a few seeds germinating, and in the second, to the ravages of slugs and beetles, and the disadvantages generally under which the young seedlings labor to obtain roothold and subsistence.

I have been struck with these disadvantages to which the plantlet is subject as compared with the adults of the same species. The climatic and other conditions must be very favorable to its growth, or it will soon perish. Not so the old plant, whose most recently formed roots generally penetrate close to their junction with the stem the mass of old and effete roots, and being themselves beneath them in contact with the tree trunk or branch, thereby not only living under their shelter, as well as that afforded by the stems and leaves, but actually in a great measure subsisting on the welcome material formed by their decay. No wonder that the old plants whose vitals are usually thus well protected should be able to survive, as we frequently see them do, periods of protracted drouth to which the very young of the same species would in all probability succumb.

I have now indicated the general conditions under which the majority of epiphytic Orchids live and thrive in a wild state in Jamaica. It will thus be seen,—that Peregrine's remarks on Orchid composts, quoted at the outset of this paper, are sound and reliable. In conclusion I scarcely need to suggest that beneficial results are likely to follow from treating epiphytic Orchids to rain water that has filtered through a body of leaf-mould. Nor, perhaps, need I point out that pieces of porous limestone might probably be beneficially substituted for ordinary crocks and layers of sphagnum for many of the Orchids cultivated in pots under glass. Even irregular blocks of such limestone might advantageously take the place of clay pots in many instances.

As for growing many exquisite orchids in our south Florida hammocks and gardens on tree trunks, we probably can also grow them on the honey-combed limestone rock of the lower east coast. At least it would be a valuable experiment to use pieces of this limestone rock in the compost usually put into the pots when planting orchids.

South Florida is the only place in our country where we are able to grow these wonderfully noble and aristocratic plants in the open air, provided some protection is given should the weather reach near the freezing point. Of about 50 species and hybrids of the finest orchids in my hammock at Naples not one specimen was injured during the past two winters (1927, 1928), when Mango Trees and evergreens were somewhat injured and some of the tender *Ficus* species were cut down to the ground. I grew all my orchids with many tropical bromeliads, partly in pots and boxes and partly on tree trunks. Those on the trees, after they have sent their network of roots along the crevices of the trunk, scarcely need any attention at all. They grow exposed, flower and seed regularly and are always pictures of health.

Since it became generally known that hundreds of the most exquisite orchids can be grown successfully in the open air in south Florida my correspondence has become so large that I find it impossible to answer all inquiries. The fact that Mr. Fennell of Homestead, Fla., grows thousands of them in his lath house, and that Dr. John Seeds also takes care of thousands in his garden at Miami has acted as a sensation to northern plant lovers and gardeners.

It is a peculiar fact that Mr. Theodore L. Mead's work as a hybridizer of orchids for the past 35 or 40 years has not met with the wide recognition it should have found. But Mr. Mead, whose home is at Lake Charm in Seminole County, grew his plants under glass. I have grown orchids,—mostly Cattleyas, Laelias, Vandas and Aerides,—in my lath house at Gotha. All were in pots or baskets. They grew exceeding well during the months from March to November. When one of the cold spells came I huddled them together and covered them with thick layers of Spanish Moss. I scarcely ever lost a plant, but I soon found that this covering with moss, pine-needles and cedar branches mutilated the leaves.

When I decided, after the big freeze, early in February of 1917, to start again my pioneering life 250 miles south at Naples in Collier County, I had particularly my commercial crop, the fancy-leaved Caladiums and the orchids in mind. I had seen wonderful masses of Cattleyas, Dendrobiums and Phalaenopsis in Prof. Chas. T. Simpson's garden and hammock on Biscayne Bay in full bloom. All were tightly fastened to the trunks of large, dense forest trees where they flowered with the greatest vigor. I especially admired *Phalaenopsis schilleriana*, a most wonderful beautiful orchid with mottled leaves and brilliant and fragrant flowers from the Philippines.

When I started my "Garden of Solitude" at Naples I fastened tightly to the rough bark of many trees—mostly Red Maple—quite a number of *Dendrobium nobile, Dendrobium phalaenopsis, Dendrobium thyrsiflorum* and many of the hybrid Cattleyas and Laelias from Mr. Mead. All grew well, even on the stems of the Cabbage Palm, soon forming big clumps. One of the hybrid Cattleyas in 1928 had seventeen flower-trusses. A *Renanthera coccinea* on a Cabbage Palm has grown 15 feet tall and forms a mass of stems, leaves and healthy succulent roots in the crown of the palm. It begins to flower in March and the large trusses of vivid red blossoms are extremely showy.

I have a fine lot of [*Papilionanthe teres*] in a cypress box, 4 feet long and 2 feet wide, planted in a compost of osmunda fiber, mixed with charcoal, broken pots and some sphagnum moss. The [*Papilionanthe*] flowers most profusely in April. In similar boxes I grew masses of Dendrobiums, Aerides, Saccolabiums, Cattleyas, Laelias, Catasetums, Coelogynes (*C. pandurata*, etc.) and *Ansellia africana*. All these orchids have never suffered from cold in

Collier County, though we had in January, 1927, and again in January, 1928, quite a little frost in this region. I never have succeeded with Cypripediums, but all the Calanthes and [*Phaius tankervilliae*] do exceedingly well. None of the Odontoglossums, Masdevallias and other orchids from high mountain regions can be grown in Florida.

While I roamed around in the Big Cypress near my present home I often discovered immense specimens of *Cyrtopodium punctatum* in the very tops of tall cypress trees. There are not many of these giants found in the woods, though smaller clumps are not rare. I had to fell two of the trees in order to get the entire plant. One of them consisted of several hundred long and healthy pseudo-bulbs, and the second one was scarcely of lesser size. "When in full bloom in April this orchid is very beautiful. The long spikes,—often 3 feet long,—show hundreds of open yellow flowers, blotched with brown. It is known as the "Bee-Swarm Orchid." There are also quite a number of Epidendrums. The common [*Encyclia tampensis*] has a very handsome flower, though the blossoms are small. *Epidendrum anceps,* [*Encyclia cochleata*], and *Epidendrum nocturnum* are very common, but of late the forest fires have almost eradicated them in many parts of the cypress swamps. One of the most interesting orchids around my place is [*Polyrrhiza* or *Polyradicion lindenii*]. It has no leaves, only masses of stout yellowish-white roots which cling to the trunks like an octopus. The flowers are large and pure white. They are most conspicuous on the smooth grayish-white trunks of the Royal Palms. In the Cape Sable region, and also in Royal Palm Park, we came across masses of [*Oncidium undulatum*] and [*O. floridanum* or *ensatum*], the first one an especially large and showy species with stems 5 and 6 feet long.

The cultivation of orchids possesses a singular charm, different in many aspects to that belonging to any other class of plants. It has a peculiar fascination which few who have ever experienced it have been able to resist. In my greenhouse in Milwaukee I had a most wonderful collection of orchids—hundreds of them,—and some in very large specimens. I began only with a few and soon found that the only limit to my wishes and possessions was to be found in the length of my purse. Yet to have a good collection of orchids it is not necessary to spend much money. These plants are, however, since the Federal Horticultural Board has put an embargo on them, four or five times more expensive at present than when I started my collection in 1890. At that time I could buy a nice *Cattleya mossiae* or a *C. trianae* for about $1.50 each; at present they cannot be purchased for less than $5.00 each. Some of them are ten times as high.

Orchids are therefore much rarer at present than they used to be, and their culture is for this reason confined to the wealthy and to the passionate lovers of these plants. Years ago, when big importations of orchids reached New York, it was quite a simple matter to purchase a whole box of various species for about $50.00. There were sometimes 100 or more plants in such a consignment. They were dry and often looked of little promise, but most of them, when properly treated, began to grow and formed in time beautiful specimens.

In bygone days it was supposed that because orchids mostly came from tropical countries, great heat was necessary for their culture, and no one can estimate the tens of thousands of orchids which perished from hot treatment and know the choice species which thus may have been lost. As a general rule the majority of orchids do not require a great degree of heat, and many of them do exceedingly well in a common lath house in south Florida, provided they are grown on benches, in boxes or pots or even on tree trunks, and also provided they are carefully cared for as to watering. Cold winds must be kept away from them. During the dry season, from March to June they never should dry out completely, but need a limited amount of moisture all over. During the rainy season they usually take care of themselves.

There is a large class of cool orchids, such as the Odontoglossums and Masdevallias, for which our Florida summers are too hot, and for this reason alone they are of difficult culture. There are also many orchids, natives of low and hot regions of the tropics, which require great heat and moisture. But I am not exaggerating when I say that I have found the majority of orchids as easy to grow as a Rose or Hibiscus. There are only a few fundamental rules to be observed.

There is peculiar satisfaction in orchid growing; it is a series of surprises. Some of the genera are so eccentric that as yet botanical science has failed to ascertain the rules which govern them. If we have a collection of Caladiums, of Pandanus or Dracaenas, or any special genus of tropical plants, we can (a few special cases excepted), tell accurately just what the plants will do. They will develop the same kind of leaves and flowers as their parents, any variance being in size or abundance of bloom or leafage or in color effects, directly traceable to special cultivation. But who that has a *Catasetum* can foretell what it will do or put limit to the eccentricities of flowering which it may develop. As any orchidologist knows, in *Catasetum* we cite an extreme case, but all the allied genera of Orchids, in no way related to *Catasetum*, surprise one with startling developments. The time may come when all these seeming eccentricities may be reduced to rule, and a good deal of progress has already been made by those who have recently given attention to the subject. Every year is adding to our knowledge, but we have yet much to learn in regard to orchids. [Nehrling drew upon an 1894 article in the *Mayflower* written by the late Mr. Edward S. Rand, who spent many years on the Amazon at Pará in Brazil; Nehrling here cites Rand without a page reference.]

If one only requires a show of flowers let him get a few Cattleyas such as *C. trianae, C. labiata* var. *mossiae* and var. *mendelii, C. skinneri, C. bowringiana;* Laelias,—*L. anceps, L. purpurata, Lycaste skinneri, Dendrobium nobile* and some Oncidiums of the freest flowering species. All these he can grow with a moderate amount of attention. I have found the following also of easy growth in extreme south Florida: *Aerides* is a beautiful genus of Indian and Malayan orchids. Compared with our tropical American Cattleyas and Laelias their flowers, which are produced on long tail-like drooping spikes, are not very showy. The individual flowers in the spike—white and rosy-red,—are, almost without an exception, of an enchanting fragrance. This fragrance and their lovely growth has made them exceptional favorites of mine. I have only *Aerides odoratum, A. crispum, A. fieldingii* (Fox-brush Orchid) and a few others not identified. All grow and flower in my lath house without any extra care. [*Ascocentrum ampullaceum*] with fragrant rosy-red flowers in dense drooping spikes also does well.

Some of the Angraecums, with their long conspicuous spurs, and mostly winter-flowering, also do quite well. I have had *A. sesquipedale* from Madagascar. It has flowers like a great white star, more than a foot long. This orchid was brought back by the late Rev. Dr. Ellis from his first voyage. It was examined by Darwin, who said that there must be in Madagascar butterflies or moths with sucking proboscis sixteen inches long, otherwise the flower could not be fertilized and would in time become extinct. Entomologists laughed at him, saying that such an insect was an impossibility, yet on returning from his second voyage Dr. Ellis brought the moth.

Thus wonderful are the adaptations of nature. The orchid does well in south Florida, though it should have some protection during very cold weather. There are quite a number of fine Angraecums, some of them very fragrant. As the showy orchids which have a commercial value elbow out almost all the rest, however beautiful and fragrant they may be, all these species, known as *Aerides,* Saccolabiums, Angraecums, Phalaenopsis and many others should be taken in hand by specialists and private plant lovers in order to preserve them. The present day florists grow plants only for their commercial, not for their ideal value,—only such things that are most showy or are most easily grown and sell best. The old time gardeners held a much more different and ideal viewpoint.

The species of the genus *Phalaenopsis* belong to the most brilliant genus among orchids. As they are expensive they are not often found in our south Florida collections. Prof. Chas. T. Simpson had a big mass of them on the trunk of one of his hammock trees where it flowered profusely. Unfortunately this was stolen. Mr. R. F. Deckert has a fine specimen in his lath house and Dr. John Seeds also has it. Mr. Theodore L. Mead has a fine plant of it under glass, and there may be others. It is a most beautiful plant with red fragrant flowers. The species mentioned is *P. schilleriana.* The fine white flowered *P. amabilis* is now and then seen. On account of the high price of these orchids and their extreme scarcity I never had the good luck to add them to my collection.

Great satisfaction can be obtained by confining one's self to the culture of one or two genera. For instance, the [Paphiopedilums] or Lady Slippers, of which hundreds of beautiful species and varieties are known,—a number which with the host of hybrids yearly produced will soon be increased to thousands. A collection only consisting of Cattleyas, with the allied genus of *Laelia,* or one of Dendrobiums would be most satisfactory, and such is the number of species in either of these genera that one, by careful selection, could have a perpetual show of beautiful flowers.

When orchids are grown under glass, unless one has unlimited space and chooses to pay indefinite coal bills and many gardeners, there is a limit to their cultivation, but when one lives in a climate where all one has to do is to build a lath house, or to fasten them to tree trunks or hand them up on the branches, and for a great part of the year to trust nature by the daily showers to take care of them, the temptation to form a large collection is very strong, for almost the only expense is the first cost. Our orchids give us many pleasant surprises. All are generally examined once a day, yet often a flower-spike will be unnoticed, and one morning we see on one plant in the distance a mass of color where there was none the day before. Some orchid has expanded in the warm night and in full beauty is greeting the rising sun. How the buds so often elude my searching eyes is a mystery, for the plants are carefully examined. My excuse is that the buds of orchids are often of about the same color as the leaves; perhaps too, if a plant looks generally well, it may not be rightly examined. Another reason may be found in the very rapid growth of the flower-spike of some species. On the other hand, some orchids with long flower-scapes take so long to develop the flower from the time of the first appearance of the spike, or sheath, that it seems as if life was not long enough. Many of the Oncidiums, like our fine native *O. luridum* and grand *Cyrtopodium punctatum,* take months before they open their first flowers on the long spikes. I have had [*Laelia tibicinis*], which showed its spike for five months before it bloomed.

Many orchids have transient flowers. Those of the Sobralias last usually only one day; Stanhopeas and Coryanthes from 2 to 5 days; Catasetums and allied genera a little over a week; Cattleyas and Laelias from a few days to three weeks; Dendrobiums from a week to months. We have had *Dendrobium dearei* last in full beauty two months, and *Dendrobium* XSuperbiens last about two weeks, and, as on a strong plant new buds are constantly produced by elongation of the branches from the main flower-spike, the plant is practically never out of bloom. Calanthes keep in perfection until, if such a thing were possible, one is tired of seeing them.

If, however, the flower of an orchid is fertilized it fades almost immediately. The purpose of color and fragrance in our orchid is to attract the insect by whose special ministration fertilization is effected, and thus the production of seed for perpetuation of the species is secured. This effected, the flower fades and the seed pod swells very rapidly. Where the plants are grown in the open the flowers attract multitudes of insects. How often have I found a choice *Cattleya* and other showy orchid which I had expected to enjoy for days or weeks had been fertilized within a few hours after it had opened, and the petals immediately began to droop, and before night all beauty was gone.

In my orchid collection no less attention is paid to the smaller species, which often possess more curious form and strange adaptations than do those with large and beautiful flowers. To the gardener and florist who desires orchid flowers for sale or for decoration those with showy flowers alone are desirable, but for the true lover of flowers, who wishes to study their wonderful structure and admire beauty other than that given by size and color, there are a host of orchids which are of the greatest interest.

Many of these orchids are of small habit and have insignificant flowers. These, under a glass of even moderate magnifying power, are quite as wonderful as many of the large-flowered species. The time is coming when these miniature orchids will receive the attention which they so richly deserve. I do not, however, intend now to treat especially of these curious little orchids. My object at present is to call attention to some well known species, especially noticeable for singular form and curious structure.

The first which I like to bring before the reader is one which, in the beginning of the year, is beautifully in bloom. It is a *Cycnoches*—Swan Orchid—a species of a family of which the generic name signifies a swan, the long arching column of the flower resembling a swan's neck. The genus is South American, allied to *Catasetum,* and like all the genera of that affinity, is as yet imperfectly elucidated. [Rand in the *Mayflower,* 1894, p. 6.]

The specimen in question is *Cycnoches loddigesii,* it bearing the name of a famous English horticulturist, who was one of the first introducers of orchids, well known about eighty years or more ago, and thus one can see how long this plant has been known to botany, yet even now it is rarely seen in cultivation, though by no means rare in its native country.

The plant has short, fusiform pseudo-bulbs, from the top of which spring 4 to 6 broad lanceolate leaves. The flowers, which are 4 to 8 in number, are in a drooping raceme from near the top of the pseudo-bulbs. They are very large, being 4 inches broad by 5 inches from the top of petals and sepals. The former are brownish, the latter beautifully marbled with green and, broadly expanded with the curving column, they give the flower some resemblance to a swan. The thickened head of column resembles the head of a snake, and has an uncanny look. The lip is broad, trowel-shaped, whitish, spotted with red dots. The flowers last about a week in perfection, and are very fragrant. That which I have described is the male flower. Most plants of the *Catasetum* group produce male and female flowers which are of totally different aspect, and of many species only the male flower is known. A more curious flower than this *Cycnoches* would be difficult to find. Perhaps it cannot be called especially beautiful, but certainly the flower is most attractive.

There are other species of *Cycnoches,* all of the same bird-like appearance. *C. [egertonianum]* var. *aureum,* a native of Central America, has great golden flowers, while *C. loddigesii* is a native of Guiana; *C. pentadactylon* comes from Brazil. This noble orchid is found in the Amazonian region, but not on the lower river in Brazil, where it is called *Baw-nilha,* or vanilla, from the delicious fragrance of its flowers. The pseudo-bulbs are, in large specimens, very long. We have seen them a yard high, not measuring the broad, arching leaves. The male flowers are in slender, drooping racemes from near the top of the pseudo-bulb, often fifty in number, the racemes being over a foot long. They are white, densely covered with reddish-purple spots. The column and the expanded petals give the flower a bird-like appearance, but it is not as pronounced as in the flowers of some of the other species. The female flowers are rarely produced, though occasionally we have had both forms on a plant at the same time. They are of great substance, more than 2 inches in diameter, pure white, reminding one in general appearance of *Angraecum eburneum* var. *superbum.* They look as if carved out of ivory. They, too, have the same powerful vanilla-like fragrance of the male flowers. They are always produced from near the base of the pseudobulb. This *Cycnoches* we consider one of our choicest orchids. It is rare to find plants as large as that we have described, but even the smallest specimens bloom, bearing spikes and flowers in numbers proportionate to their size. We have had little plants with pseudo-bulbs not an inch long give 2 or 3 flowers, but the flowers on the small plants are always, as far as we have seen, males. In fact, the proportion of male to female flowers may be approximately stated as five hundred to one.

I have had *Cycnoches egertonianum* var. *aureum* and *Coryanthes loddigesii* in my collection, and I have now a few unnamed Catasetums from Honduras. All thrive under the same treatment given to the Cattleyas. They are best grown in pots in a mixture of osmunda fiber, charcoal and pot crocks. The drainage must be perfect. They need a good deal of water when growing, which is in our rainy season. They are very impatient of moisture during the winter months—from November to March—and are easily lost if over watered at that time. As a rule, all are easily grown, but they can scarcely be regarded as favorites with the general class of orchid growers. I have always been immensely fond of them, and their enchanting fragrance alone entitles them to be favorites everywhere where orchids are loved and cultivated.

Bulbophyllum is a genus containing many interesting orchids, mostly of dwarf stature. There are a few with large flowers, but many of the small flowering species are among the most curious of orchids. Some are fragrant, but almost all have dull-colored flowers. These little flowers are, however, very attractive to the close observer, and many show very singular adaptations. This genus has one member that has flowers which are an exception to the rule that orchids always have pleasantly fragrant flowers.

Bulbophyllum beccarii, a native of Borneo, is a species of large growth with curious brownish flowers, the smell of which is so offensive as to be almost unendurable. It would not be popular as a plant in the orchid house. The most curious of all the species is *B. barbigerum,* a plant long known, native of Sierra Leone, but very seldom seen in cultivation. The pseudobulbs are small, producing from the base a spike of about a dozen flowers. Both sepals and petals are insignificant, of a dull green color. The lip, which is long and narrow, is fringed with long dark hair, and terminates in a mass of dark filaments which move with the slightest breath. This lip is also so delicately attached at the base as to be almost in perpetual motion, and the whole flower gives one the idea of a strange, lively insect. These little flowers keep in perfection for many weeks, and one never tires of watching their quaint movements.

Coryanthes, or Helmet Orchid [to quote again from Rand],

is a South American genus of somewhat wide distribution. The flowers of some species are on upright spikes, but most are pendulous. Many of the species are Amazonian, and around Para some are very common orchids. They grow in partial shade, forming immense masses in the forks of trees. We have seen single plants so large that one would be all a man could carry. A species of fire-ant chooses these masses for its home, and builds its nest around and among the slender, ribbed pseudo-bulbs. Thus, the collector who seeks *Coryanthes* often has an experience which he does not soon forget, for at the very first touch of the plant the ants drop by myriads and swarm over everything near, and be the deficiencies of ant knowledge what they may, no one who has ever collected orchids will deny the fact that they know how to sting to perfection.

The flowers of *Coryanthes* are very large; the unopened bud is of indescribably singular shape. On first opening the petals and sepals spread out like wings, but soon shrivel, but the lip, which hangs at the end of a long claw and terminates in a pouch bearing a close resemblance to a helmet, is the curious part. There are two fleshy opposite horns communicating with glands which continually distil a honeyed liquid which drops into the pouch beneath, and thus continues until the flower fades. In Para this orchid is called "boca de leao," or lion's mouth. The colors of the flowers are generally dull brown and brownish-yellow predominating, but some have white flowers beautifully speckled with red or rich purple, and others are pure yellow. The variety of color is very great, and all, besides being intensely interesting for their curious shape, are very attractive. The flowers of all the species are very fragrant. The great Miriti Palms (*Mauritia flexuosa*) are said to be ornamented with numerous clumps of these orchids.

The well-known "Espirito Sancto" (*Peristeria elata*) looks like a dove with extended wings poised in a shrine of polished wax. The Butterfly orchid (*Oncidium papilio* and *O. kramerianum*) readily deceive a not very close observer as they float in the air on the tops of the long, slender stems. In fact, a large proportion of orchids present an appearance more or less pronounced, similar to the head and bill of a bird, and, as for antennae, tails and such adjuncts of shape, the variety is endless.

Then again, the markings of many of the flowers are veritable hieroglyphics, to the reading of which no savant has ever yet given attention. Many of the colors are so vivid and the tintings so beautiful and various that they have no rivals in the floral kingdom. We have had large experience for many years with orchids, and as yet we have to find one which does not possess attractions of beauty of color, singularity of form, grace and elegance and delicious fragrance.

Orchids are the elite of the forest kingdom. They were made for their beauty alone. Very few have an economic use. The *Vanilla*, the seedpods of which are used for flavoring, is an orchid. We have two wild species of *Vanilla* in south Florida. All are desirable as flowering plants, and they are easily grown on posts or tree trunks in half-shade. A species of *Angraecum* has very fragrant leaves when they are dry. There may be others that are useful. They are made to gratify the senses of sight and smell. Extensive as their culture now is, it has only just begun. None can tell what wonders, both of discovery and hybridization, the future will develop.

The progress made in the cross-breeding of Cattleyas alone during the past thirty-five years is truly wonderful. Truly, the Cattleyas, as they came from their native wilds in the Andes, were from the beginning regarded as the most gorgeous of all orchids. There are now many hundreds of exquisite hybrids that outrival by far their parents. The *Laelia-Cattleya* hybrids are also good, and the new *Cattleya-Brassavola* hybrids bid fair to be at the head of all. There is a future in the hybridization of orchids that no one can foretell. We are on the way of great beauty and great developments.

Vanilla: Not long ago the following inquiry came: "Does the Vanilla plant grow wild in Florida? I have seen a plant in the hammocks of Dade County, a climber, that was pointed out to me as this plant. It has bunches of greenish-white, very fragrant flowers. I would appreciate a little light thrown on this subject."

The genus *Vanilla*, belonging to the orchid family, consists of about twenty species, all inhabitants of humid tropical countries. There are two species in the rich hammocks of extreme south Florida, [*Vanilla dilloniana*] and [*V. barbellata*]. Both are very interesting, and are also in culture in quite a number of gardens. I have had them in my collection several times at Palm Cottage Gardens but a severe freeze always killed them outright. Here at Naples they are perfectly hardy in my moist low hammock.

[*Vanilla mexicana*] of Mexico [also native to Florida, unbeknownst to Nehrling] is the real Vanilla of commerce. It is in my collection also and grows well here, but never sets its pods, which contain, in their almost dust-like seeds, the true vanillin. It is in Mexico where the finest vanilla is naturally produced, as the flowers there are pollinated by certain insects. The Vanilla plant is now grown extensively in Ceylon [Sri Lanka], Java, Mauritius and the West Indies and other islands of the tropics. But in all these islands the flowers must be pollinated by hand. All the species of *Vanilla* are propagated by cuttings of the stems from 6 inches to even 10 feet long. These cuttings are either planted in the ground near trees or they are tied to a tree so that they are not in direct connection with the soil. It does not take long before they send out aerial roots, which soon touch and enter the soil and get established.

The Vanilla plants in the tropics are always trained to the trees so that the climbing stems may find a support, not only on the rough bark in growing upwards, but also in the branches to spread out. Lately trellises have been tried with good results to induce them to clamber over them. It requires at least three years for a young plant to flower and fruit for the first time, and a well established and healthy plant forty years, yielding about 50 pods annually. The pods are picked before they are ripe and are dried in the shade. The vanillin crystallizes on the outside of the pod. *Vanilla aromatica* is a native of Jamaica, Colombia and Trinidad. It has angular stems and broadly ovate leaves. But otherwise it is closely allied to the former. One of the most famous collectors of by-gone days, the late Austrian botanist, Benedict Roezl, has studied [*Vanilla mexicana*] in its native habitat in its wild state in Mexico.

I have hopes that not only the two true *Vanilla* species of commerce, but also our two interesting natives [*V. dilloniana* and *V. barbellata*], may thrive well along the lower west coast, especially at Fort Myers, if planted on such trees as the Sapodilla, the Bauhinia and some of the Showers or Cassias. The Avocado also may be mentioned and also the Otaheite Gooseberry Tree [*Phyllanthus acidus*] as supports for these really lovely and interesting climbers.

Many letters have been received during the past few years inquiring whether some of the terrestrial Orchids can be grown successfully in Florida. I have grown in rich moist ground the Chinese [*Phaius tankervilliae*] without much trouble, and in somewhat drier soil [*Bletilla striata*] did very well. These fine orchids are scarcely in the trade and they are therefore difficult to obtain. A lady in Tallahassee has grown the first-named species in quantities, and as soon as I can find out certain particulars I shall report of it to my readers. This orchid has been successfully naturalized in Jamaica, and I herewith give an account of it written by no less authority than Mr. J. Syme, many years ago superintendent of the famous Castleton Botanic Gardens in that island. He writes under the heading "*Bletia tankervilliae* at Home":

> This is perhaps the most showy of our terrestrial Orchids; and from four to six weeks ago, at elevations varying from 400 feet to 1,000 feet above sea, plants of it were to be seen dotted here and there on every grassy bank, particularly where the soil was either rich in decomposed vegetable matter or of a loamy character. And last week (some time in March) I saw it in full flower on the mountains at elevations between 2,000 and 3,000 feet. It was plentiful,—even common,—on rather dry loamy banks, where the tubers, and sometimes its leaves, were pretty well shaded from the sun by a dense growth of Bracken and Bracken-like *Gleichenia* about 2 feet in height, over which the flower spikes reared

themselves to the sun. I counted as many as fifteen strong flower spikes issuing from one tuft of tubers, and one of them bore 20 florets. It was comparatively cold up there, with a rather strong breeze blowing from the yet higher mountains. The average temperature during the night there is about 55°F. So that here the conditions of life for this Orchid are: good rich, rather heavy soil, a great amount of moisture during the season of active growth, little moisture during the day, when the plant is in bloom, but heavy dews at night all the year round; and while the blossoms are fully exposed to the sun, the tubers and sometimes the leaves, are in partial shade. I noticed that the flowers on the higher elevations were of a deeper shade of color than those on the lower.

Though this is not a very showy, but a very beautiful, orchid, it is grown in large numbers by the Chinese in Canton as a pot plant. They use the rich mud from the Canton River to grow it in and it is said that the flower-spikes often grow 3 to 4 feet high. My plant, a small clump that I had received from Mr. August Koch, Garfield Park Conservatories, Chicago, grew well in rich moist muck, where it flowered annually, but the flower-spikes never grew higher than about a foot or 15 inches tall.

[*Bletilla striata*]: A beautiful Chinese and Japanese terrestrial Orchid which has grown in Palm Cottage Gardens most beautifully in half-shady misty places, where it formed, among Marantas and other similar plants, large clumps within a few years. The [*Phaius tankervilliae*], also from southern China, formed a good companion plant to it. This *Bletilla* grows about 2 feet high. The upright placed leaves are bright green. The flowers, of a warm amethyst-purple, are produced in short racemes. It is a beautiful plant when in full bloom, and it usually begins to bloom in March. Big clumps with 5 to 6 flower-cymes are very effective. Both orchids are entirely hardy all over Florida, and should be found in every good lath house.

1. Dr. Nehrling with his *Pandanus* in Naples, Florida, 1927.

2. Henry Nehrling examining his papayas at Palm Cottage Gardens, Gotha, early 1900s.

3. Henry Nehrling and sons. Left to right: Werner, Henry, Bert, and Arno.

4. Nehrling in his "wilderness" at Naples, mid-1920s.

5. Dr. Nehrling's home at Gotha, Palm Cottage Gardens, presently the home of Florida Native Plant Society member Mrs. Barbara Bochiardy.

6. Henry Nehrling on the steps at Palm Cottage; photo by Dr. Liberty Hyde Bailey, late 1920s.

7. Henry and his Caladiums, Palm Cottage, Gotha, 1908.

8. Henry in his lath house at Gotha with *Alocasia odora*.

9. Henry and his wife, Sophie, at Gotha, 1907.

10. Flower show exhibit of Nehrling's Caladiums in Estero, Florida, mid-1920s.

Shade Trees and Flowering Trees

We live in a most beautiful state. Our climate is ideal,—never too cold and never too hot. The beauty of our landscape cannot be pictured by pen or pencil. We must see and feel its loveliness in order to understand it. The innumerable fresh water lakes, large and small, scattered over the state; the rivers with their edgings of palmettos, Magnolias and other evergreen trees and shrubs; the many deep, clear springs; the enchanting forest growth, especially in the localities where the soil is underlaid with phosphate; the charming beaches along the Atlantic and Gulf coasts; the unrivaled orange groves on the rolling lands of central Florida and the Mangoes, Avocados, Royal and Coconut Palms, the Traveler's Trees and Bananas, the glorious Royal Poincianas and the mighty Rubber Trees of south Florida—all combine to make the state a paradise for the nature lover and horticulturist. Florida is the winter home of the most cultured and educated people of our country. Tourists appear every winter in constantly increasing numbers. For many years the state has been an ideal abode for all those who love to commune with nature. And as the years come and go it will be more and more the playground of a great nation.

The natural beauty of Florida is as unique as it is lovely. Nowhere in this country can palms and other gorgeous flowering and shade trees and shrubs be used in such wonderful variety. Garden paradises can be created here that scarcely can be rivaled anywhere else. The available material is immense. It needs only a little enthusiasm, love for the ideal and beautiful, and a little knowledge to make the best of it.

Variety is the spice of life. The number of plants adapted to our soil and climate is so large that monotony can easily be avoided. Every garden should have an individuality of its own, should be different from the one next door in combination and landscape effects as well as in the selection of plants. It is the purpose of this chapter to call the attention of my readers to the most beautiful shade and flowering trees available for our Florida highways and gardens. In traveling over our fine highways by motor cars we often pass country places, town and city yards and rural homesteads entirely bare of anything like a beautiful evergreen shade or flowering tree. The native monarchs of the forest have been cut down and nothing has been put in their places. Even the century-old picturesque Live Oaks have been ruthlessly destroyed. They should have been preserved and tenderly cared for as nothing else in the whole plant world can ever take their places.

Shade trees are a necessity for Florida. Their value and importance can scarcely be overestimated. They not only enhance the beauty of their surroundings, but they render the atmosphere cooler and healthier. The Florida sun in summer—even in spring and autumn—is very bright and hot. Human abodes, be they bungalows, villas, simple farm-houses or even back-woods shanties, are immensely improved and beautified by handsome shade trees. I want to call particular attention to the fact that no native or exotic tree is more beautiful, more distinguished and noble in foliage, flower, fruit and symmetrical growth than our native Florida *Magnolia grandiflora* and Live Oak. Both are evergreens and both are easily grown. They can be used anywhere in large and small gardens, in parks and pleasure grounds, along highways and city streets. They should be given preference over any and all exotic trees. Along our high roads the natural growth along their sides should be carefully preserved. This is a most important point.

In northern and central Florida, and the west coast as far south as Fort Ogden and on the east coast as far south as Palm Beach, a most beautiful assemblage of native trees and shrubs fringe the roadsides in many places. In coming down by motor car from Orlando I have often counted at least a hundred species, among them many fine ornamental trees and shrubs. In south Florida the case is a little different, particularly from Punta Gorda southward. The landscape is low and level. There is much water and often we pass very extensive Cypress swamps. The Cypress and the Pine are, in fact, the prevailing trees. Were it not for the millions of beautiful and dainty wild flowers, and for the numerous, and often gorgeous air plants (Tillandsias) which transform many a huge Cypress into a veritable air garden, the landscape would be quite monotonous. Here it becomes a necessity to improve the highway by planting native and exotic trees of a tropical nature. Species should be selected with broad, dense dome-shaped crowns, that really shade the road, and with a rich floral display. The finest and most beautiful trees of the world are available for this region.

Without any intention to go in detail here, I cannot refrain from calling into the mind of my readers the magnificent Royal Poinciana, not an evergreen, but in all other points the ideal highway tree for extreme south Florida. The color of the large fern-like leaves is of such a light, bright emerald green that no description will enable the novice to form an idea of its unrivaled beauty. The glowing color effects of the large flower trusses in May and June belong to nature's most wonderful gifts to mankind. I do not think that the Royal Poinciana has a rival in floral beauty, when we consider its easy growth and its beautiful dome-shaped form. This is only one example among many, though the most exquisite.

As a rule only fast growing easily cared for trees should be selected. Trees of a spreading form, with upright or horizontal branches only are desirable for roadside planting. These find their proper place in gardens and parks. The same holds true of the charming trees with drooping branches, like *Ficus benjamina* and [*F. virens*] their proper place is on lawns and in parks. The East India Rubber Tree (*Ficus elastica*), a favorite with many plant lovers, is not a good roadside object on account of its immense buttressed root system. The crown, however, is one of majesty and grandeur. Our native species, *Ficus aurea* and [*F. citrifolia*], as well as the grand Australian *F. macrophylla* and the noble Asiatic *F. altissima,* are much better adapted for this purpose.

A good shade tree should have the following qualities: 1st.—It should be an evergreen, if possible. 2nd.—It should grow freely and quickly, without requiring much care. 3rd.—It should have a dense, broad, dome-shaped crown. 4th.—It should be adapted to soil and climate. High, dry sandy land is adapted to some species, while wet, undrained low land only is to be recommended for moisture loving species. 5th.—It should be free from formidable thorns. 6th.—It should not sprout from the roots.

Florida soil, as a rule, is naturally very poor. The lands have been overrun annually, in spring, by forest fires for many decades. Every particle of humus has been destroyed, and without humus no plant growth is possible. It is a futile effort to set out trees and shrubs without making the soil rich at the start. After organic matters—humus—have been added the soil becomes wonderfully responsive. The orange groves and vegetable fields are excellent examples of these facts.

No family of trees contains so many beautiful shade trees, so many brilliant and magnificent flowering members as the Leguminosae or pea family. Says Mr. H. F. Macmillan in his *Handbook of Tropical Gardening and Planting*: "That suitable shade trees thinly planted and properly attended to, have beneficial effects, physically and chemically, upon most crops in the tropics is an established fact. They help to conserve moisture and aerate the soil by means of their deep feeding roots, which bring plant food from the under strata to be returned again in the form of mulch by the falling leaves. Leguminous trees are preferable for various reasons, viz.: (1) They are usually fast growers; (2) their thin feathery foliage does not form too dense a shade; (3) their leaves have often the habit of closing up at night, and (4) many of the family have the property of collecting free nitrogen by means of bacteria nodules on the rootlets."

This family contains the most important and beautiful shade trees, not only for highway planting, but also for gardens, parks and town and city streets. I shall bring before my readers the most useful and the most superb, and mostly such that have been tested. The most beautiful member of the family for our purposes is the Royal Poinciana [treated elsewhere].

Albizia lebbek: The Woman's-Tongue Tree is a most beautiful, a most impressive tree, one of the most easily grown shade trees. One fine Sunday morning in July, 1918, I stood before a large, dense, broad specimen in one of the streets of Miami admiring its noble growth and its handsome outlines. It was full of ripe seed pods, and I began to pick a number to take home with me. While doing this two ladies passed, one of them remarking in a mirthful mood: "Do you know this tree? Are you not afraid of it? It is said to be a dangerous tree, and we call it the Woman's Tongue." The seeds I then gathered sprouted, and I have now a few nice little specimens of it in my garden here at Naples and also at Gotha.

Dr. David Fairchild of the Bureau of Plant Industry, U.S. Department of Agriculture, to whom we are indebted for the introduction of many thousands of economical and ornamental plants, speaks of it in the following interesting way:

The Lebbek is altogether the most beautiful shade tree that is extensively planted in Egypt. It was introduced from the East Indies previous to 1807, and hundreds of thousands are now planted along the roadways. As an avenue tree it is not excelled for shade and grace. The seeds are planted in seed beds, and when the young plants are one year old they are transplanted in nursery rows. Where they are allowed to remain three years. They are then "topped" to the desired height and transplanted. The first year after transplanting they need water; later they stand drouth exceedingly well. If left in the nursery rows until the trunks are 3 inches through, the three or four new branches formed make a graceful crown. The tree has endured 28°F. or possibly lower. The blossoms are sought by bees. The wood is of good quality. It grows in poor limestone or rocky soil. This one tree has transformed the roadways about Cairo into most beautiful shady avenues.

Planted out in dry, poor soil at Naples, my plants did not make any growth and finally pined away. In fairly moist soil, however, they began to start into vigorous growth at once. At Gotha they were a success on high pineland as well as on lower ground. I lost rather large specimens in the latter place by the heavy freeze of February 5, 1917, when the thermometer went down as low as 19°F.

There are a few fine large specimens at Punta Gorda as well as at Fort Myers. Mrs. Marian A. McAdow planted one out in the high school grounds at Punta Gorda, about ten years ago, which is now a very beautiful dense specimen. It ripens seeds abundantly. Says our veteran Florida horticulturist and celebrated naturalist, Prof. Charles T. Simpson: "I have a splendid specimen in my grounds, about nine years planted, that has a head more than fifty feet across and forty in height, with a trunk diameter in excess of two feet. It has attractive pinnate leaves and heads of silvery and green stamens all summer and it appears to stand well against high wind. Its leaves are retained throughout the greater part of the year, falling in the spring when the new foliage almost pushes off the old. Its broad whitish pods are, however, one of its attractive features."

Pithecellobium dulce, Montezuma's Manna Tree, Mexican St. John's Bread Tree: This is one of the best and most promising shade trees for dry lands in Florida. It is perfectly hardy, even in north Florida, as far as I know, but it is not often seen. I have raised a specimen from seed in my Orange County garden which attained a height of 30 feet in six years. Besides its value as an important ornamental tree it is highly prized for its wood, bark and pods. I am gathering together all these trees now in my Tropical Garden and Arboretum at Naples for the education and enlightenment of those who are interested in beautiful trees and shrubs, as well as for my own study and pleasure. In order to give my readers an idea about this beautiful shade tree I insert here a most valuable quotation.

Dr. E. Palmer, our best authority on Mexican plants, writes:

Fruit edible. Bark used for tanning. Wood useful for many purposes. Fine shade tree. The wood, if sawed, makes good planks for many uses and is good fuel. The bark is much used, alone or in combination, by all the tanners of Mexico. With ordinary care the bark makes a beautiful, strong, white, elastic tan—not as strong as that of Oak, but one of the safest and best tanning materials. A yellow dye is prepared from the bark.

The fruit of the tree is much sought after as food. It is very prolific and the white manna-like substance which adheres to the black seed is a favorite food with all classes, especially with those who have consumption, who eat it with the strong conviction of obtaining relief. In Colima it is so abundant that it is sold for 1 cent a kilo. At Acapulco there is an ample supply of this fruit, and in spite of all the tropical fruits on the market, it is a great favorite.

[*Samanea saman*], Rain-Tree, Saman, Guango, ["Monkey-Pod"]: Introduced by Reasoner Bros. many years ago, but rarely seen, though one of the most beautiful and easily grown shade trees. I had it for quite a number of years in my garden at Gotha in Orange County, but it finally succumbed to a heavy freeze, after having attained a height of about 30 feet, with a crown-diameter of equal size. In extreme south Florida it appears to be perfectly hardy. It is not partial to any kind of soil, but will not grow in wet undrained land. Such a magnificent, noble tropical shade tree is the very ideal for highway planting, and it should not be overlooked by those who will have charge of the ornamentation of our county roads.

Baron Ferdinand von Mueller, in his excellent book, *Select Extra-Tropical Plants,* speaks very highly of this tropical tree as follows: "The Rain-Tree or Guango, extending from Mexico to Brazil and Peru, attains a height of 70 feet, with a trunk 6 feet in diameter, the colossal branches expanding to 150 feet. It is of quick growth, and in outline not unlike an Oak. It is content with light soil, and forms a magnificent feature in the landscape. One of the best trees in mild climates for shading roadsides. The wood is hard and ornamental, but the principal utility of the tree lies in its pulpy pods, which are produced in great abundance and constitute a very fattening fodder for all kinds of pastoral animals, which eat them with relish."

The brown pods are about 5 to 7 inches long and contain a sweet, sugary pulp, an excellent cattle feed and exported from South America for this purpose. "It is called Rain-Tree," says Dr. David Fairchild, "because, after having lost its leaves during the dry season, it bursts forth into flower and leaf at the commencement of the rains."

My specimen tree at Palm Cottage Gardens flowered several times, but I did not think the blossoms very conspicuous among the dense bipinnate foliage. The corolla is yellowish-green and the stamens are light red. The flowers are grown in round clusters and their color is a deep red.

Enterolobium cyclocarpum, Monkey-ear Pod, Parota, Guanacaste: Introduced by Reasoner Bros. many years ago. Lately disseminated by the Bureau of Plant Industry. A noble, a very beautiful and a most interesting tree—one of the most strikingly ornamental tropical trees we have. It is such a noble and distinguished tree that avenues of it should be planted wherever this is possible. My own trees are still small, but there is a fine large specimen in Mr. J. E. Hendry's garden at Fort Myers, and a magnificent one in the beautiful garden paradise of Mrs. Marian A. McAdow at Punta Gorda.

Mrs. McAdow offers the following charming description of her *Enterolobium:*

> Up its rough exterior clamber and cling the triangular forms of a Night-blooming *Cereus* and the enormous yellowish and white-blotched leaves of *Pothos aurea* [= *Epipremnum pinnatum*]. At its base nestle white Spider Lilies, Crotons with brilliantly dyed leaves, while close beneath its sheltering shade grows a lusty *Bactris* palm encrusted with needle-like spines up its trunk and even on the front and back of its lovely pinnate leaves. The *Enterolobium* has been in my garden for eighteen years, and its measurements at this date are 7½ feet in circumference at my height from the ground. From there down it spreads out into great python-like roots, making it difficult to measure. Its height is at least 50 feet and the branches extend 45 feet from the trunk. It hardly seems possible that in our sandy Florida soil a tree could make a top covering an area of a hundred feet, as this one will do before the year is over. When their fine green leaves fall, these sift down among the grasses of the lawn with no litter apparent. The Seagrape and a Queen's Crape Myrtle stand in close proximity to the big tree and these two are now shedding their last year's garment and the lawn is an untidy sight until the new spring garb is donned.

This beautiful tree which I have so often admired grows on rather low land. "It has been flooded," Mrs. McAdow goes on to say, "by the salt water of the bay many times and it seldom shows any evidence of dislike for a salty diet." [She continues]:

It is a deciduous tree, losing its leaves for a month in the spring time. The new leaves, so much like those of the Royal Poinciana, are followed by short-stemmed clusters of small white flower-balls, not at all showy, but having a delicate fragrance that is pleasing on the night air, as it drifts lazily the length of the long verandah. The leaves of this tree are what I call night-sleepers, because they fold up closely just as the sun goes down and are not opened fully the following day until eight or nine in the morning. The seed pods are a dark maroon color and twist into as complete a circle as is possible and look not unlike the ears of some monkeys. Children always notice the similarity and when they find them lying underneath the tree on the lawn, pick them up and flatten them against their own ears, laughing merrily at Nature's giving ears on a tree.

No doubt many of these trees have been distributed over the state in the last 35 years, but so far as I know only three specimens can I recall to mind, although no doubt there are others that I have not run across. They take up so much room that they should be planted only in the grounds of large estates and not in city lots. I try to imagine what my baby giant will look like when it is 50 years old. Will it keep on spreading its green canopy or will it soon stop and get thick in girth like we humans do in our old age?

One of our best horticultural authorities, Mr. Wilson Popenoe of the U.S. Department of Agriculture, speaks of it admiringly as it grows in Cuba and in Central America. "A fine leguminous tree," he writes, "extensively used in the region—Santiago de Las Vegas, Cuba,—as a shade tree along avenues and *carreteras*. Of the four or five different species used on the rock road from Santiago de Las Vegas to Habana this is certainly one of the best, growing to a considerable height and branching to form a symmetrical, rounded head, deep green foliage, giving a fairly dense shade and presenting an attractive appearance. While it already has been planted in Florida, I know of no avenue in that state, and it might advantageously be propagated at Miami, I believe, with the intention of testing it as an avenue tree" (*Plant Indus-*

try No. 111 and 112, p. 907). [Leaves with 7–10 pairs of pinnae and leaflets of 20–30 pairs; *Hortus Third*, 1976.]

In my garden at Gotha large specimens were repeatedly destroyed by the occasional heavy freezes, but in south Florida it is perfectly hardy and makes an extremely vigorous and rapid growth within a few years. Wherever the Royal Poinciana thrives all these fine leguminous trees will do well.

[*Enterolobium contortisiliquum*], Timbouva: This tree, one of the most ornamental and charming of the forests of northern Argentina, Paraguay and southern Brazil, and one of the most appreciated and beloved of avenue and shade trees in Buenos Aires, was introduced a few years ago by the Bureau of Plant Industry at Washington under [Seeds and Plants Imported] No. 43455. March 30, 1918, I received a small seedling plant for experimental purposes. Almost all valuable plants which I receive are first put in pots and then sunk into the ground in place under lath cover where they are constantly under my eyes. This species was particularly cared for at first on account of its interesting habitat and history.

At Gotha almost all plants are growing with surprising vigor, and this *Enterolobium* is no exception. When I took up the collections to pack them for shipment to my new place at Naples, about 200 miles farther south, I found that it had assumed a height of over 10 feet. It had bursted its pot, and the vigorous roots penetrated deeply into the surrounding soil. Being too large for packing, I left it where it stood. This last spring (1923) I measured the tree. It had attained a height of over 30 feet, and its girth near the ground was 25 inches. Having formed a very broad, symmetrical crown and a very sturdy growth, it made a very good impression among its next neighbors, a likewise beautiful *Pithecellobium dulce*, several clumps of the exquisite Bamboo Grass—[*Thysanolaena maxima*]—now in its garb of tall purplish-brown seed bunches, overtowering the dense mass of thrifty foliage, and numerous climbing lilies (*Gloriosa rothschildiana*). The bipinnate leaves are bright green, giving a light elegant appearance to the tree. The flowers are white with a slight yellowish tinge, appearing in large heads or clusters. They are not very conspicuous and exhale a faint odor at night. The pods, formed like an ear and of a deep dark brown color, ripen here in July and August. These pods are to most people of great interest, and are called in Argentina *orejos de negro*.

The growth of this tree is very ornamental. The rather dense branches form always a shapely and somewhat open crown. In my garden it retains its foliage during the winter months, but drops it in the dry season, usually late in May. The young leaves appear almost immediately after the old ones have fallen. In its native home it attains a height of 25 meters. Its wood is very hard and is used for cabinet-work, canoes, construction work, etc. This species will be a very valuable shade tree for highways and avenues. It does not require much care after the first few years, but it requires a fairly rich soil. Its large size and luxuriant growth do not adapt it for small city lots. [Leaves commonly with 3–14 pairs of pinnae and leaflets of 10–15 pairs; *Hortus Third*, 1976.]

Dalbergia sissoo (*Amerimnon sissoo*) [*D. sissoo* is the accepted name], Sissoo: This beautiful deciduous leguminous tree was introduced into Florida many years ago by Reasoner Bros., of Oneco, Fla., but I have never seen it outside of my garden. It is perfectly hardy at Palm Cottage Gardens and thrives with equal vigor here at Naples. Lately it has again been disseminated by the Bureau of Plant Industry. The Sissoo reaches a height of 60 to 80 feet and is of a handsome form with very beautiful foliage. In spite of its being leafless during winter, it is a most important tree for highway planting, its fine broad crown being the very ideal of a good shade tree.

The flowers I have never seen. It is easily raised from seed and cuttings, and can safely be transplanted when of large size, and is of rapid growth. Being a native of northern India and Afghanistan, it may prove hardy all over south and middle Florida. The late E. H. Hart had fine specimens in his garden at Federal Point, Fla., many years ago. "Its wood is of great value, being very elastic, seasons well, does not warp nor split, is easily worked, and takes a fine polish" (Ferd. von Mueller). The trees grow most luxuriantly on high, dry, poor land. In fact, it improves sterile soils in a most wonderful way.

Dalbergia latifolia: This is also an East Indian species, known as Black Wood. It is deciduous, but very ornamental, when well grown. I have raised it from seed, but the plants were killed by the heavy freeze of 1895. I cannot speak from experience regarding its economic value, but I think it will make a fine shade tree. The wood is hard and tough, and in demand for fine furniture.

Mahogany: How many woods are worked under by thy name! Prof. Dixon enumerates no fewer than 45 kinds of timber which take the names belonging to *Swietenia mahagani* and *S. macrophylla*. At the present time it is doubtful whether any Mahogany comes from either of the regions in which these species grow. The former is found in Cuba, south Florida and St. Domingo, the latter in Honduras, Nicaragua and other central American states. Prof. Dixon, on the basis of his microscopic examinations, suggests as "a definition of Mahogany—all red or red-brown timbers in which the fibers of adjacent layers cross obliquely."

There is a beautiful illustration of a very dense and broad specimen of *Swietenia mahagani* in the *Gardener's Chronicle* (vol. 65, 1919). This tree grows vigorously and beautifully in extreme south Florida in gardens. A tall and large specimen is found in the grounds of the Royal Palm Hotel at Fort Myers and there are others at Coconut Grove and elsewhere. A well-grown specimen is a beauty, forming a noble and dense shade tree in rather good soil. The tree is known in south Florida under the name of Madeira, and the Madeira hammocks formed a most interesting sight in bygone days. Dr. John Gifford has given us a very exhaustive account of this fine and noble tree in one of his books about south Florida trees. It should be planted largely for shade along our highways.

[*Hibiscus elatus*], Cuban Bast: A most interesting evergreen, Hibiscus-like seaside tree, common in Cuba, but also found, according to Prof. Chas. T. Simpson, along the shores of Biscayne Bay. I have never seen it wild, but I admired large and beautiful specimens at Mr. Chas. Deering's now abandoned place at Buena Vista, near Miami. These Cuban Bast trees stood in rather moist and rich soil and often directly at the edge of ponds and artificial lakes. I admired their broad and spreading form, the large cordate leaves and the masses of buff-colored flowers, which changed to a peculiar brownish-red later in the day.

Mr. R. F. Deckert, the naturalist, and an expert horticulturist in this domain, sent me seeds of this and the following species, and most all of them germinated after about a week. I have now numerous young plants that flower most profusely all the time after they have reached a height of about three feet. It is easily transplanted and is a rapid grower. Though not one of the tropical evergreens that stands in the first rank along ornamental lines, it is extremely interesting and very characteristic, being well adapted as a border tree for seaside planting.

In our tropical parks, where a large variety of trees and shrubs are of importance, the Cuban Bast should always find a place. How far north it will be hardy I do not know, but I think that Punta Gorda on the West Coast, and Fort Pierce on the East Coast will probably form its northern limit in garden and beach ornamentation. The bast of this tree is largely used in Cuba for cordage. The bales of Tobacco for export are usually covered with the square slats of the flowering spathes of the Royal Palm, and are tied with the coarse but very strong, roughly twisted bast of this tree.

[*Hibiscus tiliaceus*], Mahoe, Fau: The Mahoe (another seaside tree), according to Dr. J. K. Small, probably a native of the Old World tropics, grows on the shores of the Everglade Keys and Florida Keys. This species is more ornamental than the former, and is a great success in all south Florida gardens, even in those along the sea shore and on poor and rather dry pineland. Its dark green, shiny, heart-shaped leaves remind one of those of the linden (*Tilia*—hence its specific name). In the extensive grounds of Mr. Chas. Deering the Mahoe was largely used along ponds and water-courses. Here it mostly grew in hedge-form, the shrubs standing clipping very well and is used where other plants would not thrive.

My friend, Mr. R. F. Deckert, a passionate lover of tropical trees and shrubs sent me seeds, from which I have raised quite a number of fine plants. All of them are constantly in bloom, though most of them are only 2 to 3 feet high. The flowers are bright yellow in the morning and change to a light orange in the afternoon. The next morning they are almost entirely red before dropping. It is not a tree that is much admired by the general public. Just now (Sept. 10, 1925) there are several fine and dense specimens here in my garden in bloom. I counted 25 open bright yellow flowers on one small bush, not exceeding 3 feet in height, and around it quite a number of the brilliant Catesby Lilies held their open and broad chalices up to the blue sky.

Dr. W. E. Safford, one of our great and noble scientific Americans, and years ago vice-governor of the Island of Guam, has the following to say about the Mahoe in his charming volume, *Useful Plants of Guam*:

In Guam this species is abundant. The natives make a cordage of its inner bark, nearly every family being provided with rope-making appliances. The ropes are used for halters and lines for tethering cattle and carabaos, for harness and for cables for ferrying the bamboo balsas, or rafts, across the mouths of the rivers of the east coast of the island.

The strength and durability of the ropes are much increased by tarring. If they are not thus treated and left uncared for they are soon ruined by the attack of insects. The Caroline Islanders split the inner bark into narrow strips, which they soak and scrape, and weave into breechcloths or aprons for the women. In Tahiti also mats are made of it. The wood is light, durable, and flexible and can be readily bent into any desired shape. Thus is suitable for frames of boats. The lightness of the wood fits it for outriggers of canoes. In Samoa most of the outriggers are of Fau-wood.

Cassia fistula, Golden Shower: This most beautiful tropical tree has not only flowered in the garden of Thomas A. Edison in Fort Myers, on the shores of the Caloosahatchee, but it has ripened its long most conspicuous seed pods in great profusion. Few trees are more ornamental and certainly none more strikingly attractive than this Golden Shower when in flower and fruit.

This tree is one of the wonders of Honolulu, where it is largely planted for shade, growing from 30 to 50 feet in height with a straight trunk and slender spreading branches. It has abruptly pinnate leaves, which are alternate and one foot or more in length. It bears pendulous racemes, about one foot in length, of beautiful fragrant yellow flowers, followed by very long, cylindrical, indehiscent legumes, 1 to 2 and even 3 feet in length and about one inch in diameter. They are mostly nearly straight, but sometimes are slightly curved or bent and marked with numerous transverse striations, corresponding with their flat partitions inside, dividing the whole pod into numerous cells, varying from twenty in a small pod to a hundred or more in a large one. Each of these cells contains a single, small, hard, pale brown, shining seed, enveloped in a blackish sweetish pulp.

The tree itself is a native of India, where it is also cultivated. It is likewise found, apparently in a wild state, in tropical and subtropical Africa. In the West Indies, Central America and Brazil, as well as in other parts of the Tropics, it is largely cultivated. Bulow, the celebrated traveler, who met with the tree in the garden of Cairo in Egypt, mentioned it in 1553, and it was also mentioned in 1592 by Prosper Alpinus. It was first grown in England by Miller in 1731, and good plants of it may now be seen in many botanical gardens. In countries where it thrives, and also in south Florida, the showy fragrant flowers appear in May and June and the pods ripen about the following February and March.

The economic value of this tree consists entirely in the pulp surrounding the seeds as before described. As found in commerce the pods are for the most part dry, and in this state the pulp is separated from the seed and becomes attached as a coating to the transverse divisions of the walls. These pods are shipped from both the East and West Indies, the latter supplying the bulk of our importations. The pulp is sometimes imported by itself, having been removed from the pods. The best, however, is that which is imported in the pod. Its use is that of a mild laxative either by itself or in combination with other ingredients. It can be purgative.

It has always been a wonder and a surprise to me how the great inventor, Mr. Edison, found time and leisure to bring together such a wonderfully large and varied collection of tropical trees in his charming garden at Fort Myers. It requires study and a great amount of plant knowledge to bring together such a collection. Last June I found in full bloom in this garden also the Red and Pink Shower (*Cassia nodosa*) with flowers of fragrance of a rose, and he has also the Red Shower (*Cassia grandis*) in his garden. These are also most beautiful flowering shade trees.

[*Schizolobium parahybum*]: Since 1879 I have experimented with tropical and subtropical plants, making my first attempt at Houston, Texas, and a few years later on the West Yegua, in Lee County, continuing my experiments in 1886 at Gotha in Florida. Here a large number of fine palms, many bamboos and a host of beautiful broad-leaved evergreens, partly natives, and for the most part denizens of Japan, China, Australia and southern Brazil, formed the nucleus of the at present so beautiful Palm Cottage Gardens.

The strictly tropical plants were often lost by a heavy freeze. In November, 1917, I moved a large part of my tender plants to a new place at Naples-on-the-Gulf, starting again pioneer work in the wilderness in my 66th year. The hardships that I had to overcome, the obstacles that had to be removed from my path, the disappointments that I had to contend with were legion. The soil looked good to me, but during the rainy season a very high water table makes it impossible to induce deep rooting plants to do well. Nothing could be done until the soil, even for shallow rooting plants, had been well worked and thoroughly aerated.

At Gotha everything had been different, and almost all plants started into vigorous growth after they had been planted, though the land was rolling high pine land. The only troubles were the occasional heavy freezes. I had four crops of Mangos and Roseapples, five or six crops of Amatungulas and

Caranda [*Carissa bispinosa* or *C. grandiflora*] and *C. carandas*. From 1910 to February, 1917, we had had no killing freeze, and I even had the Royal Poinciana and the Jacaranda in full bloom. A specimen of [*Schizolobium parahybum*], the subject of this sketch—a huge tree, native of Brazil,—was in full bloom in February and March, 1916. Its big erect racemes of bright yellow flowers were a sight that is deeply impressed upon my mind. In the February freeze of 1917 this and many other tender trees and shrubs were killed outright. I have had no opportunity since to add this noble tree again to my collection. It is an extremely fast growing evergreen shade and flowering tree, of very fine form and of easy growth.

My specimen was quite bare of leaves when it bursted into flower. As soon as the blooming period is over the few old leaves drop and the young feathery bright green foliage follows very quickly. Prof. Chas. T. Simpson says that even on his place at Lemon City, on Biscayne Bay, it is sometimes hurt by frosts. My impression is that it will grow and will be perfectly hardy where the Royal Poinciana, the Jacaranda and the Royal Palm can be successfully grown. This species, and also a number of others, dislike sour soils. I have found that some heavy pieces of limestone, piled around their roots, will have a beneficial effect. This is a very beautiful and a very gorgeous winter-bloomer.

Phyllocarpus septentrionalis: The discoverer and introducer of so many valuable new avocados and other tropical fruits from Guatemala and elsewhere in the Tropics, Mr. Wilson Popenoe, also succeeded in finding many most beautiful plants for the ornamentation of our gardens, among them a magnificent winter-flowering leguminous tree, a close relative to our famous Royal Poinciana. His discovery was hailed by all plant lovers in south Florida with unusual interest. Dr. David Fairchild gives the following account of it in *Plant Immigrants* (No. 200): "Of the many beautiful flowering trees cultivated in the tropics, none is more gorgeous, when in full bloom, than the Royal Poinciana. The *Flor de Micco,* or Monkey Flower of Guatemala, however, may be considered a worthy rival. At the flowering season it drops its leaves and the entire tree is covered with crimson-scarlet blossoms. So far as known, this tree has never before been introduced into cultivation. On Mr. Popenoe's last voyage to Guatemala he secured 15 pounds of seeds from which several thousand sturdy young plants have been grown for distribution in southern Florida and in our tropical dependencies."

The *"Flor de Micco"* grows in small ravines in the lowlands of eastern Guatemala. It flowers at the end of winter, and for this reason it may be of particular interest in southern Florida, where ornamental trees which will bloom during the winter season are greatly desired. The Royal Poinciana, which the *"Flor de Micco"* greatly suggests in appearance, does not flower until mid-summer here at Naples. In Estero and Fort Myers it flowers from the middle of May to July [or earlier] and even August.

Mr. Wilson Popenoe writes: "A magnificent flowering tree found in sandy loam in eastern Guatemala, at 1500 to 2000 feet altitude. It is of broad spreading habit, 45 to 50 feet high, with light green compound leaves. In January and February the tree is a mass of crimson-scarlet flowers which are borne in small clusters and are each about an inch broad."

This beautiful flowering shade tree was first introduced in 1917. I received three small seedling plants from the Bureau of Plant Industry in April, 1919. They are at present (August 1923) about 4 feet high with a broad spreading crown, looking very distinguished in their dense deep-green foliage. They are easily grown healthy plants, but rather slow growers. Undoubtedly there are many of them dispersed over south Florida, and we may hear of their flowering in the near future. My plants are growing on poor, sandy land and have never received any special care; a thick mulch of old grass and weeds is all the humus they get, and now and then some liquid manure as a stimulant. The compound leaves consist of 4 to 5 pairs of opposite leaflets or pinnae, the two terminal ones being a trifle larger than the rest. The bark is grayish, with darker longitudinal streaks. This species will unquestionably become one of our most popular winter-flowering shade trees. I can scarcely await its blooming period. I infer that it will require 6 to 8 years before this species exhibits its first inflorescence.

The two small specimens in My "Tropical Garden and Arboretum" here at Naples are growing with great vigor and promise to show their full beauty within a few years.

[*Peltophorum pterocarpum*]: In looking over my books and lists of plants I have experimented with in Florida since 1886 I find that it comprises not hundreds, but thousands of tropical and subtropical species. This experimental work falls mostly on the shoulders of the pioneers in ornamental horticulture. It is of great importance and extremely fascinating. There are successes and failures—often more failures than successes. It is a wonderful occupation, and a never ending time of hopes and anticipation to observe each particular species in the struggle for existence.

To follow one's ideals is in itself a great satisfaction. It is, however, an expensive work, and it requires a large library and much study. The pleasure that comes out of this work cannot be described in words. One has to feel its subtle touch. Happiness, satisfaction, delight, gratification, recreation, ever-present hope, and the innate assurance of an ideal life full of visions, con-templations and poetry constantly follow in its wake. These were the musings when I, on this first day of August, stood before a new tropical tree—[*Peltophorum pterocarpum*]—in full bloom. The erect, large, yellow, many-flowered panicles of this glorious tree from the Philippines were a sensation. My imagination was far surpassed by reality. This specimen is scarcely 10 feet tall. I received it from the Bureau of Plant Industry under the name, *Baryxylum inerme*, but I prefer its good old designation. It came in April, 1918, and was planted out on rather high, dry land, in poor white sand of my Naples garden. The large, erect flower panicles terminating every shoot are covered with a rusty-brown tomentum with a slight touch of chestnut color. Its vigorous growth, the distinct green color of its foliage and the large erect panicles of bright yellow, fragrant flowers combine to make this tree a marvelous object of tropical beauty. It is a unique and a first-class flowering and shade tree. It thrives well in south Florida, is evergreen, not too dense, gives a good shade and produces an abundance of showy flowers. Prof. Chas. T. Simpson in his charming park-like garden on Biscayne Bay has had the pleasure to see several crops of seeds ripen on his trees. The seed pods are dark-brown, flat and broad, with a narrow wing down one side.

"This tree," says Dr. E. D. Merrill, "is one of the best shade trees we have. The species is of wide distribution in the Malayan region, and in the Philip-pines grows in nature near the seashore." Mr. W. E. Broadway of the Trinidad Botanical Garden, near Port-of-Spain, goes more into detail. He writes: "The appearance of this tree at all times of the year is conspicuous as seen growing in Trinidad on account of its dark-green feathery foliage. When in flower this dense-leaved tree carries great weight with those who prefer a mass of bloom. The yellow flowers are arranged in large erect panicles; the corolla is hairy inside and out. The calyx is clothed with a red-dish pubescence externally and the stamens have their filaments covered similarly with rust-brown hairs, such as are also found inside the corolla; the anthers are bright yellow."

[*Peltophorum dubium*]: The Baryxylums are closely related to the Pelto-phorums; in fact, the latter is merged into the former genus by some of the younger botanists. The species under consideration is a native of Argentina, and is much used as an avenue tree in Buenos Aires. It was introduced by the Bureau of Plant Industry about 5 or 6 years ago. My specimen is about 10 feet high and consists of several stems. The leaves are very conspicuous, dark green, a little wavy and, of course, compound. It flowers very profusely, each shoot being terminated by a large erect panicle of bright yellow blossoms reminding strongly of those of [*Peltophorum pterocarpum*]. My specimen though only about four years old, it flowers this year for the first time, being in full beauty at the beginning of September. It is one of those trees that is easily accommodated, growing vigorously on high, dry sandy land. A little fertilizer now and then is appreciated and a good mulch of fallen leaves is essential for its welfare. A large forest tree in the province of Rio de Janeiro and Minas Gerais, Brazil.

Triplaris americana, a beautiful new flowering tree: Several years ago I received a few small plants from the Bureau of Plant Industry under the name of *Taraktogenos kurzii*, the Chaulmoogra Oil Tree. The plants made a most vigorous growth and were, from the beginning, very conspicuous and beautiful. Dr. Paul C. Standley, when visiting my garden at Naples in the winter of 1927, expressed his doubts about the correct naming of the plants. They looked familiar to him, botanically known as *Triplaris americana*. In a letter from him, which I received May 2, 1927, he writes as follows:

> You will remember that I brought away a leaf of the supposed Chaul-moogra Tree, which I thought was something else. Upon comparison with herbarium specimens I find that it is, as I thought, *Triplaris americana*. While this is not as interesting as the Chaulmoogra from an economic standpoint, it is a much better tree from a horticultural point of view, and I have never seen it in cultivation before. The Triplaris trees are either staminate or pistillate. The pistillate specimens are very fine indeed. They have great masses of bright red flowers, which last for several weeks. Each fruit is provided with three wings of such a nature that when the fruit drops from the branch, it spins about like a parachute as

it falls to the ground, hence the name Volador applied to the tree in some Spanish counties. In its native haunts the hollow branches are nearly always inhabited by savage ants that bite painfully.

Dr. Standley sent me a lot of fine seeds which he had collected in Salvador, Central America, and I now have quite a number of nice young seedlings. My oldest three-year-old plants are now about 15 feet high and very healthy. None of them suffered during the heavy freezes early in January, 1927, and again Jan. 2 and 3, 1928. It thrives well in moist, rich soil near my Cypress hammock. So far it has not flowered. It is a distinct and distinguished looking tropical tree.

Parkia timoriana [possibly *P. javanica?*]: As its specific name implies, this stately tree was first discovered in the island of Timor, but it has since been found in many of the islands—Malaya and the Philippines included. My specimen here at Naples, protected somewhat by a group of Pines, is one of the most conspicuous trees of my arboretum. Even people with a very limited interest in ornamental horticulture are impressed by its sturdy, tall, upright growth and its singular beauty. It reached a height of 10 feet within a year, having formed so far only a single stem and no side-branches.

The leaves are very long, broad, flat, bipinnate, fern-like and of a very bright green color. Their appearance is very distinct. It was introduced from the Philippines a few years ago by the Bureau of Plant Industry, to whose credit we must put the introduction of so many valuable new plants. In its native home it is a very large tree, and is strongly buttressed. Its growth is said to be very regular and of fine outline, the large, broad open crown being very wide-spreading. It prefers good soil, deep, rich and well drained, though my specimen grows vigorously on dry, poor sandy land. It is heavily mulched and supplied now and then with a little organic fertilizer. The wood is valuable, being light and durable. It is used for packing-boxes, paper pulp, etc.

Mr. P. T. Wester, connected with our Miami Experiment Station for a number of years, and also now occupying a similar position in the Philippines, gives the following account: "A very large leguminous tree, often 115 feet high, with a wide-spreading crown, compound fern-like leaves and dense, pear-shaped panicles of small yellow and white flowers. The pendulous black pods, 18 inches long, contain seeds which are roasted and used for coffee. It does very well in south Florida and is exquisitely beautiful, especially when young; quite tender, and should be planted, if possible where protected by large trees."

Lagerstroemia speciosa, the Queen's Crape Myrtle: This glorious flowering tropical tree was introduced by Reasoner Bros. many years ago, but it is still rare in our south Florida gardens. Mrs. Marian A. McAdow has a fine large specimen in her most interesting garden at Punta Gorda. I have a fine small tree in my Naples place. It should be in every good garden where brilliant tropical flowering trees are grown. It is a native of India, and has been lately sent out by the Bureau of Plant Industry under the name *Lagerstroemia speciosa* [more recently erroneously as *L. flos-reginae*].

Mr. J. Lowrie gives the following description of the home of the Queen's Crape-Myrtle in the *Garden*:

> To see this queen among flowering plants when in bloom is truly a grand sight. . . . This plant is a wonderfully interesting object when in a cultivated state in the gardens of India, but the wonder and interest deepens greatly when it is seen in a state of nature. The jungles of India abound in flowering trees and shrubs of stately dimensions and varied and splendid hues, but few approach in beauty this Lagerstroemia, when the trees are seen at the right season and in quantity, their beauty simply defies description.
>
> In Malabar it is seen to perfection, both as a cultivated plant and as a wild one. Its habitat in that province is a limited belt of forest stretching along the base of the Western Ghat range at no great elevation, and where the annual rainfall is heavy and the temperature high. I can well remember with what delight and astonishment it was that I first came across this plant in its native wilds in the heyday of its florid pride. I had traveled overnight from the seacoast to the foot of the Ghats, and after a pause started on horseback at daybreak to climb the mountain pass. First a bamboo-belt of considerable depth was passed; then came a belt of deciduous hard-wooded trees, interspersed with group of Cycads of rare growth and beauty, with Tree Ferns and trailing *Calamus* peering from recesses in the giant evergreen forest above, from which issued a noisy mountain stream of the purest water.
>
> The trees forming this belt included the Teak Tree; a species of *Terminalia, Dalbergia,* and strange enough another species of *Lagerstroemia* named Benteak, a fine timber tree with polished silvery bark; the noble [*Bombax ceiba*], with its crown of scarlet glory, and others. Mingled with these grew this Lagerstroemia in abundance, lighting up the forest with

its splendid flowers. Long and earnestly did I gaze on that scene, till the increasing heat of the sun warned me that I must seek a higher altitude. More than a score of years have come and gone since that morning, yet the glory of that jungle tree is as fresh in my memory today as it was then.

After securing a large bunch of the flowers I resumed my journey, but not without many a "long, lingering look behind," till I entered the evergreen forest, and the Lagerstroemia belt was lost sight of. The soil in this belt is neither rich nor deep, stones and boulders covering the surface, with a ferruginous subsoil, the elevation above sea-level being perhaps from 250 to 300 feet. The heat at this elevation in Malabar at the foot of the Ghats is very great at all seasons, but such temperature, it would seem, is not absolutely necessary for the development of the plant.

In Malabar I never found the plant growing in a state of nature save at the altitude and position described above. But in a cultivated state it is a common plant in gardens at sea level all along the coast of Malabar, and also in gardens and plantations at from 2500 to 3000 feet. At the higher elevation I have seen the plant growing and producing an abundance of flowers on the poorest of soils, on grassy hills with barely 6 inches of poor soil. This Lagerstroemia, as far as I know, is not included among the sacred plants of the Hindus, but the natives are extremely fond of decorating their persons with its beautiful rose-colored flowers, and are always careful in its cultivation and presentation.

I have had the Queen's Crape Myrtle for many years at Palm Cottage Gardens. It made a fine vigorous growth, but was always cut back by the occasional hard freezes. It always sprouted again from the rootstalk, but never flowered. It is at home, however, in our south Florida gardens.

[*Jacaranda mimosifolia*]: When in full bloom in April the Jacaranda is one of the glories of our south Florida gardens. In spite of its great beauty it is, however, not seen as often as its merits entitle it to. I have had it in full bloom at Palm Cottage, but it suffered severely during the occasional heavy freezes. Another fine tree of it, though rather small, flowered profusely in the grounds of Bishopstead, an old garden paradise—now extinct—at Orlando. Last April I enjoyed the beauty of quite a large specimen in a garden at Avon Park. One of the hotels there is called "The Jacaranda" because a very large specimen was the main feature of the surrounding garden. The largest and finest Jacaranda in the state grows in the wonderful garden of Mrs. Marian A. McAdow at Punta Gorda. In good well drained soil, rich in humus, phosphoric acid and potash, this fine blue-flowered tree grows with great vigor. Being a native of northern South America it is a real tropical tree, but it can stand more frost than the Royal Poinciana. It usually is a sheet of blue in April and when its last flowers drop the first brilliant red blossoms of the Royal Poinciana expand.

E. André, a well-known botanical traveler, saw it in full bloom in January, 1876, when crossing the half-woody plains of the River Guatiquirs, one of the chief effluents of the Rio Negro, a very important tributary of the Orinoco.

These immense savannahs, or llanos, form a part of the region known as the territory of St. Martin, situated at the foot of the eastern slope of the great Andes of Colombia. The vegetation of the thickets which lined the natural depressions (canyons) was luxuriant; Palm trees (*Mauritia flexuosa*) spread abroad their fan-like foliage, while the thorns of the stems protected them from the assaults of the monkey tribe. *Bactris, Aiphanes* and *Geonoma* were the least important among the family of palm trees, at once so noble and so elegant. *Bertholletia* (Brazil-nut trees), Cedrelas and Cecropias supplied a thick and grateful shade, while the undergrowth, composed of many Myrtaceae—Eugenias especially—sheltered in their turn quantities of Heaths, Orchids, Bromeliads and Aroids.

The forest-floor was starred with beautiful flowers on a background of *Selaginella* with fronds of emerald-green. Abruptly I drew rein in front of a tree of which the inflorescence surpassed in brilliancy that of all the surrounding vegetation. At once I recognized *Jacaranda mimosifolia*, long since introduced into European gardens, but so rarely blooming in our hothouses that its flowers are unknown to most of our gardeners. The tree I refer to might be some 60 feet in height and its straight strong branches were terminated in great panicles of brilliant violet blue flowers, the obliquely tubular form of which gave them a certain similarity to those of Gesneriaceae. The corollas were so abundant that the soil around the stem of the tree was strewn with them. It was then about the close of the dry season.

The best description of the Jacaranda I ever read comes from Mrs. Marian A. McAdow. I quote it in full:

The glory of the garden this 8th day of April, 1923, is the Jacaranda tree. It has been showing its blue color for two weeks, but today the ground is covered with a mottled blue carpet of fallen blooms over which a myriad of bees hover, seeking the last remaining drops of nectar the blue flasks hold. The tree is leafless, but at the end of every branch and twig nods a bunch of violet-blue bell-like flowers dangling and shaking their song of spring in every breeze that blows. This is a South American tree and there are different varieties of it, one being white and the others various shades of blue. My Cleveland garden has its first blooming specimen this year and it is slightly different from my Punta Gorda one. The throat of the new one is filled with silky hairs of a whitish color. The leaves of the Jacaranda tree are quite as interesting and beautiful as the flowers. These are what is known as double-pinnate and this makes them resemble the formation of the leaves of the Tree Fern and often one hears the Jacaranda called the fern-tree.

The leaves which at their best measure three feet in length and taper down in size toward the tips of the branches, are arranged in whorls around these and this tends to carry out the semblence to the fern-tree. The leaves do not appear until the flowers have fallen and they reach their greatest period of development and beauty during the latter part of the rainy season. The bunches of bloom contain from forty to ninety flowers each and these measure two inches in length and one in width. They have a sort of silky texture, which, with their unusual color for a tree, draws enthusiastic attention whenever the blooming season is on. This will last until the Royal Poincianas show a blush of color and, where one wishes to keep up a constant display of bloom in the garden, this attractive tree should be planted to fill in the gap between March and May.

In my trips over the state I see many fine specimens, but I am always told that they do not bloom. As mine never fails, I must lay this absence of flowers to starvation. My own noble specimen receives at least one hundred pounds of fertilizer every year in February not to mention the ashes and bone meal it gets benefit of from the dwarf palms that live underneath its sheltering arms. Not far from it grows another of its kind that was planted by a plant lover who came here before my time but this tree blooms only at rare intervals and then bears but few flowers. These two trees came from the Royal Palm Nurseries, but I have another tree in the rear of my garden which bears a much more exquisite leaf, but has not yet bloomed. This came from Dr. Franceschi's gardens near Santa Barbara, California. In my Cleveland garden are 20 trees which are from four to six years of age. The seed of some of these came from South

America and some from Lady Hanbury's garden in Italy. The latter have a reddish petiole to the leaves which gives them a marked and different appearance from the other members of the Jacaranda family.

The perfume of this flower is obnoxious to some persons, but to me it resembles faintly perfumed honey. There is no doubt about the variation in the sense of smell in different individuals. Our own changes with the passing of years. Once upon a time I detested the odor of the Guava. Today it lures me like one of the perfumes of paradise. This morning my large tree was measured. Its trunk at the ground was seven feet three inches around. At four feet from the ground it branches into two parts, one being five feet and six inches around and the other two feet and nine inches. Its height is at least fifty feet and the branches extend thirty-two feet from the center of the trunk. It was planted in 1899 and in 1900 a cow broke the young plant off a foot from the ground. This forced it to branch low down and it was well it did for this tree grows up so fast that it tends to produce tall slender growths that are easily broken by the wind. Are you satisfied with this development of the Jacaranda tree in Florida? If you are, plant one. It will give you many happy hours of lovely companionship.

Jacaranda caerulea: To the uninitiated this species could easily be mistaken as belonging to the fern family when not in flower, so remarkably alike in their divisions are the leaves to those of numerous ferns. The corymbose flowers are provided in enormous quantities at the same time, and they are of a bluish-purple color. The tube of the corolla is white and hairy within and glabrous without. The trunk of the tree is smooth, owing to its grayish bark peeling oV in flakes. Many specimens are now flowering in the gardens of Port-of-Spain, some leafless, others only partly so. The tree is quite common throughout Trinidad, and forms a striking feature in the landscape during this season of the year—March. [Source likely W. E. Broadway of Trinidad.]

As far as I know this fine species has never been introduced into our state, though it very likely would do well and flower profusely in south Florida.

Jacaranda acutifolia, from Peru: Violet-blue in terminal and axillary panicles. One or the other of these species may turn up in our south Florida gardens. There are two distinct forms or species in the Punta Gorda region [other than Mrs. McAdow's?].

Tipuana tipu: Quite a large number of beautiful flowering and shade trees have been introduced from Argentina. Several years ago I was struck with the fine form of *Schinopsis lorentzis,* the celebrated Quebracho, and the beautiful Timbouva, in the Miami Experimental Gardens. Another grand shade tree from the same country is the Tipu, my specimen grown in my home grounds at Gotha, near the Timbouva, having attained a height of 30 feet in four years. It is a very dense tree, but of the finest ornamental form imaginable. When Dr. David Fairchild saw the two trees at Palm Cottage Gardens last April (1923), side by side, he was struck with the beautiful picture. It grows on rather dry, poor, sandy soil, and has received no care after the first year.

Time will prove that this fine species will be one of the best and one of the most easily grown shade trees for central and south Florida, being especially adapted for highway planting. Dr. Fairchild wrote the following note for *Plant Immigrants* (No. 8, p. 22): "A leguminous tree from the Salta, of great value for avenues. It grows in very dry localities in the Chaco. Will stand 25°F. Branches a trifle unruly. Recommended for avenues in Florida."

It is a large tree, 50 meters high, very ornamental and supplies excellent timber. My tree has flowered several times during the past few years, but having been absent from my old home, I had no opportunity to examine the inflorescence. I have been told that the flowers are scarcely noticeable.

Pterocarpus indicus, Padouk: A most beautiful shade and flowering tree, a native of Burma, but cultivated throughout India, southern China, the Malay Archipelago and the Philippines as an ornamental. I have raised many fine plants from seed received from the Botanical Garden of Buitenzorg, Java. It seems to be perfectly hardy here at Naples, near the coast, thriving well in moderately moist rich soil. Its growth is healthy and quite vigorous. It is described as a very ornamental tree, bearing a profusion of pale yellow, sweet-scented flowers in March and April, followed by circular button-like pods. According to Dr. C. V. Piper, who saw this species in Singapore, it is "a beautiful shade tree, Elm-like in form, but with drooping branches and abundantly planted in the Malay Peninsula."

The following is adapted from "the Annual Smithsonian Report" of 1915: "A large forest tree with drooping branches, the trunk often being provided with broad buttresses. The leaves, 8 to 10 inches long, are composed of from 5 to 9 ovate leaflets, 2 to 4 inches long. The standard and wings of the yellow Papilionaceous flowers are fringed on the margins. The tree has been introduced as a shade tree in many tropical localities. Cups are made of the beautiful flesh-tinted wood, which turns water yellow, orange and finally blue. The valuable timber and cabinet wood furnished by this tree shows pale red lines of growth and large conspicuous pores."

Colvillea racemosa: This is another magnificent flowering tree, a native of Mauritius and Madagascar. It was named in honor of Sir Charles Colville, first governor of the island of Mauritius. I have raised it from seed received from the Calcutta Botanical Garden at various times, and Dr. Geo. S. Stone of Fort Myers has also grown it from seed. At Palm Cottage Gardens it made a most beautiful growth and did not suffer at all from cold, but it must be said that while I had it no killing frosts occurred. I lost my three plants here at Naples, not by cold, but supposedly by something injurious or something lacking in the soil. So far, I have not been able to replace my loss. All explorers and all lovers of beautiful trees are unanimous in their praise of this tree, bearing in the early fall "large, erect, close racemes of bright scarlet flowers, presenting a very showy appearance." The leaves are twice pinnate and quite handsome. This *Colvillea* assumes a height of from 30 to 40 feet, and the crown is elegantly formed and spreading. The stem is always straight. In my lath house at Gotha it grew most vigorously in dark, moist soil, rich in leaf mould.

Attempts should be made to introduce this magnificent flowering shade tree again to south Florida, where it undoubtedly will thrive as well as the Royal Poinciana from the same region. My experiments have shown beyond doubt that it will do well if properly treated. It evidently dislikes new, sour soil.

[*Delonix regia*], Royal Poinciana [Flamboyant]: What a world of brilliancy, nobility and sublime grandeur is embodied in the name, Royal Poinciana! There is no other tree that can compare with it. When in full bloom it is one of the wonders of the tropical world. No description, not even the brush of the artist, can do it justice. A native of Madagascar, it has been introduced into every tropical country of the world. Everywhere it is highly prized. Poets have immortalized it, sages and philosophers have lauded its form and idealized its dazzling beauty. South Florida has the good fortune to grow this jewel of the plant world to perfection. It does not display, however, its splendor during the winter months. In June it is usually in its full glory, although some flowers may be seen in May, and quite a number as late as July. The tourist and winter sojourner, therefore, has no opportunity to enjoy one of Florida's most wonderful sights. Even without its showy flowers the Royal Poinciana is a tree of perfect form and gigantic outline, a most valuable shade tree. Its immense crown is broad and dome-shaped. The only fault it has, if fault it be, is that it sheds its leaves in winter. But even when deprived of its foliage it challenges the admiration of the lover of nature.

When I saw the Royal Poinciana for the first time in full bloom, at Fort Myers, I was overwhelmed. The impression was a deep and lasting one. I could not find words to express my feelings. I could only bow in appreciative reverence. The immense bunches of dazzling scarlet flowers lie over its dome in broad masses, not evenly disposed, but here thicker and there thinner, showing patches of the lovely bright, light green foliage. This disposition gives additional value to the large pinnate leaves, delicately shaped after the manner of the Jacaranda and some Acacias, and of the softest, loveliest bright green, and the tree which is of forest size when fully grown, is always shapely. It puts its perfection together for the months of May and June, and then it outrivals everything else in the plant world. One has eyes now for these flowers alone. The Hibiscus, so plentiful in all our gardens, pale their now ineffective fires. They are swept out of sight as stars before the sun. The display is wonderful.

Seen from a distance, the huge flower trusses are of a dazzling scarlet color, a color so vivid and so entirely its own that it is impossible to describe it. Not even a faint idea can be derived from a description. A flame, to which they sometimes have been likened, and even the tints of the rainbow and the brilliancy of a sunset as seen on the beach of the Gulf, cannot give a correct idea of this wonder of colors. I have often picked a single flower to examine its composition more closely. Though large, its form is very delicate, reminding one of a noble orchid. There is also a very conspicuous diversity of tints. Seen from a distance the color is a solid mass of brilliant scarlet, but viewed at close range we find in the center of the blossom, bright yellow, and even violet and rosy shades. The single blossom is a revelation, showing an entirely new beauty which only those who take the pains to study it closely may find.

The Royal Poinciana is of massive and beautiful growth, forming one of the very best shade trees imaginable. In every respect it is a gem,—one of the greatest gifts Nature has ever presented to us. It is easily grown and cared for. A very little attention when young is all it requires. Instead of finding here and there a specimen, it ought to be largely planted as an avenue tree in cities and towns, and it should line miles upon miles along our south Florida highways. Mr. Edgar Wright of the *Florida Grower* was so charmed by its beauty that he urged, years ago, to plant Royal Poincianas on a large scale along our highways, and he even offered seed free to all who would follow his advice.

Seen in winter, deprived of its feathery, delightful green foliage and only showing its long, empty dark-brown seed-pods, we may admire its massive broad form, its huge limbs. Its real value, however, its unrivaled splendor is hidden away until the proper flowering season has come again.

Why this wonderful tree, the real king among them all—a royal member of the plant world—has been so sadly neglected is undoubtedly due to the fact that it does not flower in the winter season and that it is not an evergreen. We have, unfortunately, lost our course in planting our gardens and in forming fine avenues. In most instances we only keep them tidy during the winter time and look for winter flowering plants only to delight our tourists and winter sojourners. Many northerners—in fact all of them—who own winter homes here very naturally care only for the plants that offer a display of an abundance of bright flowers during the winter months. But all those who have made Florida their permanent home and who enjoy the beauty of our breezy summer months, should see to it that the floral display is evenly distributed over all the seasons. Along the lower East Coast many of the tourists and winter residents stay long enough to obtain a glimpse of the floral display of the Royal Poinciana.

Spathodea campanulata: The subject of this sketch is a native of tropical Africa, belonging to the Bignonia family. It is one of the most beautiful flowering trees of the tropics, being well established in all the fine gardens of the lower east coast, but as yet I have never seen a single specimen at Fort Myers or elsewhere on the lower west coast, except a few small specimens in my own garden at Naples. My plants came from the Bureau of Plant Industry, Washington, D.C. Dr. B. T. Galloway, of the U.S. Department of Agriculture, was struck with its beauty in Java, where it is one of the most beautiful flowering evergreen trees, being there in bloom almost throughout the year. He obtained seeds and introduced it on a large scale. The honor of its introduction belongs however, to Mr. W. M. Matheson, of Coconut Grove, who brought it in earlier from Jamaica.

My late old friend, Dr. E. Bonavia, sent me, almost forty years ago, the following description from India: "This is a tall tree with unusually dark green foliage, interspersed with masses of scarlet bell-shaped flowers turned upwards. At a short distance they look like bunches of scarlet Pelargoniums. The tree is a perfect marvel of the vegetable world, and matched only, I think, by [*Delonix*] *regia*. Its common name is 'Flame of the Forest.' An avenue of Spathodeas, full grown and in full bloom, would be a subject on which to write a poem. The charm of this tree is that it flowers in winter. Will no one try to immortalize himself by planting such an avenue at Bangalore?" And I beg to add: Will no one erect for himself a lasting monument by planting such avenues at Fort Myers and all the pretty little towns along the lower west Gulf coast?

The *Spathodea* has an individuality entirely its own. It is a most beautiful tree, evergreen, dense, of fine form and of rapid growth. The brilliant flowers appear in dense clusters during the winter months. The color is of the brightest scarlet. A cluster of them in a vase forms an exquisite table decoration. With some attention the tree is easily grown in good rich soil. When the soil is very sandy and dry a large hole should be filled with muck and old stable manure, well mixed, and some top soil added. When in full growth good application of well decomposed organic manures and even a little chemical fertilizer is appreciated. This tropical gem is rare yet, but no doubt the Everglades Nursery will have it for distribution if there is a demand for it. Seeds ripen abundantly in the gardens of Coconut Grove and elsewhere on the lower east coast. The ample pinnate leaves show a peculiar glossy deep green color. They are smooth to the touch. The leaflets, of which each leaf numbers from 12 to 15, are lamellate. In its native habitat the tree assumes a height of from 50 to 60 feet.

Spathodea nilotica. This beautiful species is a native of Uganda, British East Africa, the upper Nile and Congo regions. About twenty years ago I read with much interest a charming book, *The Uganda Protectorate,* by Sir Harry Johnston (two volumes, New York, Dodd, Mead & Co., 1902). A very beautiful plate of *Spathodea nilotica* and a fascinating description aroused my enthusiasm. At that time I did not dream that some day this noble plant would be under my care. At present there are quite a number of healthy young seedlings growing in my garden here at Naples. "Some of the forest trees of Uganda," says Sir Harry Johnston, "offer magnificent displays of flowers. There is one, *Spathodea nilotica*, with crimson scarlet flowers larger than a breakfast cup and not very dissimilar in shape. These flowers grow in bunches like large bouquets, and when in full blossom one of these trees aflame with red lights is a magnificent spectacle." And in another place he says: "We walk under canopies of richly foliaged trees, many of them celebrated for their brilliant flowers, like the . . . magnificent *Spathodea*, whose flowers are of the shape and almost of the size of Roman lamps and of a vivid scarlet, so that the tree looks as though it had been hung with crimson lights for some illumination."

Last year the director of the Botanical Garden, at Entebbe, Uganda, had the kindness to send me a package of fresh seeds, which soon germinated after sowing. Quite a number of fine seedlings were the result. Some of them were given to various enthusiastic plant lovers on the east coast and Fort Myers, and all are growing thriftily. The young plants look very much like *Spathodea campanulata*, but the leaves are very hairy and rough to the touch, showing also a very conspicuous brownish hue in their green color. The plate in Sir Harry Johnston's book seems to indicate that the color of the flowers is of a much deeper scarlet. As the Bureau of Plant Industry also distributed this brilliant species, there is hope that it soon will be an inmate of many south Florida gardens.

The family of Bignoniaceae, to which the *Spathodea* belongs, comprises a large number of extremely ornamental plants, among them many climbers. [*Pyrostegia venusta*] is one of our most gorgeous winter-flowering vines. Among trees, all evergreen and all extremely handsome, though not often seen in our gardens, the following deserve our special attention: *Jacaranda mimosifolia*, the Jacaranda, with immense bunches of beautiful blue flowers, of which a fine large tree is found in Mrs. Marian A. McAdow's famous garden at Punta Gorda; *Kigelia pinnata*, the Sausage Tree, so named on account of its pendant sausage-like seedpods; *Parmentiera cerifera*, the Candle Tree; *Millingtonia hortensis*, a gem of the Indian flora with fragrant white flowers, not yet introduced; *Crescentia cujete*, the Calabash Tree, of which there is a fine specimen in Mr. Edison's garden; [*Radermachera sinica*], from Hong Kong, represented by a good tree in my garden at Gotha, in Orange County. The flower-trusses stand upright. The single blossoms are bell-shaped.

Magnolia grandiflora! How charmingly poetical is thy name! How many pleasant memories of southern life, of the sweet song of the mockingbird and cardinal, the oriole and nonpareil, dost thou recall! I have listened underneath thy glorious crown to the call of the chuck-will's-widow when the evening was falling, and pleasant reminiscences of the days of my boyhood, spent in the cool and idyllic woodlands of Wisconsin, entered my mind, while I inhaled the sweet perfume of thy immense chalices. How often does thy name remind me of my excursions along the Gulf and in the romantic land of the Creoles and Acadians! I have seen thy unrivaled beauty on the banks of the Mississippi and the Chattahoochee, on the Suwannee and the St. Johns, and I have rested in thy shade on the beautiful shores of Mobile Bay. I have admired thee near the tomb of the immortal Washington, the father of this great country.

How I longed to see thee in all thy splendor in thy native Southland, when, in the days of my youth, I read the glowing descriptions of the great Audubon, and the adventures of Bartram! And when I at last saw thee on the picturesque banks of Buffalo Bayou in the flowery month of May, in all thy glory and splendor, my enthusiasm and my admiration were boundless. All my anticipations were far excelled. *Magnolia grandiflora*! The most beautiful tree in the world; no picture and no painting can do thee justice; no description,—and be it ever so glowing,—can give an idea of thy natural and noble beauty. How does thy elegant and refined form imbue the marble statues of the sculptor with life and beauty and stateliness! Thou has found a second home in the classical soil of Italy and in the temple grounds and quaint gardens of Japan, but in thy native land thy admirers have to point out thy beauty and stateliness, thy glory and magnificence in foliage, flower and fruit to those lovers of nature who could so easily cherish and admire thee near their homes! No other tree can take thy place, *Magnolia grandiflora*! Thou alone art designed to impart to the simple cabin, as well as the cozy cottage and the pretentious villa, a refined splendor and beauty entirely thine own. And when they carry me to my last resting place, thou shalt shade my grave in the beautiful Southland with thy glorious foliage, and the mocking-bird and cardinal shall sing the song of hope and love and eternity in thy flowery branches!

The true home of *Magnolia grandiflora* extends from North Carolina and Arkansas southward, reaching its greatest perfection along the Gulf of

Mexico, especially in the alluvial soil of Louisiana and Mississippi and on the St. Johns, where grand specimens, seventy to eighty feet high, may be seen. Its southernmost limit in Florida is the Manatee River. Growing naturally in moist soil rich in humus, in company with Tulip Trees, Pecans, Hickories, Live and Water Oaks, Sycamores, Liquidambar, Hollies, etc., its trunk and branches are often festooned with a dense growth of *Smilax laurifolia, Bignonia capreolata,* Trumpet Creeper and Grape Vines. In Florida we often find it in company of the princely Cabbage Palm. Growing in groups and frequently adorned with masses of Carolina Jessamine, Bignonias and Moonflowers and their trunks covered with ferns, the picture is a decidedly tropical one.

The Magnolia, which is also known as the Big Laurel and the Laurel Magnolia, has been called by a well-known German dendrologist, "the most beautiful evergreen in the world," and those who fully appreciate the ornamental value of the tree will agree with me that this is no exaggeration. When I first saw it in its serene beauty on the banks of Buffalo Bayou at Houston, Texas, it seemed as if I had been carried away into another sphere, into a fairyland. The sight was such a grand one that it far exceeded my expectations. The largest and finest trees, however, I found on the banks of the Mississippi, in Louisiana, on the shores of beautiful Mobile Bay and along the banks of the St. Johns—trees almost a hundred feet high, with glorious crowns of dense foliage.

Over a hundred years ago, the famous botanical traveler, William Bartram, gave the following account of the Magnolia as he found it on the banks of the St. Johns in Florida:

> Behold yon promontory, projecting far into the great river, beyond the still lagoon, half a mile distant from me; what a magnificent grove arises on its banks! How glorious is the Palm! How majestically stands the Laurel, its head forming a perfect cone. Its dark green foliage seems silvered over with milk-white flowers. They are so large as to be distinctly visible at a distance of a mile or more. The Laurel Magnolias which grow on this river are the most beautiful and tall That I have anywhere seen, unless we except those which stand on the banks of the Mississippi; yet even these must yield to those of the St. Juan, in neatness of form, beauty of foliage and, I think, in largeness and fragrance of flower. Their usual height is about one hundred feet, and some greatly exceed that. The trunk is per-

fectly erect, rising in the form of a beautiful column, and supporting a head like an obtuse cone. The flowers are on the extremities of the sub-divisions of the branches, in the center of a coronet of dark green. They are large, perfectly white, and expanded like a full blown rose. They are polypetalous, consisting of fifteen, twenty or twenty-five petals; these are of a thick coriaceous texture, and deeply concave, their edges somewhat reflex when mature. In the center stands the young cone, which is large, of a flesh color and elegantly studded with a gold-colored stigma that by the end of summer is greatly enlarged, and in the autumn ripens to a large crimson cone or strobile, disclosing multitudes of large coral-red berries, which for a time hang down from them, suspended by a fine, white silky thread.

Like other trees, the Magnolias attain their full beauty only when stand-ing alone. In the woods, where they have to struggle for existence with other trees, large specimens show a rather grotesque appearance, and do not sug-gest what they are capable of in more favored situations. They only show their full beauty in parks and gardens and in fields and pastures where they are allowed sufficient space to develop their inimitable glory. Here another important point has to be recorded: The Magnolia grows with a particular freedom on high and dry land, where the aromatic network of feeding roots are pushing their way in all directions. In all the finer gardens of the South, this tree is never absent.

There are magnificent specimens in New Orleans, specimens that must have been planted eighty or even a hundred years ago. The most beautiful Magnolias I ever saw were two specimens standing in an old antebellum garden in Montgomery—on the Noble place, if I remember rightly. The lower branches of these dense pyramidal trees were touching the ground and had a spread of about sixty feet, the tops rising to a height of about sixty-five feet. They were perfect in form. Behind them stood the quaint old home, built in plantation style, with broad front verandah, resting on strong rounded and ornamental pillars. I never saw again such strikingly beautiful specimens. They should be carefully preserved by the present generation as landmarks of a romantic old time. I was told that they had been planted about fifty years ago.

Though the Magnolia attains its largest size and greatest beauty in the South Atlantic and Gulf States, I have seen healthy specimens as far north as

Louisville, Washington, Mount Vernon and even in Philadelphia, but so far north, though always attracting attention wherever seen, they cannot compare with the grand beauty of growth, density and luxuriance of foliage with those farther south. They flower beautifully, but their foliage is more scant and smaller and the growth is more open. I have varieties in my garden from these northernmost localities which show the same characteristic here.

The type has foliage five to six inches long, smooth and shining, dark green above, clothed with a rusty brown tomentum underneath. In garden varieties the leaves are sometimes only four inches long, while in others they attain to a size of ten to fifteen inches, often strongly nerved, or undulated and crinkled. They are always glossy on the upper side,—in fact so glossy that they seem to be covered with glass when the sun strikes them. The underside of the leaf varies considerably. In some forms it is whitish or gray, in other forms spotted with a dark color, and in a third class only a trace of brown is noticeable. The most beautiful variety in my garden has large, dark green, glossy foliage, with an underside densely covered with orange-brown, and the wind moving the branches to and fro gives the tree a magnificent appearance, the contrast between the glossy, deep green and the light orange-brown being an indescribably charming one. The new leaves are enclosed in a sheath which is covered with whitish hair, but in some varieties it has a very striking rosy color.

The bark is smooth, gray, resembling that of the Beech. The wood is rather soft and light. The flowers range from a pure white to a milky-white, changing to leathery-brown when fading. They are beautifully cup-shaped before they open, eight to nine inches in diameter when fully expanded, and strongly and deliciously fragrant. In some of the garden kinds they measure from twelve to fifteen inches in diameter. Aside from its easy growth in gardens, its noble form, its grand foliage, its beautiful flowers, the Magnolia has an aristocratic appearing form, its long blooming period and other important characteristics adding considerably to its value. I have had them in flower in my garden from the beginning of spring to the middle of November.

When I began to plant my garden in the orange belt of Florida, near one of the innumerable small clear glades, *Magnolia grandiflora* was the first tree that was set out. This was in November, 1891, and the largest specimen has attained a height of twenty-five feet. It looks grand on the side of a fine

Cocos australis [= *Butia capitata* or *Syagrus romanzoffianum*] and a very huge specimen of a hybrid Phoenix Palm (probably between *P. sylvestris* and *P. canariensis*). Only a few trees out of several dozens, gathered in the hammock woods, survived. All the rest died, due to not planting them properly. In transplanting Magnolias from the woodlands the crown should be cut down entirely and only the stump should be planted. This will throw up shoots in the spring which should not be removed, but left as they appear. These will, in a few years, form bushy, vigorous trees provided with branches up from the ground. It must be kept in mind that only a Magnolia is beautiful and valuable which grows in a natural way and whose branches almost touch the ground.

In 1892 and '93 I collected all the different varieties of the Magnolia I could obtain in the different parts of the country, and I raised a large number from seed which I procured from the finest trees in Louisiana and Florida. In 1893 and '94 I sent large consignments of pot-grown plants to Florida. They were set out with the ball of earth, in which they grew, in November, and all started a vigorous growth in the following spring. At present they are from five to seventeen feet high and pictures of beauty.

All these Magnolias flower when quite small, and for this reason they may prove valuable pot-plants in the North. To me their foliage is much more beautiful than that of the Rubber Tree. They bloom from late in March to the middle of November, their main flowering period being the months of April, May, June and July. The flowers never appear in masses. They are scattered sparingly over the dark green foliage, pervading the air with the sweetest perfume. In the early morning hours and at night the huge blossoms are half-closed. In this cup-shaped form they look particularly beautiful. During the bright sunshine of midday, they widely open their petals and bees and other nectar loving insects swarm among them. The fruit-cones are at times also very attractive. They are covered with a dense tomentum, which is at first whitish-gray, then assuming a rosy red, and finally a very striking dark red color. When the cells in the ripe cones burst open and the bright red aromatic berries are seen in large numbers, or when they hang down on silky threads, among the large glossy foliage, the picture is an exceedingly charming one. Mocking-birds, woodpeckers, blue jays, fish crows, and a little farther north, thrushes, catbirds, and many other birds are very fond of these oily, aromatic fruits.

In our southern gardens the Magnolia should have a much more prominent place than it now occupies. It is particularly effective in connection with fine architecture, and there is no better tree in existence to be used near the house. There should be planted less China Trees and Water Oaks and more Magnolias. It is not particular as to soil, and in favorable places it is of very rapid growth. Even in the apparently poor sand of the hilly country of Florida, it finds a congenial home. The spreading varieties should never be planted closer together than twenty or thirty feet. The more columnar kinds may be planted much closer. Pot-plants should always be chosen if immediate success is looked for. Of course, the named kinds can only be increased by grafting. The Magnolia groves around the lakes of northern Italy have a world-wide fame. In Florida, where the gardens abound in a host of evergreens, the groups of Cabbage Palms and Magnolias—at present more imaginary than real—should gain the fame of unrivaled beauty and magnificence.

Eugenia malaccensis [= *Syzygium malaccensis*]: Commonly known as Malay-Apple, this is a native of tropical Asia and highly prized as an ornamental. Many years ago, in 1878, I found an interesting and puzzling account in the *Garden* (London): Lindley, in his *Vegetable Kingdom*, mentions an indigenous and solitary species of apple as found in the Sandwich Islands. As I said, this account puzzled me for many years, as no botanical name was given. I also knew that no real apple is found in the tropics. What could it be? Finally—only a few years ago—Dr. David Fairchild's description of a trip to Panama solved the riddle. He mentions the Malayan Apple (*Eugenia malaccensis*) as one of the most beautiful ornamental "flowers in which the stamens and not the petals make the display. Few experiences are more thrilling to a lover of flowers than when he first walks under the branches of a Malay Apple Tree, and finds the whole interior of the tree filled with a scarlet carpet made up of myriads of stamens."

When I saw the name of *Eugenia malaccensis* I at once was aware of the fact that this beautiful tree belongs to the Myrtle family and that I was well acquainted with it and its history. I had received the seeds repeatedly from the celebrated Botanical Garden of Buitenzorg, Java, and there were growing in my collection at Naples quite a number of thrifty seedlings. I also knew that Mr. E. N. Reasoner of Oneco, Florida, had fruited it successfully several years ago.

The great beauty of this tree when in foliage, flower and fruit has been often referred to in English horticultural periodicals. With me at Naples the

Malay-Apple grows quite well and will form, within a few years, a most beautiful ornamental tree. The fruit seems to vary a good deal, some varieties being of little value, while others are described as most delicious. The seeds from which my plants were raised came from the most valuable varieties in Java. It requires good rich soil and a moderately moist position. It is closely related to the Rose Apple [*Syzygium jambos*] and to the Jambolana [*Syzygium cumini*], and I have planted the three species in one large group.

In my collection I have a few other beautiful Eugenias. The Rose Apple, [*Syzygium jambos*], is now found in many gardens of south Florida. It is a beautiful dense tree and very ornamental. The leaves are long, narrow, Oleander-like and when just appearing, of a beautiful red color. The flowers are pure white and very showy. The fruit ripens here early in June. It is deliciously rose-scented, and is used by some people in connection with other fruits in preserves, and is also candied. Being rather dry and very strongly aromatic it is only cherished in its natural state by children.

Eucalyptus ficifolia, the Scarlet-Flowered *Eucalyptus*, a Gum Tree: A correspondent inquires: "Is there a real fine-red-flowered Eucalyptus, and has it ever been introduced into Florida?"

The species mentioned in the above headline is a beautiful red-flowered Eucalyptus, but I never have seen it, and never was successful to make the seed germinate, though I have received several times packages of seeds from the Melbourne Botanical Gardens, through its director, the late Mr. Wm. R. Guilfoyle. Mr. Guilfoyle has the following to say about it:

> This was first discovered several years ago by a Mr. Maxwell (a most enthusiastic plant collector) at Broker Islet, Western Australia; and also upon the ridges of Mounts Roe and Mitchell, which are not far from the Frankland River. It forms a large shrub, or small tree, 15 feet in height, and often produces its flowers before it has attained a height of 5 feet. It is a rapid grower, will stand an enormous amount of drought and exposure to drying hot winds, and may justly be considered one of the most valuable acquisitions in the way of ornamental plants which has ever been introduced into the Colony of Victoria. Out of the 150 kinds of Australian Eucalypti enumerated by Baron von Mueller, who named this species when Director of the Melbourne Botanical Gardens, it is questionable whether there is any other which blooms so profusely, or produces its flowers at such an early stage of growth.

Several individuals of this magnificent tree are at present (February

1. *Bromelia balansae,* type genus for Bromeliaceae.

2. *Bixa orellana,* Annatto fruit, seed coating used for dye.

3. *Bixa orellana,* Lipstick-Tree flower, also called Annatto.

4. *Acalypha hispida,* female flowers of Chenille-Plant.

6. *Cestrum elegans,* relative of Night-blooming Jessamine (*C. nocturnum*).

5. *Cassia fistula,* Golden-Shower, fruits a source of senna.

8. *Hibiscus rosa-sinensis,* Common Chinese Hibiscus.

7. *Podranea ricasoliana,* Pink Trumpet-Vine.

9. *Antigonon leptopus,* Love's-Chain, Corallita, Coral-Vine.

10. *Alpinia purpurata,* Flame-Ginger, a gingerwort.

11. *Phyllocarpus septentrionalis,* Monkey-Flower, in Naples.

12. *Aechmea mariae-reginae,* a Nehrling favorite, male plant.

13. *Ixora* hybrid, a yellow cultivar, possibly *I. speciosa.*

Upper left: 14. *Triplaris americana,* "Long John" from El Salvador, according to Standley.

Above: 15. *Delonix regia,* Royal Poinciana, Flamboyant, from Madagascar.

Left: 16. *Peltophorum pterocarpum,* Yellow-Poinciana, from Southeast Asia.

Below: 17. *Delonix regia,* "the real king among them all," according to Nehrling.

18) the "pride of the garden." The numerous massive bunches of bright orange-scarlet, standing boldly above groups of varied tropical leafage, are seen from many parts of the grounds. The foliage of the plant itself is dark green, and somewhat resembles that of another beautiful species— *Eucalyptus calophylla*—which bears large creamy-white blossoms. This also is indigenous to West Australia. In its native haunts *Eucalyptus ficifolia* fairly clothes some of the hills, and the effects produced, even in the hazy distance, are grand in the extreme, somewhat resembling huge masses of fire. The tree remains in bloom for several weeks, first abundantly, and ought to make a valuable conservatory plant in climes where it would not be sufficiently hardy for outdoor cultivation. Though I have on several occasions forwarded seeds of it abroad, I have not heard whether any of them have germinated. Upwards of seventy specimen plants have been recently purchased by me from Mr. Brunning, of the St. Kilda Nurseries here, which have been distributed over the lawns of the garden, some in clumps, others in groups, together with various golden-yellow Australian Acacias and purple flowering Rosewood of Brazil (*Jacaranda mimosifolia*), all of which bloom at the same time. In the course of another year or two, therefore, the gorgeous contrasts of color which will be produced during our summer season can be better imagined than described.

The late Mr. Guilfoyle was, for many years, one of the most valuable and interesting correspondents of the writer.

7

Fig Trees

No trees in all the great plant kingdom can vie in size, form and massive grandeur with the Ficus or Rubber Trees, these weird giants of the tropical forests. They are beautiful in their way—extremely beautiful—but their beauty is very characteristic, impressive and awe-inspiring. They are shrouded in mystery and their dense bewildering growth makes them objects of never-ceasing surprise and superstition, particularly among the natives.

There are taller, loftier trees. The great Sequoias of our California mountains excel them by far in height and supreme magnificence. None of the Figs grow taller than 150 feet; 35 to 70 feet is their average height. It is the immense spread of their crowns, the intricate masses of air-roots, the gigantic buttressed trunks that combine to make them the most wonderful objects of the tropical plant world. Banyan-like Fig Trees occur in Queensland, Lord Howe's Island, Samoa, Guam, Mexico and in South America.

Their spread is so enormous, their density so dark green and bewildering, their intricate masses of air-roots so wonderful that they act like magic on the mind of the natives who suppose that the spirits of the departed have taken up their abode in them. They look with superstitious wonder and awe at these giants—even with fear, avoiding to walk under such a colossus during the night.

A few weeks ago a rare and most beautiful tree attracted my attention,— a tree on the highway,—a most exquisite dense shade tree. This happened at Punta Gorda, a city renowned for its handsome and rare trees, such as the Council Tree (*Ficus altissima*) in Mrs. McAdow's garden. While motoring along the Highway No. 5, just outside of Punta Gorda, and near the turn towards Arcadia, I noticed on the right hand on the edge of the sidewalk and close to a ditch, a most impressive tree, very dense and of a fine form—one of the most beautiful trees I ever have seen. Its characteristic light gray bark, with a slight touch of cinnamon-brown; its very dense leaf-masses and its upright and vigorous growth,—beautiful, strange and exotic—aroused my enthusiasm.

The World's Most Sacred Tree

When returning a week later my wife and I stopped and we examined this stranger more closely. I saw at once that I stood under the shade of an exceptionally beautiful specimen of the Peepul, or Sacred Fig (*Ficus religiosa*), the most sacred tree of India and Ceylon [Sri Lanka]. It is a young tree and therefore not of large size as yet, but it is a picture of vigorous health and unique beauty. I think it is not taller than about 25 feet and its crown-diameter is about 20 feet. A little distant from the main trunk and close to the wall of the ditch I noticed several vigorous young sprouts. These undoubtedly can be used for propagating purposes. The leaves are quite large, reminding somewhat of the Poplar, but having the characteristic long, pointed appendix.

I was unable to learn from whence this Peepul Tree came and when it had been planted. I surmise that it is one of the late E. N. Reasoner's introductions. It is very rare in gardens, and I never before have seen it anywhere along the West Coast. There used to be a lovely specimen in the courthouse grounds of Fort Myers, but it unfortunately was cut down by someone who had not a shadow of an idea of the beauty and rarity of this real tree aristocrat. Mr. Geo. Hendrie, a winter sojourner from Hamilton, Canada, has a fine specimen in his grounds at Naples, and I have a small plant in my Naples garden. There are quite a few large Peepul Trees along the lower East Coast.

The trunks of this Sacred Fig, when young, are round and smooth, but in age they exhibit perpendicular ridges and hollows alternately, presenting the appearance of cloistered columns of Gothic cathedrals, the ashy color of the bark tending to favor the illusion, as resembling that of gray stone. The leaves are almost 6 inches in length, and of a dark shining green; their stalks being rather long and slender cause them to have a tremulous motion with the slightest breeze, like those of the Aspen, and the rustling sound thus created adding to the impressive effect.

The fruit is not larger than a cherry, and of a purple color when ripe. Though not unwholesome, this fruit is not considered edible. Roxburgh, in his *Floral India*, speaks in terms of wonder of the great size of *Ficus religiosa*, stating that it is found over all India, even on the mountains, but that it is most common near houses, where it is systematically planted for the sake of the deep and grateful shade which it yields.

The Peepul or Sacred Fig has been cited as an emblem of the vastness and unchanging character of India. The duration of the Oak and other long-lived forest trees is, in fact but a span compared with the perennial life of the Sacred Fig, some well known specimens of which are calculated to have endured for at least 3,000 years.

The foregoing, adopted partly from an article in the *Garden,* came to my mind, when seeing and admiring the beautiful healthy specimen of the *Ficus religiosa* at Punta Gorda. Long may it live and delight its owner! Many thousands of tourists, among them undoubtedly numerous nature lovers, pass this tree in their autos. May it appeal to them, as it appealed to me and my wife, as one of the most distinct and beautiful wonders of the plant world.

Though the family resemblance is very pronounced in most species each one has an individuality entirely its own. Some display in their dense growth an elegance and grace that finds no rival among trees. Others are characterized by their forests of trunks, all belonging to one and the same tree. No wonder that the simply minded of the natives regard them with superstitious awe, and some of them are even sacred to the Singalese and the highly civilized Hindus. To the latter the Peepul is one of the most sacred of all trees,—perhaps the most sacred. It is an object of particular veneration to the worshipper of the powerful god, Vishnu, the Destroyer, as it is supposed by many that he was born among its branches.

From the following interesting details respecting the Peepul Tree, written from Benares (by an unknown author), which is not only the holiest, but also the oldest city in India, a vivid idea may be gained of certain phases of Indian life:

> Close by here is a more than usual sacred growth of the peepul, a patriarchal tree whose once stalwart limbs, drooping under the weight of far-spreading boughs, were supported by a block of solid masonry built under them. Being Saturday, an ever-changing procession of grave elders, matronly women, young men and maidens, were walking round and round the tree, chanting a low strain. Every time they passed a par-

ticular point in its circumference they threw on it with their hands water taken from the Ganges and carried in their *lotas*. Some varied their performance by throwing marigolds or grains of rice. It seemed a particularly dull game of follow-my-leader, but it is a serious religious function, and good Hindus would not see Saturday's sun go down till they had walked 108 times around the Peepul Tree, laved its trunk with holy water, or cast upon it some offering of food or flower. A goat had discovered the richness of the land, and, climbing up the masonry browsed upon the flowers, whilst the pigeons coming down in swarms, picked up the rice, nobody saying them nay.

In the North-Gallery at Kew a picture represents a Nepalese temple and Peepul Tree, with blue pigeons, which are sacred to Krishna. In Ceylon the Singalese call it *Bogaha,* or the Tree of Buddah. It is accounted the most sacred of trees, and is held in such estimation in the district of Kandy that the form of its leaves is only allowed to be painted on furniture employed exclusively for the gratification of the king. In countries where Buddhism prevails the Peepul has become a consecrated object and may be seen on the roadsides, about houses and temples and in towns, protected by masonry over which shrines are placed for homage. All of them are eager for a single leaf, but no one would dare to pluck it from the tree, for it must fall in full maturity to yield its highest merit. When one of them falls there is a pious scramble among the multitude to get it, and then the solitary leaf is borne away in the happy bosom of the successful competitor.

There are many very old trees of the Peepul in Ceylon, and one of them is said to be over 2,000 years old. Several years ago my son Werner came home from Miami, telling me most enthusiastically that he had seen a tree there, a most wonderful tree, a tree so beautiful and distinct, so dignified and refined that no other tree could compare with it, and he took from his pocket a leaf of the Peepul. I have heard others go into raptures over its beauty. The more you see of the Peepul the better and more intensely you like and admire it. I have always found that the possessors of this tree are especially fond of it and that they always point it out to you with much pride.

It appears to me that the Government Experiment Station has distributed the Peepul largely in and around Miami. On the West Coast it is rare. In growth and form and in foliage it is extraordinarily distinct and impressive. Its crown, though not so broad and gigantic as in many others, is of peculiarly graceful form, and its leaf is a gem. It is of a very bright green color, nearly cordate in shape with the apex lengthened out to a long tail-like process. It attains a height of 75 feet in India. The largest I have admired at Miami did not exceed 25 feet in height, but they were scarcely more than fifteen years old. My specimens grow in rather poor and dry pine-land soil. They do splendidly here, but they need to be well fertilized and cultivated. Along the East Coast they thrive luxuriantly on the evidently poor limestone rock.

Cuttings do not root freely, but large trees may be transplanted with little trouble during the rainy season, although the greater part of the roots have to be cut off. When large Peepul Trees have been transplanted a forest of young plants springs up from the roots left in the ground, forming excellent and abundant material for propagation.

The Great Banyan

[*Ficus benghalensis*] of India is so gigantic and determined in its growth as frequently to cover from its starting point of a solitary plant whole acres of land, beating back and overpowering its less energetic associates. A fine sketch now before me shows a Banyan Tree which has covered from one patriarchal stem several acres by the simple process of throwing out from the arms of its extended branches roots, which gradually but surely find their way to the earth, and firmly attach themselves to their natural element, forming auxiliary stems in position. Without such aid the heavy load of leathery foliage would inevitably crash to the ground.

I have never yet met with an uninteresting species of *Ficus*, from the small Ivy-like [*Ficus pumila*] to the fruiting Fig so well known in horticulture and commerce. The Sycamore Fig forms the avenue from Cairo to Shubra (Mohomid Ali's princely garden in Egypt). The India Rubber Fig, too, so well known in its dwarf state as one of the best additions to our tropical and subtropical gardens. The Sacred Tree of Buddha (*F. religiosa*) is found near every Buddhist temple in Ceylon and India.

An almost historical Banyan grew near Colombo, in Ceylon, at Colpetty, giving the name of Banyan House, Banyan Villa, etc., to most of the residences in its neighborhood. This tree had evidently covered a widespread area of land, but as civilization has grown in its vicinity it had been cut back for the merchants, residences and villages that form the west-end portion of Colombo. This patriarch stood on the border of the government road from Colombo to Point de Galle, was upwards of 30 feet in circumference at its base and was supported by a few air-root stems upward to 60 feet in height. It had, no doubt, witnessed the decadence of the Portuguese and Dutch Governments in that island, but in the winter of 1867, during a heavy gale of the northeast monsoon, it came down, fortunately doing no greater damage than knocking down the portico of Banyan Tree house, where I was then staying, upsetting about a hundred Coconut Palms in its fall, and blocking up the mail road to Galle for about ten days. [Peter Wallace?]

Something must be done in diminishing the monotony of our southern counties, which have been deprived by the woodsman's axe of their original Pine forests and of their giant Cypress trees. I have now preached for quite a number of years the gospel of the *Ficus* species, of palms, etc., and I see from my correspondence and from actual doings, slowly, but surely, that the best and most intellectual people are making my ideas their own.

Sycamore of Scripture

Ficus sycomorus (*Sycomorus antiquorum*): What is a Sycamore? A short while ago I received a letter from a plant lover at Kissimmee from which I quote the following sentences. "As you perhaps know, there are quite a number of fine Sycamore Trees planted for shade and ornament along the streets of Kissimmee, and it is taken for granted by many of our people that they are the true Sycamores of Scripture, while others assume that the name is wrong and that they should be called Plantain Trees. I am of the opinion that the true Sycamore of the Bible does not grow at all in Florida, and that it is vastly different from what we have here. I would be under obligations to you if you would be kind enough to give some information about this most interesting subject.—J. M. P."

The fine and large deciduous trees you have at Kissimmee, and which are often called Sycamore, are not identical with the one under that name in the Bible; they are not even distantly related. They belong to the Plane Tree family (Platanaceae) and are very common along streams and in moist lands, particularly on the Wabash and other parts of the middle west. Dr. John K. Small calls it Plane Tree, Buttonwood and Button-balls, and omits the name

Sycamore entirely. The real Sycamore, however, is a Ficus or Rubber Tree—
one of the most famous trees in the world. I cannot refrain from quoting
from my manuscript:

Pharaoh's Fig Tree. A native of Arabia (Yemen), Egypt, Abyssinia, Nubia,
Syria, etc., one of the most famous of all trees and one of the most admired.
It is an inhabitant of the hottest and driest countries in the world. On account of our humid climate it does not seem to thrive very well in Florida.
"This species of Fig," says Dr. David Fairchild, "is grown largely along the
northeast of Africa as a shade tree. Giant specimens are to be found in Alex-
andria and Cairo, and at Biskra. The trees are beautiful shade trees, and
make wonderful avenues in these dry climates where irrigation is practiced.
The fruits are small, about the size of a pigeon's egg, and are sometimes
eaten by the Algerian Arabs. I do not know how low temperatures it will
stand, but probably not more than a temperature of 18° or 20°F."

> Tourists having visited Cairo will be familiar with the remains of the
> celebrated tree at Matarieh (ancient Heliopolis and Scriptural Urr) in
> the Coptic Garden, now over two centuries old, but the original of which
> is, traditionally, the tree under which Joseph and Mary rested during
> their visit in Egypt. It is an evergreen in its native country, but in the
> climate of Alexandria is often leafless for a month or two in February and
> March. The fruit is borne from May to September in large bunches on
> the main branches and stem, never on the leafy ones, the figs being of
> a yellow or tawny color when ripe edible, but of a poor flavor. (R. M.
> Bloomfield.)

It appears to be a fact that there are good edible varieties of the Sycamore
Fig. "Seeds and Plants Imported" (No. 51). From the same valuable publication (No. 42) add the following supplementary item:

> From the wood of the Sycamore of Scripture, the "Tree of Life" have been
> made by the ancient Egyptians their mummy cases. They are still in good
> condition after thousands of years. But we must remember that the cli-
> mate of Egypt is extremely hot and dry. It is a true Fig Tree, and was
> introduced into Egypt, probably from Yemen, on the east coast of the
> Red Sea, in very early times. It bears figs of inferior quality, which are
> inhabited by the fig insect (*Sycaphage crassipes*). These figs are not fit to
> eat unless their tips are cut off to let the fig insects escape. From the time
> of Pliny even the Egyptian boys have operated on the Sycamore Figs,

using a kind of thimble made of iron plate ending in an iron finger-nail. These figs are borne on small leafless fleshy branches arising directly from the trunk, and it is the practice to beat the trunk of the tree with a hammer to increase its fruitfulness.

I hear that there is a fine, large and dense specimen growing on a shell-mound, near Chokoloskee, and there may be others. The leaves are "ovate, obtuse, cordate at base, four or five-ribbed on both sides, entire, repand, or slightly angular, glabrous and smooth; petioles and branchlets slightly hairy" (Nicholson 1887).

My garden at Naples is replete with rare tropical plants, but so far I have not succeeded in making a beauty spot of it. Lack of means and insufficient help have prevented it. The collection contains a vast number of new and rare tropical plants, many of which I introduced myself. My specialties during the past ten years were great clumps of tropical bamboos and tropical shade trees. I have always been struck by the massive grandeur of the Ficus or Rubber Trees, these dense and weird giants of the tropical plant world. I have at present over a hundred named species and about twenty-five un-named ones in my collection. There are new ones constantly added, mostly raised from seed. In my opinion there are no finer and denser and larger growing shade trees in existence. I have just received a set of most exquisite photographs of *Ficus* species, taken by the famous keeper of the Arnold Arboretum of Harvard University, Mr. Ernest H. Wilson, also known as Chinese Wilson, the most successful plant hunter of our time. One of them represents [*Ficus subulata*], or a rather large specimen of the species growing near Pretoria, South Africa. It is so magnificent that the natives call it "the wonderboom." Its crown measures 300 feet in diameter and its beauty and dense growth are almost incredible.

Strangling Habit of the Fig Tree

I have called the Fig or Rubber Trees a mysterious group, and now I must add that the entire family is a very surprising one. The mystery and suspicion are enhanced by the way these trees come into existence. We know that the great majority of them are stranglers. All of them bear small berry-like figs in great abundance. Being soft and of a peculiar sweetness, they are eagerly sought by many small birds. Birds deposit the tiny seeds in their excrement in the top of a large forest tree or a palm. This seed usually germinates immediately, if it happens to fall into a fissure of the bark, where the rains cannot wash it away. The young plant is at first small and weak. A tender, soft string-like or even thread-like root is formed which closely adheres to the bark of the host and grows downward. After it has reached the ground it changes its modest and harmless character at once. It rapidly increases in size and thickness, soon looking like a rope or cable. Other roots follow in quick succession, cross each other, encircle the trunk of the host with a dense network and finally choke it to death. It soon dies, rots and falls to dust. Only the hollow cylinder of the Fig Tree stands proudly erect, filling out gradually the empty space with a solid mass of its own wood. It is now a forest tree like all its neighbors, occupying the place of its host whom it has strangled to death. We are able to observe this strangling process quite often in our south Florida hammock woods. Prof. Charles T. Simpson has given us a vivid account, beautifully illustrated, of this extremely interesting strangling habit in its various stages in his charming book *In Lower Florida Wilds*.

Many Rubber Trees form along their stout horizontal branches thread-like roots, swinging in the air and finally reaching the ground where they soon take firm hold and form additional trunks. The Banyan of India (*Ficus benghalensis*) is particularly famous on this account, but there are many other species in various parts of the tropical world with exactly the same habit. These often enormous side-trunks,—10, 25 and even 50 and more feet away from the main trunk,—serve as props to keep the heavy horizontal branches in the proper position, and to insure the entire tree against the ravages of typhoons.

The root-system of a large number of these trees is so enormous, so powerful, so far reaching and so aggressive that they only should be used in places where space is of no consideration. They are excellent for highway planting. The parks and plazas of Cuba, and particularly of Mexico, are famous for their dense and beautiful various Fig Trees.

The most celebrated shade tree we know of is a Fig Tree—the Sycamore of the Bible, of ancient history and tradition. Beautiful myths have clustered around it since ancient days. The grandest monuments of architecture have fallen to dust and ruins. But the grand and dense Sycamore (*Ficus sycomorus*) has remained.

The Hindus of India have had, from ancient times down to our present day, their own peculiar species. The Banyan and the Peepul, or Sacred Fig Tree (*Ficus religiosa*), must be particularly mentioned in this connection. The southern Chinese have their indigenous species (*Ficus impressa* [?] and others), and the natives of western tropical Africa enjoyed the cool shade of another beautiful species—*Ficus vogelii*. We know that the ancient Americans, the Mayas, Toltecs and Aztecs, had attained a very high civilization. Their monumental buildings, buried under a dense growth of tropical vegetation, show it a thousand fold. They also used their most conspicuous and handsomest trees for ornament and shade and some of the Fig Trees, like the Sayula Rubber Tree [*Ficus pertusa*] are in great veneration up to this day. The wonderfully dense avenues of this Sayula Fig Tree are among the grandest sights in the landscape of Mexico.

There is, for instance, the species called here the Cuban Laurel [*Ficus microcarpa*], really an Indian tree, but the most popular and prominent shade tree in Cuba. The leaves are of a very deep glossy green, Laurel-like and very dense. The Weeping Rubber Tree (*Ficus benjamina*), planted so much for shade at Nassau, in Bahama Islands and in Jamaica, has similarly deep green small foliage, but its dense branches droop gracefully to all sides.

Flowering and Fruiting of the Fig Tree

All the species of the genus *Ficus* are devoid of flowers, or rather, the flowers are contained inside of the fig-like fruit. This fruit, mostly small and usually of a dark-red color when ripe, is soft and juicy and is much relished by many birds, monkeys and domestic animals. It is not used very much as human food, as it is quite tasteless, though often sweet and of a peculiar flavor. When in full fruit most all of the species display an additional charm, as many small birds are then seen among the dense foliage, and the red fruit itself is quite ornamental. The species with large clusters of fruit along their trunks are very conspicuous when bearing their abundant harvests of figs.

There are, as far as we know, few species with good edible fruits. The Sayula Rubber Tree ripens its sweet berry-like fruits abundantly in Mexico where they are sold in the markets, and our Bureau of Plant Industry has repeatedly mentioned among its plant immigrants species bearing good edible fruits. None of these wild Figs, however, can be compared with our commercial Fig (*Ficus carica*) which supplies one of our most delicious fruits and which has been cultivated extensively since the time of Christ. Hundreds of acres are planted with it in Mexico, California, Texas and other southern states.

At Fort Myers I have seen *F. elastica* in full bearing and also *F. lyrata,* and in both cases the figs become soft when fully ripe. Not in a single case did any of the seed taken from these fruits germinate. After many experiments I have found the cause. Our native *F. aurea,* which bears abundant crops of berries several times during the year, always supplies seeds that sprout easily when properly planted, and also the seed of about a dozen Mexican species germinated without much difficulty.

When the fruit in our Florida species has set and reached almost its natural size, I found frequently a tiny, hard, swift and very active little insect in them. At first, really for years, I supposed this little insect to be injurious, but finally I came to the conclusion that it crawls or slips into the quite hollow interior of the flowers within the young fruit to pollinate them. Only on account of this pollination the large crops of fruit and the abundant fertile seeds can be explained. I do not know the name of this insect, and I never have seen a report of this fact made by other observers. I arrived furthermore at the conclusion that all our exotic tropical Fig Trees bearing in my garden, have only abortive seeds because they are not fertilized by the proper insect.

It seems to me that each species must have its particular small wasp-like insect that crawls inside of the fig to pollinate it. As long as these insects are not introduced we never can expect full crops of soft figs containing fertile seeds. This observation of mine was corroborated by a letter of recent date from Dr. H. L. Lyon of the Hawaiian Experiment Station at Honolulu. He writes: "We succeeded in introducing from Australia the wasps associated with *Ficus macrophylla* and *F. rubiginosa,* so our local trees of these two species are now supplying us with viable seed and I can send you as much as you may desire. We have made several attempts to bring in the wasp of *F. retusa,* but as yet, they have not become established on our trees."

It was discovered ages ago that the famous little fig wasp, known as *Blastophaga grossorum,* breeds within the Capri-fig "and is able to cross-pollinate the flowers of the invaluable Smyrna Fig which otherwise will not perfect fruit."

Species of Figs

There are two specimens of our native Florida Banyan or Rubber Tree in the Naples Hotel grounds. They are wonderfully impressive, dense, broad and thrifty specimens—worthy of a trip from distant localities to see and enjoy them. A native Banyan, as most other trees, is an eyesore, when not well grown. Mr. Peter Schutt took particular pains to fertilize and cultivate them, when he had charge of the Naples Hotel, and the success was an immediate one. The hurricane in September, 1926, almost ruined the trees. All the large limbs were broken, so that only—so to speak—two skeletons were left. But nature in her work is a powerful and a loving mother. The damage was soon repaired and the trees are now as beautiful as ever. Mr. van Gelder, of the Hercules Power Co., who usually spends part of his winters at Naples, was so impressed with the beauty and nobility of these trees that he took various photographs of them, two being before me while writing these lines.

We have our so-called native Banyan Tree [Strangler Fig] (*Ficus aurea*). If well grown and cared for this species makes a wonderfully beautiful and dense shade tree, as the two specimens in the Naples Hotel grounds abundantly demonstrate. But the most famous and the most wonderful is the real Banyan Tree of India. "Among the many striking features of tropical vegetation," writes Peter Wallace, "none are more interesting than the Fig family, which has from early history been mentioned in connection with religious and secular usages."

The common name of this group of plants is not only Ficus or Fig—a term that applies to the fruit only—but also Rubber Trees, and in fact they all deserve that appellation, as all of them are full of milky sap which oozes out more or less profusely when wounded or cut with a sharp instrument. The first commercial rubber was obtained by the English from *Ficus elastica*—the real India Rubber Tree, now so much grown as an ornamental pot plant. This tree was largely cultivated by experts in Assam and Burma, until the Pará Rubber (*Hevea brasiliensis*) was discovered and planted by the millions in India, Malaya, Ceylon, etc. This belongs to a very different family—the Euphorbiaceae—and yields not only much larger quantities, but also a better quality of rubber. The Mexican and Central American *Castilla elastica* is closely related to the Figs and is still used to a great extent in the manufacture of this commodity.

The so-called boom in Florida has destroyed many a beautiful garden paradise—places that neither time nor money can replace or bring back again. Such a garden paradise was the old Heitman place at Fort Myers, where the most beautiful Sapodillas and the densest and largest specimen of the Tamarind in the state grew. There also was a [*Ficus racemosa*] or cluster Fig, about 70 feet high and always provided with clusters of fruit along the trunk and the big limbs. The lust for filthy lucre has destroyed this most fascinating spot.

The most conspicuous and beautiful of all these trees stands in the grounds of the late Capt. Gwynne on First Street,—a specimen of the Fiddle-leaved Rubber Tree—a marvel of dense beauty and of fine form. Its leaf-crown must be at least 35 or 40 feet in diameter, though its height scarcely exceeds 30 feet. It shades in a most lovely way a large part of the sidewalk. There was a most lovely specimen of the Sacred Rubber Tree (*F. religiosa*) in the courthouse grounds, but a crude specimen of a city politician who knew nothing and was nothing, had given orders to cut it down, because it stood too close to another common tree.

The largest and finest Cuban Laurel [*F. microcarpa*] grows in Dr. John Gifford's garden at Coconut Grove, and there used to be two enormous specimens of the same species in Chas. Deering's place at Buena Vista. A variegated form of the common India Rubber often delighted me when I strolled around at Miami. It was a large, dense and very symmetrical tree. A wonderful specimen of the Sycamore Fig is found in the old government experiment garden at Miami. The most exquisite Weeping Rubber Tree (*F. benjamina*) is scarcely represented in our gardens. There is a fine umbrella-like tree of it in one of the gardens at Olga near the Caloosahatchee. The avenue of these trees planted by Mr. Geo. Dorner, about 10 years ago, at Boca Grande has gained a wide reputation.

Very few of the Ficus will grow as far north as Sanford. Many of them are very tender. During the four nights of heavy frosts in January 1927, and the last one, March 4, when the thermometer went down to 25°F., quite a number of my species were killed to the ground in my Naples garden, and a few were lost entirely, among them *F. benghalensis*—the Indian Banyan. Though cut down to the rootstalk, the following have not suffered in the least: [*F. microcarpa*] (the Cuban Laurel), *F. benjamina, F. wrecklei, F. macrophylla, F. rubiginosa, F. altissima*, [*F. virens*], *F. saemocarpa, F. infectoria, F. elastica*, and *F. religiosa*.

Mrs. Marian A. McAdow has reported that it is always very cool, even during the hottest days, under the shade of her giant *F. altissima*. I have found that there is no better and cooler place to rest and dream than under my dense Cuban Laurels. In addition to this characteristic cool shade there are scarcely any mosquitoes or other insects under the canopy of the dense foliage and branches. I always find a harbor of safety under the dense foliage, when mosquitoes, horse flies and sand flies are particularly troublesome. Snakes scarcely ever are found underneath the trees and the climbing snakes are never found in them. I always hold the opinion that birds would find perfect protection against their many enemies in these dense trees, but they are rarely found in them, except when they are searching for the berry-like fruit. Never have I found a bird's nest in one of my trees, with the one exception of a nest of the mocking-bird in the dense top of the Werkle Fig. Why these trees with their masses of closely-set branches and foliage, in my opinion so ideally adapted for nest building, are not selected for this purpose is a mystery to me.

Devoid of flowers, Fig Trees in tropical countries support a host of charming epiphytes, such as Orchids, Bromeliads, Aroids, Gesneriads and Peperomias. Dense masses of ferns not only decorate their trunks, but also the large horizontal limbs.

I have never found epiphytes—bromeliads, orchids and ferns—upon the trunks or branches of our native Banyan (*F. aurea*), though they thrive well enough if tightly fastened to the bark with wire. Dr. C. A. Purpus of Zacuapam, Vera Cruz, Mexico, states in one of his extremely interesting and instructive letters that many of the ordinary forest trees are covered with air-gardens to the breaking point, but that the Fig Trees only occasionally show a few scattered clumps of Bromeliads or Orchids. Dr. B. P. Reki writes me on this point: "The assumption that Orchids and Bromeliads do not grow on Fig trees is certainly incorrect. I have found them abundantly on these trees, particularly the latter."

The root-system of a large number of species is so enormous, so dense, so far-reaching and so aggressive that they only should be used in very large gardens or parks,—never in small ones. All of them have most beautiful dense, evergreen, glossy foliage, which in some species is very large, thick and leathery, and in others small and elegant, while some have very thin leaves.

Ficus afzellii: This may be *F. eriobotrioides*, said to be a native of South Africa [it is a synonym]. I received my specimen from my friend, Mr. August

Koch, head gardener of the Garfield Park Conservatories, Chicago, one of the most ideally designed and beautiful garden paradises in this country. This rubber tree is a very vigorous grower, quite hardy and promises to become a large tree. The leaves are from 15 to 20 inches long, narrow in their lower part and broader towards the apex, of a rather light glossy green color and veined with creamy white, and the mid-rib is almost white. Nothing is known of the history of this fine and distinct species.

Ficus altissima, India and Java: This is called the Council Tree in Java because the chiefs in olden times are said to have held their councils underneath its enormous leaf-crown. A most beautiful dense evergreen shade tree. The much undulated leaves are very large,—12 inches long, 8 inches broad,—glossy, rather light green, with a whitish mid-rib and veins. One of the largest and finest shade trees I have seen, a marvel of beauty and of gigantic aspect, is one of the features of Punta Gorda. Planted some years ago by Mrs. Marian A. McAdow, it has attained a great height and immense leaf-crown. It is covered during the early summer months with abundant crops of bright red small figs, the size of cherries. When in Punta Gorda, I never fail to admire this wonder of the plant world. One day last summer I not only observed mocking-birds, cardinals and blue jays in its branches, searching for the berry-like fruits, but I was surprised to see an entire family of the little graceful spider monkeys. They were so tame that they came close to where I stood. It was a beautiful and entirely tropical picture.

A large specimen of *F. altissima* ripening its bright fruits in abundance is a most beautiful sight, and I hope that this species in bearing is just as fine, as the small figs are said to be of a bright orange color.

Ficus aurea, Native Rubber Tree [Strangler Fig]: This is a common forest and shade tree in south Florida. At Naples-on-the-Gulf it is a feature as an avenue and shade tree. There are three magnificent specimens, decorated with orchids and *Tillandsia fasciculata,* in front of Bamboo Cottage, and two enormous and very symmetrical specimens in the rear of Hotel Naples are the delight of every plant lover. As this species stands the salt spray quite well, it has been planted in groups in Gen. W. B. Haldeman's beautiful grounds along the beach, being particularly effective as a background to the many large Coconut Palms in front of the place.

In our woodland it usually begins its life as an epiphyte and strangler, sprouting from seeds dropped by birds in the top of a forest tree. The small "dark red" [yellow], soft and sweet-tasting figs are ripe here in April and May, and then the tree swarms with birds,—not only residents, but especially migrants, among them beautiful warblers who find their table well set when they move northward. Seeds are deposited everywhere. The seedlings are very vigorous, with large leaves,—much larger than in the old trees, showing a very glossy light-green color, with a distinct red-brown mid-rib, and very ornamental. Within six or seven months they frequently attain a height of 8 feet in rich soil, and are well branched from the bottom. Well grown Florida Rubber Trees must be placed in the list of first-class shade trees. They never grow tall, 30 or 40 feet being their extreme height, but their crowns are dense, broad, of dome-shaped form and very dark green. Their roots, though sometimes buttressed, are not so aggressive as to interfere with sidewalks. In order to have a good shade tree, the lower limbs, which eventually will attain an enormous size, must be removed. This broad evergreen tree is very serviceable for highway planting, and as it can easily be obtained in all sizes from the woods, it can be planted in large numbers, together with our noble Live Oaks which can be had in fine, dense little specimens in all scrub lands along the highways.

Ficus benghalensis, India: This species and *F. indica* are the real Banyan Trees of India, belonging to the wonders of the plant world. Their growth is enormous, and their immense buttressed root system destroys many a fine old temple in the land of the Hindus. The two species are so similar that even some botanists regard them as identical. I have both species in my collection, and I find that they are undoubtedly distinct as garden plants, though none of them, as yet, has attained a large size. The native home of this Banyan is the sub-alpine tract and the lower slopes of the Himalayas. One tree soon forms a forest of stems, all connected with each other. It grows vigorously in south Florida, and will be a fine shade tree for highways, as it can easily be kept in check by cutting off the long air roots.

F. benjamina, Weeping Rubber Tree, Weeping Fig: Unquestionably one of the most beautiful, noble and elegant shade trees in existence. Being a native of India, it is much planted in gardens, parks and along highways in the West Indies, Bahamas, in India and Singapore. Mrs. Marian A. McAdow, who was struck with its marvelous beauty at Boca Grande in this state, says that it is as dense as [*F. microcarpa*], showing a drooping habit, and being unusually charming when its new growth is made. It belongs to the small-leaved section of the genus, and is particularly adapted for lawns, for larger gardens and as an avenue tree. The leaves are 2 to 4 inches long, shortly stalked, and of an ovate-oblong, acuminate form, thin and glossy green.

[*Ficus citrifolia*], Poplar Leaved Rubber Tree: A native of south Florida, but not found at Naples, where *F. aurea* is abundant everywhere. It is more open in growth than the Florida Banyan and is excellent for planting along highways, and even as an avenue tree in cities. Being a very rapid grower, it ultimately attains a height of 35 ft. It bears small "bright red" figs which are eagerly sought by many birds. The growth, as in most Fig Trees, is very symmetrical, and handsome specimens are formed within a few years. Prof. C. T. Simpson says that while *F. aurea* "quite commonly begins its life as an epiphyte, [*F. citrifolia*] usually grows throughout its life in the ground." Then follows a very interesting discourse, illustrated with fine halftones, on the strangling habits and peculiar growth of the two species. A very fine large banyan-like specimen of this species is illustrated on page 391 of his very interesting and scholarly book, *In Lower Florida Wilds*.

Ficus elastica, Common Rubber Tree, India Rubber Plant: Scarcely any pot plant, palms included, is so widely and so well known, so much cherished and loved as this Rubber Tree. It is grown by the hundreds of thousands annually, and always finds a ready sale. It is probably familiar to more persons, even in our northern states, than the one which supplies the fruit for our tables. Few persons who have had it for years in their rooms would imagine that it forms one of the giants of the forest in its native home,— upper India, Burma, Assam, etc. Old trees are veritable wonders of the plant world. They usually show immense buttressed roots. These undulating buttresses which run along the ground are very striking features and must tend to prevent the trees from being overthrown by hurricanes.

Beautiful small specimens are found in many a garden in Orlando, Winter Park and Sanford. Often a heavy frost cuts them down, but they always sprout again from the vigorous root-stock. In south Florida from Punta Gorda southward, the India Rubber Tree can be grown to perfection. In Fort Myers there are some gigantic specimens, one of them with a leaf-crown almost 100 feet in diameter, which shows in a very conspicuous way the buttressed root-system, though the trees are scarcely over twenty years old.

The early history of the India Rubber Tree is very interesting. The way in which this remarkable tree became known to botanists and horticulturists was very singular, as related by Roxburgh, the father of Indian botany and the founder of the Calcutta Botanical Garden, in his *Flora Indica* (Vol. III, p. 543). Towards the close of 1810 a Mr. Mathew Richard Smith of Silhet sent Roxburgh a vessel, there called a *turoung*, filled with honey in the very state it had been brought from Pundua or Tuntipoor Mountains north of Silhet. The vessel was a common, coarse basket, in the shape of a four-cornered, wide-mouthed bottle, made of split rattan, several species of which grow in abundance in the above named mountains and contained about two gallons. Smith observed that the inside of the vessel was smeared over with the juice of a tree which grows on the mountains. Roxburgh was therefore more anxious to examine the nature of the lining than the quality of the honey. The *turoung* was accordingly emptied and washed out, and Roxburgh then found that it was very perfectly lined with a thin coat of *caoutchouc*. Young trees were rapidly procured through Mr. Smith, and cultivated in the Botanical Garden of Calcutta.

In 1815, five years after its discovery, it was in cultivation already in England, and it soon spread over the continent, its hardy nature enabling it to bear smoke, dust, gas, wet, and drought better than most other plants. It soon became a common and favorite ornament in sitting rooms and other parts of the dwelling houses all over the civilized world. Although it will bear a great deal of rough treatment, it repays a little care by producing leaves as much as 2 feet long, but for indoor decoration it should be kept in small pots, in moderately rich soil, or it will soon outgrow its space. It is indeed, remarkable how long this tree, which attains gigantic dimensions in a wild state, may be kept healthy and ornamental in a mere handful of earth.

All the Fig Trees exude a milky sap, the rubber of commerce. It varies in quality, some species yielding a very poor rubber, others a fine and valuable product. This species stands at the head of all Fig Trees in this respect, and is planted for this purpose over large areas in India and elsewhere, though the Heveas and Castillas, [the former] not related to this genus at all, produce at present the best rubber in quality as well as in quantity.

Ficus elastica 'Variegata': A very ornamental and distinct variety of the former, with creamy-white or golden-edged leaves. The variegation extends mostly over the edge for about an inch, but it often covers most of the upper part of the leaf. The center is deep glossy green. It is a most beautiful and characteristic variety, a vigorous, tall grower, very dense, and of a very symmetrical form. Not yet common in gardens, it should be extensively planted wherever fine foliage plants are in demand. Several years ago I came upon a large specimen of this variety in Miami. It was so large, so dense, so finely formed, and its variegation was so pronounced that for quite a while I stood spellbound before it. The tree was about 25 feet high and its round crown was of about the same diameter. The roots were not buttressed, and no damage was done to the concrete sidewalk nearby. It will very likely prove to be a valuable avenue tree.

Ficus indica, the Banyan Tree of India: One of the most celebrated trees in existence. The many enormously large specimens in India belong to the wonders of the world. As far as I know, this species was introduced by our Bureau of Plant Industry a number of years ago. The specimen in my collection here at Naples is small yet, but its vigor indicates that it soon will be a feature of the place. The leaves are oval, deep glossy green, and remind one very much of those of *F. benghalensis,* a very closely allied banyan. There can be no doubt that it will grow well in south Florida, but in consideration of its immense growth and spreading habit by air roots, it is a tree only for parks and large estates. When room in a very large garden is of no consequence, it also may find a place. Writing about the Botanical Garden of Calcutta, J. H. Veitch in his *A Traveler's Notes,* says: "The great banyan is a fine sight. Its main trunk— 48 ft. in circumference—106 years old (in 1896); in 1886 it had 232 aerial roots, many of them large enough to form a trunk of a fine tree. Now there are, of course, many more. The space covered by this gigantic tree is about 70 yards through. The tree is in good condition, and apparently growing as freely as ever, and as there is little vegetation in the immediate neighborhood, there seems to be no reason why it should not go on for a long time. Philodendrons, Anthuriums and other creepers grow over its main stem and along the principal arms."

Often germinating on the walls of the old temples of the Hindus, and sending down to all sides its enormous roots, many a precious building is destroyed or rent apart,—buildings which have seen untold generations of a highly civilized people.

Ficus macrophylla, Moreton Bay Fig Tree, Moreton Bay Rubber Tree: A native of the coast regions of eastern Australia, from Queensland to New South Wales. Perhaps the grandest of Australian avenue trees, and one of the most majestic and noble shade trees in existence. An avenue in the Adelaide

Botanical Garden, planted many years ago by its director, the late Robert
Schomburgk, is the delight not only of the Australians, but of all the travelers, who promenade under its deep shade. The trees are dense, with immense dome-shaped crowns and quite tall and very broad. Having been
introduced by the Bureau of Plant Industry scarcely more than ten years
ago, this species has not yet been widely distributed. I have in my new place
at Naples-on-the-Gulf two fine young specimens, about 8 feet high, which
were planted four years ago. They are very vigorous in growth, dense and
shapely in habit, and are adorned with an abundance of large rather deep
green, shining leaves, oblong in form, pointed at the apex, 10 to 15 inches
long, 4 to 6 inches broad, and showing a distinct light green mid-rib. As I
have not yet seen a large specimen of the Moreton Bay Fig here in Florida
nor anywhere else, I of course cannot speak from my own experience. Judging from my own small specimens, however, I feel safe to predict that this
species will be in the near future one of our grandest and most beautiful
shade trees. Scarcely any other tree is so easily cared for. It grows best in
moderately moist soil, and it does well in dry and even rocky places, though
its growth in such situations is rather slow.

[*Ficus microcarpa*], Cuban Laurel, Indian Laurel Fig: Only a poet-natu-
ralist can do justice to this most elegant, graceful and noble species. I saw it
first in Punta Gorda. I was spellbound. Never before had I seen a tree so
ideally beautiful, so densely deep green, so noble in aspect and growth. It
was an entirely new, a most delightful beauty. Its picture followed me like a
beautiful, dream. Mrs. Marian A. McAdow had told me that she had a great
surprise in store for me. She pointed out to me this tree, and gave me its
name.

I immediately made an attempt to add it to my collection, but in vain.
Only after a few years had elapsed I was fortunate to obtain six little plants.
They were set out on my place here at Naples. Two of them in moist soil,
have attained a height of seven feet in four years, and they are as much in
diameter—perfect pictures of beauty, and so dense that I know of no other
tree that I can compare with it. The leaves are very small, laurel-like, very
deep green and glossy. Those I planted out on higher, drier and poorer land
only grew fairly well. They are as tall, perhaps, as the others, but they are not
as dense and only show a rather narrow crown. During July the largest
specimens ripened quite a number of deep yellow, soft figs, the size of a

small cherry. All the specimens I planted will be great ornaments of my place in the wilderness. Those on the poor land have been well fertilized and they at once responded.

This fine species is excellent for avenue planting, for gardens and as a shade tree for highways. Dr. John Gifford says: "A beautiful shade tree in Nassau (Bahamas) and Key West. Also common in Cuba. A very satisfactory tree for roadside planting."

Wherever the English founded colonies in the tropics they immediately also founded botanical gardens,—in India, Ceylon, China, the West Indies, Australia, etc. Many of them have a world-wide fame, and these gardens have distributed plants and seeds liberally. I have a large number of plants, not only at Palm Cottage Gardens, but here at Naples, that I raised from seeds received from the Botanical Garden at Hong Kong. In this garden the late J. H. Veitch found a fine specimen of the Indian Laurel. He writes: "Perhaps the biggest tree in the garden is a [*Ficus microcarpa*] with numerous large aerial roots, ranging from 3 to 9 inches and sometimes more in diameter. These have been conveyed in bamboo canes filled with earth from the branches above to the exact spot required, or to the one which seemed most likely to offer sufficient support to the tree, the same method pursued with banyans in India. On these roots are many *Phalaenopsis* rooting freely. Mr. Ford (the director) found he could not do much with them in a house, so he transferred them to this tree with marked success,—possibly another proof that epiphytes succeed better on living than on dead wood." I am quite certain that we can grow a large number of the most beautiful orchids, bromeliads, ferns and aroids on the trunks and large branches of quite a number of different Rubber Trees, after they have attained a large size. Though called "Cuban laurel," this Fig Tree is a native of East India and the Malayan Archipelago.

Ficus nympheifolia: Habitat not known. Comes very likely from West Africa, though Nicholson gives Caracas as its home. Among all my plants, trees and shrubs this noble rubber tree is one of my special favorites. It is so distinct from all its congeners, having such beautiful round, large, glossy leaves, as shiny as if just varnished and looking always so dignified and refined that I almost feel justified to place it at the head of all the large-leaved species. There are large magnificent specimens in the grounds of Dr. John Gifford, Coconut Grove, and on the estate of Mr. Charles Deering, Buena Vista, Fla.

It is a rapid grower in rich moist soil, but it also thrives well in poorer and drier soils. No one as yet knows how tall it will grow. As the species is still rare and has heretofore not been grown under the most favorable conditions, we are ignorant about its final size and aspect.

In 1890 I received the type from a reliable horticultural firm in Erfurt, Germany. I was informed that it originally came from Kamerun, West Africa, and that it had been named provisionally *F. "macrophylla"* (the true *F. macrophylla* is an Australian species and very distinct). Having cared for it for a while in my greenhouse in Milwaukee, I sent it down to my place at Gotha, where it was planted out on high pine land. It made a vigorous growth from the start in the fall of 1891 and up to 1894, but was killed to the ground in the big freeze of February, 1895. When the rainy season began quite a number of strong shoots pushed up from the root-stock. It had been planted on rather sloping ground. There it stood, a most charming sight, and there it still stands, though repeatedly killed down by the various freezes since.

In 1919 I sent about ten young plants which I had raised from cuttings to my place at Naples where all are now growing well, two of them in rich moist soil having attained a height of ten feet in three years. The almost perfectly round leaves, 6 to 12 inches long and 5 to 9 inches wide, are strongly nerved with whitish lines and of a deep glossy green color,—the darkest, most polished green I have ever seen in any plant. The very young leaves are of a lighter green suffused with coppery red. They are a little pointed at the apex and the petiole is scarcely 2 inches long. The underside is of a lighter, duller green. The bark is smooth, grayish-white. A most singular characteristic is that after a frost the leaves shrivel up immediately and exhale a strong perfume that reminds of that of the Tonka Bean.

Prof. Charles T. Simpson of Lemon City and Biscayne Bay is very proud of a fine specimen in his collection. His plant originally came from the National Botanic Garden in Washington. It seems to differ somewhat from mine.

[*Ficus pertusa*] Wercklé's Rubber Tree, Costa Rica. Collected by the well-known botanical collector Carlos Wercklé at El Coyolor, and introduced by the Bureau of Plant Industry. "This is," says Mr. Wercklé, "different from the rest of the genus in its being of superb form. It is a very large and very dense tree, of exceptionally beautiful color, and is evergreen. Nearly all the other species are bare for a longer or shorter time during the dry season. Fruit very much liked by birds, and always full of little parrots. Fruit and leaves very small. One of the most beautiful of Tropical trees." (*Plant Immigrants*, No. 130, p. 1124).

Through the kindness of Dr. Fairchild I received in 1919 two small plants of this interesting species from the Bureau of Plant Industry. In November, 1920, I planted them out in my Solitude Garden at Naples, and one of them is at present 7 feet high and almost as much in diameter, very dense—as dense as the Cuban Laurel Rubber, and as beautiful, though the leaves are of a lighter duller green and when young strongly suffused with coppery red. They are also a little larger. The finest and largest specimen in my garden grows on high and rather dry pine land, the much smaller one on moist mucky soil. Both were planted at the same time and received the same care, and both were of the same size. The one on moist sour soil is scarcely 3 feet high, but very healthy and robust.

Ficus pandurata: Said to have been introduced from the mountains of Kamerun, West Africa. It is scarcely in cultivation more than twenty-five years. The leaves are somewhat fiddle-shaped, large, leathery, glossy deep green and wavy-edged. Up north it is largely grown as a pot plant. In south Florida it is perfectly hardy, thriving with great vigor and soon forming large fine specimens. There are several in the gardens of Fort Myers. The largest one on the main street, almost opposite the grounds of the Royal Palm Hotel, is a dense and fine tree about 25 feet high with a crown 12 feet in diameter, and a clean trunk of about 10 feet in height. For several years it has borne its crop of figs. Each is about as large as a small plum and when ripe is of a deep crimson color, and very soft. As this is a very distinct, large-leaved, dense shade tree it should find a place in every good garden. As an avenue tree on city streets it is most valuable, as its growth is not aggressive or over vigorous. In fact I believe that this is the finest and most beautiful of all Rubber Trees for street planting. For lawn planting it is of particular merit on account of its large leaves and its fine form.

[*Ficus aspera*], Variegated Rubber Tree, South Sea Islands: One of the most showy foliage plants of our northern conservatories and botanical gardens. A well grown dense specimen always attracts the attention of even those who cannot be called plant enthusiasts. Specimens 10 to 15 feet high are not rare, and they are as striking as can well be imagined, the numerous red fruit contributing to the beauty of the effect. It is rarely seen in Florida, and I am unable to say what size and form large specimens may show.

Years ago I had a thrifty dense plant, about 7 feet high, in my lath house at Gotha, among Caladiums and other foliage plants. The soil was rich and moist. Late in fall it bore numerous small figs of a beautiful red color. I lost it by a heavy freeze and have not succeeded to grow it since. "It is so hard to keep free from root-knot and other insect pests," says Mr. E. N. Reasoner. "It is a very pretty thing in damp soil, under the sun, where it loses a good deal of its variegation." A good lath house is a valuable adjunct to every good garden in Florida. Many of the finest and most delicate shade-loving plants can only be grown in such a structure, and here this fine variegated Rubber Tree would find a congenial home.

Ficus pseudopalma, Philippine Islands: Introduced by the Bureau of Plant Industry, this is a strikingly distinct species, thriving well in south Florida. My small specimen was lost in transplanting, but Mr. J. E. Hendry, Jr., of Fort Myers has a plant about 12 feet in height, showing a single unbranched stem, tipped with leaves about 2 to 3 feet long and only a few inches broad. Would make a fine lawn plant.

Ficus rubiginosa (*F. australis*), Port Jackson Fig, Narrow-Leaved Rubber Tree, Australian Banyan, New South Wales, Australia: In 1893 I had, for the first time, an opportunity to see a dense well grown specimen of about 15 feet high, of the Australian Rubber Tree (as it was called on the label) in the glasshouse of Lincoln Park in Chicago. I was charmed with its unique beauty of form, is density of growth and its small abundant foliage. The head gardener was kind enough to present me with a small plant, which I sent to my place at Gotha, Fla. In the freeze of 1895 the specimen, being small and not in good health, was killed outright. A few years ago it was introduced and distributed by the Bureau of Plant Industry, and I obtained a good sized specimen, which grows luxuriantly on my place here at Naples. The numerous handsome leaves are 3 to 4 inches long, shining green, oblong, on petioles about an inch long, obtuse at the point and the base, and covered with a rusty-brown down on the underside of the young leaves.

The late J. H. Veitch in his *A Traveler's Notes* describes a large specimen in the Adelaide Botanical Garden thus: "Near the entrance is a *Ficus rubiginosa,* for 50 feet from the ground and upwards, a round of solid somber green, its somewhat small branches radiating from eight main stems, several of which reach the utmost height of the tree. It is an impressive object." And in another place he calls it "a truly magnificent tree." It is one of the hardiest of all the rubber Trees and one of the very best for street and highway planting. The beauty of the foliage and its dense growth are sufficient to make this one of the most attractive of trees, but its charm is enhanced by the abundance of its small red figs, the size of a cherry, first green, becoming light red and ultimately deep crimson. They are eagerly sought by numerous small birds. The ground is frequently covered with the fallen fruits which are eaten with avidity by chickens, turkeys, guinea hens and quails.

[*Ficus nekbudu*] Kaffir Fig, South African Rubber Tree: Introduced by the Bureau of Plant Industry about ten years ago, and collected by Mr. O. W. Barrett, an enthusiastic plant man, who gives the following account: "A medium-sized tree of the open bush, from Zululand to Somaliland. Prefers sandy soil. Almost evergreen, except in long drouths. Thick bark used, when beaten out, for clothing, etc. Appears to wear well. Roots well from cuttings. Fruit worthless." This is supplemented by the following: "A flat-topped or rounded tree, single stemmed by nature, but often cultivated to the extent of being cut off at the ground so to produce four to six coppice branches without knots, and of rapid growth, from which to obtain fiber; this after preparation, is used as cloth." (*Seed and Plants Imported*, No. 26, p. 14.)

Several years ago I had the good fortune to receive six nice young plants from the Bureau of Plant Industry. After having set them out on my place here at Naples in various dry and moist spots all began to grow most vigorously, though they seem to do best in drier soils. It is one of the large leathery-leaved species, and at first sight and superficially viewed, it reminds one of *F. altissima*, but closer examination reveals the fact that it is very different. It is a very strong grower. One of my specimens has a broad flat top. The others are more rounded in form, but I believe that the flat crown will be the rule. Small thread-like air-roots of a brown color are abundantly produced from the base of the big branches near the trunk. The leaves are long,—12 to 14 inches long, 6 to 7 inches wide—bright green, distinctly nerved with white and showing a conspicuous ivory-white midrib. It is easily raised from cuttings. In fact, it is so easily propagated that many nice young plants are frequently seen in the gardens of Fort Myers and elsewhere.

[*Ficus auriculata*] (S.P.I. No. 30, p. 44): A middle-sized tree found on the lower slopes of the Himalayas in northern India, rising to an elevation of 6,000 feet and extending from Assam to the valley of the Indus River." This is a very ornamental and well known species with broadly ovate or rounded leaves 5 to 15 inches long, 4H to 12 inches broad. It is said to assume a height of from 10 to 25 feet, and would make a fine ornamental for our tropical gardens. Veitch saw a bush in Calcutta with a spread of 20 yards. It was very striking with its large leaves.

This species of fig was named by the late Dr. Walich in honor of the illustrious Roxburgh, for many years superintendent, and to a large extent the founder of the Botanical Garden at Calcutta, and the father of Indian botany. [*F. auriculata*] is a native of the lower and outer Himalayas, from Nepal to Bhutan, being found at elevations of from 1,000 to 3,000 feet. It is a tree from 15 to 25 feet in height and with a wide-spreading head. The leaves are large. The most striking feature in the tree, however, is the great abundance of its handsome russet figs. These Figs are carried in enormous bunches on the stem, especially near its base, and smaller bunches on the main branches. The mass of figs borne at the collar of the stem weighs often a hundred weight. It is a remarkable spectacle and one which produces a sensation in every lover of plants and fruits. The fruit, however, although eaten by the unfastidious Indian laborer, is quite unpalatable to a European, being insipid and sloppy. (Gardener's Chronicle)

Ficus ulmifolia, Los Banos, Philippine Islands (S.P.T. No. 35, p. 46): "A good edible form of the Philippine Fig. Occasional individual trees of this small Fig give very sweet and palatable fruits. Figs for moist, hot countries are a great desideratum." (C. F. Baker). This should be tried as a fruit tree in our south Florida gardens. It is evidently a species combining beauty with utility.

[*Ficus deltoidea*] Mistletoe Fig, India and Malayan Peninsula: A very distinct and beautiful species. The shining green elliptic leaves are about a foot long by 6 inches broad, covered with a thick coat of silky hairs beneath, the underside being of snowy whiteness.

Ficus [*benghalensis*] 'Krishnae,' Krishna Bor: Regarded as sacred by the Hindus. A remarkable Rubber Tree which has the leaves turned backward and the edges joined so as to form a cup, with the upper side of the leaf forming the outside of the cup. Fruit axillary, solitary or sometimes in pairs. Its large, showy, peculiar cupped leaves will undoubtedly make this most distinct species popular.

Fig Trees of Mexico

Since I began to get interested in the species of the genus *Ficus* in the early nineties of the last century they have obtained a firm foothold in my mind. And the more I penetrated into the depths of beauty of giant forms and of dense masses of foliage, of mystery and awe-inspiring grandeur, I have been unable to retrace my steps out of the labyrinth of new forms and new names. The more I occupy my mind with their study, the firmer is their hold on me, and the more intense my interest.

This interest dates back to the time when the late C. G. Pringle published his notes on some of the Mexican species in *Garden and Forest* (1893). About the present species he had the following to say: "Another wild Fig is less restrained in its habitat than *Ficus jaliscana* (correct name *F. petiolaris*) [Pringle's aside], for it is common on the plains about the city whose name it bears, as well as by the riverside in the great barranca. It attains in this situation immense proportions. In drier and open situations it forms low wide-spreading tops. It is an admirable shade tree with its dense foliage of lanceolate leaves, and its fruits, which are nearly an inch in diameter, are of use as food for pigs and other animals."

Long before I came in close contact with this highly ornamental species as a garden plant I had been intensely interested in its introduction to Florida, and I had made many attempts to obtain seeds or young plants. I had always failed until I became acquainted with Dr. C. A. Purpus of Zacuapam, Huatusco, Vera Cruz, Mexico, the celebrated botanist and botanical collector, who sent me fresh seeds of this and other Mexican *Ficus* in the fall of 1925. These seeds germinated readily, and I have now almost a dozen beautiful dense small trees of this Guadalahara Fig in my collection. They are densely foliaged and provided profusely with branches from the ground up. The deep green, somewhat glossy leaves are large and leathery, oval-oblong in form and quite hairy when young. These young specimens are so attractive that I anticipate in this new introduction a real gem among shade trees. In many parts of Central America and Mexico it is a favorite avenue and lawn tree, being very broad in form and of dense growth. The edible fruits are quite large and abundantly produced. Evidently it is well adapted to the climatic and soil conditions of Florida. My small specimens have not suffered in the least by our heavy frosts early in January and again March 4

(1927) which proved so disastrous to tropical plants along our lower West Coast.

In a letter to the author, Prof. Paul C. Standley, the acknowledged authority on Mexican and Central American shrubs and trees, and particularly on the various *Ficus* species, writes as follows: "I think I can get seeds of *Ficus glaucescens*. It is very common in Central America, an easily recognized form (there are some others closely related) because of the very large fruits, often two inches in diameter. They are not bad to eat." In Mexico, from Vera Cruz to Sinaloa, it seems to be very abundant and is often found around the houses of the inhabitants and along streets and country roads as a shade tree.

I have lately, May 9, received from Dr. Harold L. Lyon, Forester and Botanist of the Hawaiian Sugar Planters' Experiment Station, 28 new *Ficus* species in beautiful small healthy specimens. This brings up my collection of *Ficus* to over 115 species. These, with many tall palms, flowering trees and Bamboos, will convert the landscape in Collier County, and also in Lee County—monotonous as it is now—into a veritable tropical paradise.

A few days ago the writer received a very interesting letter from New York from which the following is quoted:

A friend of mine in Florida who is acquainted with the fact that I have resided for years in Mexico, prospecting for oil, and who also knows that I had had my temporary home for a while in the town of Sayula, sent me a copy of the *American Eagle*, in which you refer to the Fig Tree avenues of that interesting place. I am no botanist, but I am extremely interested in what you say about this wonderful broad, dense tree under the shade of which I have often rested. I may add, too, that the fruit, though small, is sweet and edible and can be converted into an excellent jam. It is sold in the markets and is much used in the Mexican household. You call it the Sayula Rubber Tree, but the natives call it 'Nacauli' and 'Comuchini'.

To resume, this is the most beautiful and the densest shade tree I ever have seen and the avenues formed of it and the specimens in the parks are most wonderful trees. There are many other such trees with milky sap (*Ficus* sp.) in Mexico, some of them with large shiny leaves and all very dense and beautiful,—often equally beautiful to the Sayula species,—but I only know the native names of some of them. The old Mexicans, before the conquest and in the times of Montezuma, planted them for ornament and use. Their wood is no good, but it has been used in making paper, even hundreds of years ago. You reside in Florida and I own land in the state—in Highlands and Polk County. There are not many shade trees in Florida, the Live Oak being perhaps the best, but even this is far behind the various Mexican Fig Trees for shade.

I am glad that, according to your statement, you have this Sayula Rubber tree and several other Mexican species in your collection. I made an attempt to obtain a copy of Dr. Standley's book on the subject, but was informed that it is out of print. Could you not give me a list of these trees and where they are to be found? I am leaving again for Mexico soon and I shall try to study them and get specimens for my Florida holdings. They are, however, quite tender, but I think should succeed where the Assam or Indian Rubber does well. About all of them are beautiful ornamental trees and very valuable for shade but I know not their botanical names. If you succeed in adding these trees of Mexico to the list of shade trees in Florida you would do a great work for the state,—much more valuable to future generations than most millionaires have done and could do.

In reply to the above I can only say that I personally know very little of the *Ficus* species of Mexico. Dr. C. A. Purpus of Zacuapam, Vera Cruz, and Dr. B. P. Reko, Guadalajara, have given us valuable bits of information about some of the species. For about 35 years I have tried to obtain plants or seeds of the fine species that the late Mr. Pringle described in *Garden and Forest,* but I only recently succeeded to add about four to my collection, raised from seed that Dr. C. A. Purpus had the kindness to send me.

I have most beautiful and lovely species raised from seeds that came from a celebrated botanist, Dr. C. A. Purpus, of Zacuapam Huatusco, Vera Cruz, Mexico, and I shall be supplied with seeds from various fine species from Oaxaca, Mexico, coming from Sr. Emilis Makrinius, Cafetal Couerdio, Oaxaca. My friend, Mr. August Koch, the creator of that wonderful plant paradise, Garfield Park Conservatories, in Chicago, usually takes care of these tropical seeds.

I am alone here in my little shack, being scarcely more than a camp but I never feel lonesome. My books and my plants are my best companions. There are many visitors—kindred spirits—all interested in my plants and my work, and there are red letter days—days when Mr. and Mrs. Thomas Edison call, or when Dr. David Fairchild with Mrs. Fairchild and others make their appearance. There are red letter days of a different nature, however. Such a day came on May 9, 1928—my 75th anniversary.

There were no letters, no congratulations and not one of the members of my family turned up. The world seemed to have forgotten me. But early in the forenoon came a neat and large box, containing a beautiful collection of *Ficus* species, almost all new to my collection, from Honolulu, Hawaii, an addition to my *Ficus* assemblage, from Dr. Harold L. Lyon, Botanist and Forester of the Hawaiian Sugar Planters Association. There were 28 species, the names of many of them being quite unfamiliar to me. All of them immediately began to grow and they all now promise to be very soon features of our south Florida landscape.

About the same time I received from my friend A. Koch in Chicago: *Ficus* sp., from Mexico,—5 species; *F. fulva, F. parietalis, F. kallicarpa,*—a dense vigorous climber. *F. platyphylla* and *F. capensis.* The seeds of the first two were collected by Dr. David Fairchild in India. The climbing species as found by him in Sumatra and the last two in Nigeria, tropical West Africa.

Dr. C. A. Purpus, a botanist who sent me seeds of at least 10 or 12 Mexican species, says in one of his letters: "Down along the coast in the *barrancas* of the *tierra caliente* I found a *Ficus* which I at once pronounced as a wonder of nature. There is growing one of these trees near La Antigua on the coast, which forms a forest of pillars. I never before saw anything like it. This is a real Banyan of Mexico."

In Part II of his excellent and valuable work *The Trees and Shrubs of Mexico,* Prof. Paul C. Standley gives a complete list and accurate scientific description of all the species of *Ficus* so far known from Mexico—23 in number.

Climbing *Ficus* Species

The tree-like Ficus or Rubber Trees have been frequently mentioned in these columns. The climbers of the genus are equally interesting, and very beautiful. Some of them grow on tall trees of the tropical forest, festooning the trunks and branches with a network of fine branches and foliage. In the summer of 1926 Dr. David Fairchild collected seeds of two of these climbers in the forests of Sumatra and sent them to the writer. Only one of them—a still undescribed species—germinated, and there is now a fine small plant in the writer's garden at Naples. As there are no facilities in my garden for treating tropical seeds successfully, I sent others to my friend, Mr. Aug. Koch, at

Garfield Park Conservatories, with the result that many fine Ficus and other trees are now the pride of the Tropical Gardens and Arboretum at Naples.

[*Ficus sagittata*] 'Variegata': This is a very beautiful variety, but it is rarely seen, as none of our nurserymen has thought it worthwhile to propagate it. It is dwarf and bushy in height, with pretty mottled foliage, gray-green and white. It appears to be a strong grower, and is a highly attractive plant. In 1897 shortly after its introduction, it received a first-class certificate from the Royal Horticultural Society of London. Its native habitat is the [Himalayas to Philippine and Caroline islands].

Of the small creeping kinds of Ficus that we have now in our gardens, and which are particularly valuable for clothing walls, chimneys, board fences and for similar purposes, by far the best known is *Ficus stipulata* [= *F. pumila*] or *F. repens*, as it is frequently called, and the still smaller variety of it 'Minima,' which is exceedingly neat in growth. Besides these there is a larger and looser growing species,—[*F. sagittata*],—whose leaves are each from 2 to 3 inches long and an inch wide.

The curious manner in which the upper portion of [*Ficus pumila*] will change its entire appearance, as soon as it overtops its support, created quite a sensation when this first happened in Palm Cottage Gardens. The beautiful network of small leaves, closely pressed against the board wall surrounding my plant-house, was most attractive. As soon, however, as the wall was covered and the upper twigs reached the top the stems grew as thick as a pencil and the thin fine leaves became large,—six times as large as the old ones,—deep green and leathery, and there appeared numerous large pear-shaped fruits, dry, hollow inside and of no value. Several members of the scientific staff of the Bureau of Plant Industry visited my garden and took a number of photographs of the changed tops, as well as of the fruit. I feel inclined to think that others also will undergo this change when they become large enough to outgrow their support.

The climbing or Creeping Figs form a class by themselves, being different in growth, form and in their uses from all other species of *Ficus*. All of them, as far as I have experimented with them, are extremely interesting, very dense and beautiful. My knowledge, however, is limited, not having been able to obtain more than six or seven species. Only one of them (*F. repens* or *F. stipulata*) [both = *F. pumila*] proved perfectly hardy at Palm Cottage Gardens, while all the other species were very tender, being killed outright by the first heavy freeze—18° and 20°F. At Naples most of the tropical species will undoubtedly be entirely hardy in well protected spots, in hammock woods and under lath-house cover. All of them are most impressive and beautiful ornaments for walls, pillars, chimneys and tree trunks, being particularly effective on tall palm stems, which they festoon with elegant foliage masses. I was always delighted to see the dense wreath-like branches hanging down from the top of one or the other tall palm.

Years ago—in 1903 and 1904—I had the pleasure of seeing most admirable specimens of [Ficus villosa], [F. punctata], [F. sagittata] and [F. pumila] forming most charming decorations of many a massive palm trunk in Horticultural Hall, Philadelphia. It grew on the tall stem of a palm and festooned it in a most beautiful way with drooping branches. The common creeping Fig [F. pumila] was my first acquaintance. It interested and impressed me at first sight, and it still belongs to my favorites in the plant world. I saw it first on the walls of the beautiful Metairie Cemetery in New Orleans in 1891. It formed a dense network of closely appressed small branches and masses of small foliage. The pillars forming the entrance were also covered from top to bottom with this fine Ficus. I have had it for many years in my garden at Gotha.

Several species and varieties with the habit of the one just mentioned have been introduced into cultivation in Florida, and though scarcely known as yet outside of a few gardens, they will very likely find favor with many plant lovers. I shall only briefly describe the species that I have had in my garden, and which proved to be very interesting.

[Ficus sagitatta]: I obtained this fine creeping Fig, and the still finer variety, F. radicans var. variegata, in 1897 from England. Both grew well in my greenhouse in Milwaukee, and were a perfect success in my garden in Florida, as long as there were no killing freezes. The names of these two forms are rather confusing, "Thus F. radicans appears to be a garden name for a plant of which a flowerless specimen was collected by Sir Joseph Hooker in Chattagong and still unnamed in the Kew Herbarium. The name radicans had been given by Roxburgh to the species known to botanists as Ficus rostrata, which is quite distinct from F. radicans of gardens. This name may therefore be retained for the plant under notice, at any rate until it can be determined botanically. Some cultivators confuse this plant with F. repens but the two are quite distinct in habit and leaf characters."

There are many beautiful climbing species in the tropical forests, especially of Burma [Myanmar], India, etc., some of them of great beauty, but I only succeeded to obtain the one mentioned. A fine unnamed species was raised from seed collected by Dr. David Fairchild in Sumatra.

[*F. sagittata*]: Stems creeping, smooth, wiry, green when young, dark brown when old, rooting freely, and bearing at intervals of about an inch alternate leaves with whitish stipules. Petiole half an inch long. Blade lanceolate, cordate at base, 3 inches long by 1 inch wide, light green. An evergreen, useful for covering walls, pillars, etc., in warm glasshouses. The variety *variegata* has leaves prettily marked and margined with milk-white.

"This is the plant popularly known as *F. repens*, a smaller-leaved form of it being known as *F. minima*. It has ovate, obliquely cordate leaves from 1/2 to 1 inch long, in its creeping or barren stage, and much larger, lanceolate-cordate in its tree or flowering stage." [probably Dr. King, director of the Calcutta Botanic Garden]

I have had this creeping Fig for many years—since 1893—in Palm Cottage Gardens, where it is growing most vigorously, forming a very effective decoration on the west wall of my tropical plant-house. It took possession of the rough boards immediately after it had been planted, covering in the course of time a space 125 feet long and 7 feet high. The small leaves are thin, of a pleasant light green color and are closely appressed, or lie flat, on the boards. In this form it is a most lovely creeper, its masses of small wiry branches which adhere tightly to their support by their fine rootlets, and its dense small leaves forming a very effective mosaic of bright green.

A most peculiar and characteristic change, however, takes place as soon as the plant outgrows its support and overtops the wall. An entirely new plant seems to have been formed. The new shoots grow upright, are quite stiff and woody, and the leaves become large, heart-shaped, wavy dark green and very leathery. The milky sap is now very abundant and is said to form very good rubber. The fruits now also make their appearance. They are large, hollow, pear-shaped, greenish-white and of the size of a small peach. When my large specimen fruited for the first time in 1905 it created a sensation among plant lovers and experts, and there was much doubt expressed whether or not this large-leaved woody upright form, full of conspicuous fruit, could be identical with the small-leaved plant closely attached to its support. People came from far and near, even Washington, to see this Ficus in fruit and in its large-leaved garb.

Though not at all a common plant in our Florida gardens, being hardy all over, it is met with only now and then in choice collections. There is, for instance, a fruiting specimen in the beautiful grounds of the Koreshan Unity at Estero, Fla. Years ago I gave a fine small plant to a lady friend of mine at Orlando. She set it out at the foot of a rather large Live Oak. It at present covers the entire trunk with a network of its fine foliage, and soon will reach the top. It would be a still more impressive picture if planted at the trunk of a tall palm.

[*Ficus montana*]: Oak-leaved creeping Fig, a native of Burma and Malaya. I received my plant from Mr. Montague Free, of the Brooklyn Botanic Gardens. It grows exceedingly well in my tropical garden and arboretum at Naples, Fla., forming dense bushy masses. The long wiry branches being flat on the ground, take root at once and form excellent propagating material. The leaves are dark green, small and are much lobed, reminding one of dwarf Oak leaves. If planted on a wall I think it soon would form almost as dense masses as our common creeping *Ficus*. It is a very tender species, but my plant did not suffer in the least by our exceptional cold weather early in January, 1927. Being a very rare plant—my species being the only one I know of in Florida—no definite opinion as to its size and behavior can be expressed at this time.

There are many other climbing species of *Ficus* found in the oriental tropics, and many of them are of great beauty, festooning the tallest forest trees with their masses of drooping branches. None of these species appears to be injurious to the tree it grows on. Dr. Fairchild found another fine climbing Fig in Sumatra and sent me seed, but they failed to germinate.

Shrubs

The plant lovers of south Florida,—in fact of all Florida,—are constantly searching for plants that flower during the winter season. I am frequently requested by correspondents to supply them with lists of such winter bloomers. Fortunately there are many hundreds of them, but they are difficult to obtain, as only comparatively few are propagated by our nurserymen. Some of the very best such as the Brunfelsias, the Winter Sweet [*Acocanthera oblongifolia*] and *Toxicophlaea thunbergii* [?], with corymbs of beautiful and very fragrant flowers, cannot be found outside of botanical gardens. The very showy *Sparmannia africana,* the gorgeous [*Burchellia bubalina*], the distinguished *Alberta magna* and the superb *Calodendrum capense,* all first rate winter flowering shrubs, are looked for in vain in catalogues. The Chinese Hibiscus stands easily at the head of flowering shrubs blooming constantly summer and winter, and the Turks-cap is quite as profuse a bloomer, though much less showy. *Bauhinia,* particularly *B. purpurea,* is a most beautiful flowering shrub or small tree, the large purple and white orchid-shaped flowers being always objects of admiration during the tourist season.

More Winter Flowering Shrubs

Gardenia jasminoides, Cape Jasmine, Gardenia: The genus was named after Dr. Alexander Garden of Charleston, S.C. In the Gardenia we have another plant aristocrat of the highest rank from China. In the South it is almost as much appreciated,—and in many localities even more so,—than the rose, being one of the most exquisitely and powerfully fragrant.

When well grown it is an ideal garden ornament, attaining a height of 4 to 6 feet, of dense upright growth and with rather large shiny ovate, deep evergreen, leathery leaves and opening its waxy-white, intensely fragrant double flowers in May. It is an old popular shrub in the southern gardens, having been introduced very likely during colonial times. With the Camellia and the Rose, the Gardenia belonged to a trio of the most fashionable flowers during ante-bellum days. Its glorious fragrance was particularly valued and the pure white color of the waxy double flower was another point in its favor, though not as perfectly regular as those of Camellia. Though I had seen it under glass in the North, I was never particularly struck with its appearance. In May, 1879, I had the first opportunity to enjoy its beauty in almost every garden at Houston, Texas. The effect was not only very delightful, but I was charmed with its dignified and noble appearance, its wealth of powerfully fragrant flowers. I saw that the gardens were replete with it. Everywhere, wherever planted, it added a peculiar charm to its surroundings.

From New Orleans, Mobile and other Southern cities large consignments of cut Gardenias are sent north, finding a ready sale wherever offered. But it is the fresh Cape Jasmine, just cut, that seems to be the incarnation of perfection, with its delicious perfume and pure waxy whiteness. When I started my garden in Florida I selected, besides the many beautiful native plants, the most charming Chinese and Japanese trees and shrubs I had so often admired and raved over in the halcyon days of my life. The gardenia, in quite a few distinct varieties, belonged to the very first I planted. They have always been in the vicinity of my home in Florida, though they did not thrive without careful attention in the dry, poor sand. In my garden at Naples, where the soil is moister and richer, they grow most vigorously and flower abundantly. A well drained spot rich in humus and fairly moist is what they require. I have a small plant here, only about 3 feet high, from which I cut over a hundred fine large flowers last May and June. Healthy plants in vigorous growth suffer little from the attacks of insects, but neglected and weak specimens soon fall a prey to quite a number of injurious pests. The white fly is particularly bad, as it leaves a black soot on the beautiful foliage. Healthy out-of-door plants suffer rarely with these pests. My plants have never been troubled in the least by any of them.

The name Cape Jasmine is as inappropriate as many other plant names, as the species is a native of China and not of the Cape of Good Hope. The plant was first brought to England in the middle of the eighteenth century by an English sea captain who met with a bush of it in full flower, somewhere near the Cape of Good Hope. He brought the whole plant in a pot to England, where it soon became known as the Cape Jasmine.

Phillyrea vilmoriana: Dr. Alfred Rehder of the Arnold Arboretum regards this as synonymous with *Phillyrea decora* [*P. decora* is accepted at present], a most beautiful evergreen, large-leaved shrub from western Asia. I have had this jewel among shrubs for many years in my collection at Gotha, where it grew best in half shade and in rather sandy soil. It usually flowers in May. One cannot overlook it when in bloom as its fragrance always attracts attention. The odor reminds me of Waldmeister, yet it is more powerful. The white Jessamine-like flowers are produced in axillary clusters, and contrast well with the dark green foliage. The leaves are fully 6 inches long, and about 1½ inches broad. This fact, combined with the perfect globular form the plants develop, make it one of the most desirable evergreens we can grow in Florida. It is easily raised from seeds and can also be grown from cuttings.

Dombeya wallichii: This most exquisite of all our midwinter bloomers is one of the most gorgeous and distinct plants ever introduced into this country. Whenever a fine large dense bush, covered with its large, globose, deep pink, drooping flower-heads is for the first time seen it creates a sensation. People rave over its unique beauty, so different from anything else that we are accustomed to see among plants. Nothing, indeed, can excel it in massive and impressive beauty and grandeur, when in full bloom. But the showy flowers are not its only good qualities. Its growth is vigorous, dense and upright, and its very abundant leaves are large, cordate, angular lobed and of a deep green color. Even without flowers the dense foliage alone is sufficient to rank it as a first-class ornamental. When I saw it in flower for the first time in Horticultural Hall in Philadelphia, in March, 1904, I was spellbound. The fragrant flower-heads covered the shrub from top to bottom. I at once became aware of the fact that human imagination could not depict such a wonderful sight even in its most vivid dreams. What a wonderful garden plant this would be in Florida! I scarcely dared to think of such a possibility. The label, attached to the plant, gave its old name *Astrapaea wallichii*, and Madagascar as its native country. I immediately looked it up in the botanical and horticultural literature, but could not find much. When I went home in April I took a small rooted cutting with me. Planted out in rich, rather moist soil, in the rainy season it immediately began to grow, and it flowered in the winter of 1906 for the first time. A few years later it was killed outright by a hard freeze. It had reached a height of 5 or 6 feet in my garden at Gotha in Orange County. Being a true denizen of the African tropics it is not able to stand more than a few degrees of cold. Our queen of flower trees, the Royal Poinciana, and the Traveler's Tree hail from the same region. All three plants are hardy from Punta Gorda on the west coast, and from Palm Beach on the east coast southward.

The finest and largest specimen I ever found in south Florida grew in the garden of Dr. Geo. W. Tyrrell, on the south bank of the famous Caloosahatchee near Turner's Point. It was an extremely conspicuous object as seen from the road,—one of the most superb bushy trees I ever have seen. When I passed the place in June the flowering season was over but its upright, dense growth, and its abundant large, deep green leaves at once revealed the fact that this Dombeya is a gem among broadleaved evergreens and that it is perfectly hardy in south Florida. Unfortunately this specimen was killed by the floods last summer (1922). It was planted in an open square near the highway, and it formed one of the wonders of the plant world for the tourists from the northland, coming and going from Fort Myers to LaBelle.

This Dombeya should be in all good gardens. In order to develop its full beauty it must have sufficient space. It is an excellent plant for the open lawn where it can spread and grow into a perfect specimen, and where alone it is able to exhibit its full beauty. Never should it be planted among masses and groups of other shrubs and trees. It is also well adapted for the borders of artificial ponds, or for the banks of brooks and rivers, and for the edge of lakes, provided the land is high and well drained. The picture of the masses of brilliant flowers among the background of dense deep-green foliage overhanging the border, is extremely fascinating. On high, dry pineland it also grows vigorously if planted in mulch supplemented with some old cow manure. Watering in such situations during the dry season becomes a necessity. It roots easily from cuttings, soon forming impressive specimens.

Two of the greatest botanical and horticultural authorities of the last century, Dr. Lindley and Sir Joseph Paxton, are unanimous in their praise of this Madagascar plant. Discovered and introduced by the Rev. Ellis, one of the most celebrated botanical collectors and travelers, the genus *Dombeya* received its name from Joseph Dombey, a botanist of the eighteenth century, who accompanied Ruiz and Pavón in their travels through Peru and Chili.

The name *Astrapaea,* the first one in use, comes from *astrape* which means lightning, in allusion to the brightness of the flower. There are about thirty or more species belonging to the genus *Dombeya,* all natives of the Mascarene Islands and south Africa. In addition to the one alluded to in the above we grow in our south Florida gardens a second species, [*Dombeya tiliacea*]. The flowers are also borne in crowded corymbs at the ends of the shoots. They are of a beautiful pink color and exhale a very delicate perfume, reminding of that of the May flower and the Freesia. The leaves are large, deep green, smooth cordate, acuminate with from three to five palmate lobes. The growth is more open and straggling and not so dense and upright as in the former species. It attains a height of about 10 feet. It is not as common in our gardens as it should be; in fact, I have seen it only in very few places, though it is a most beautiful and conspicuous winter-bloomer. One of my specimens here at Naples commenced to flower at Christmas time and on March 10 following it was still in full bloom. Like all the Dombeyas I have tried, it grows easily in deep, rich, well drained soil, being a very striking shrub at all times, an evergreen with large impressive foliage of a deep green color and a gem as a winter bloomer.

[*Dombeya tiliacea*]: Under the name *D. natalensis,* I have grown a shrub at Palm Cottage Gardens for several years with much success. On account of its pure white and very fragrant flowers, opening in great masses during the winter months, and with its large lobed leaves, it soon became one of my special favorites. It was introduced years ago by Dr. Franceschi of Santa Barbara, Calif., and found its way also to Florida. I found it quite tender and lost it after a few years of very vigorous growth by the heavy freeze of 1917. By banking all these tender plants with two feet of dry sand around the stem they can be saved, at least partly, from heavy freezes, and can be grown as far north at least as Sanford, where I have seen magnificent specimens treated in this way. The following interesting and beautiful species should be introduced into our gardens:

Dombeya burgessiae: This is a most beautiful evergreen shrub from the Cape of Good Hope. It was under my care for several years, having raised it from seed received from the Botanical Garden in Natal, South Africa. My specimens were all destroyed in the freeze of February, 1917 (at Gotha). Though showing a very strong family resemblance, it is nevertheless very distinct from all the rest in foliage, growth and floral display. The leaves are bright green and covered with dense hairs, being 4 to 5 inches broad and from 6 to 8 inches long. The flowers are large, with spreading white petals, marked at the lower bases with a bright rosy tint, which also extends up the veins into the center. They appear in large, drooping clusters during the winter season, exhaling a very delicate and extremely captivating perfume.

[*Dombeya burgessiae*] is from Tropical Africa. The flowers are white and very fragrant. The leaves are described as cordate-ovate and velvety to the touch. There is a fine cross (*D.* ✕Cayeuxcii) between this species and *D. wallichii*, which has been described as a "magnificent hybrid with pendant, many-flowered umbels of a beautiful pink, finely veined."

South Florida is a horticultural paradise. Nowhere else in this great country can gardens and parks be found of such beauty and magnitude as here. There are hundreds of beautiful palms available. The number of tropical shrubs and trees, one more beautiful than the other, for the decoration of our gardens, is very large. There are hundreds, or I might say as well, thousands to select from. The Crotons, in single specimens and in masses always are a revelation. Nowhere will *Pandanus* or Screw Pines, these wonderfully impressive denizens of the tropical world, grow with such luxuriance and beauty. It is unfortunate that the glory of the Royal Poinciana displays itself late in May and in June, when the tourist season is over.

Brunfelsias

My dear plant lovers: Stop, read and remember. I have a message for you. I am now introducing to you a number of real plant aristocrats, plants that flower in winter, with mostly blue flowers, exhaling a most delicious perfume, and hardy all over the peninsula, from Sanford southward. The writer has, since almost forty years, studied and introduced these plants—many thousands of them,—but he had neither the appliances nor the means to propagate them on a large scale. Among this material are many new and rare plants of great promise. To mention only one group I like to call the attention of my readers to the beautiful Brunfelsias.

Brunfelsia is a genus of about twenty [40] species found in Brazil, Central America and the West Indies, some 8 or 10 species being in gardens at the present time. Almost all of them are winter-flowering plants. They are among the gayest and most striking of tropical plants, but are by no means so extensively grown as their merits would lead us to expect. Most of the species have been under cultivation for over a century, several of the best having been introduced between 1840 and 1850, a period when many of the floral treasures of Brazil were unfolding their beauties in European, and particularly in English gardens. *Brunfelsia americana,* a native of the West Indies, was cultivated by Philip Miller in the Botanical Garden at Chelsea as long ago as 1735. Although this species has creamy-white or creamy-yellowish flowers with some purple stripes, all the others are of some shade of blue or purplish-blue. The flowers are frequently very sweet scented, the corolla being wide and spreading, dividing in five lobes, and having a long tube. Although on first opening the flowers are of the intensest blue, they gradually become paler, until at last they are almost white—a character which is common to all the species.

A strong recommendation of these plants for ordinary garden use lies in their easy culture and free-flowering qualities. Unlike many of the choicest of indoor plants, they require no special treatment to induce them to bloom, a clean healthy growth carrying with it a certainty of flowering. They are propagated readily by cuttings, which should be taken from the new growth as early in spring as possible. A point of special importance in their culture is that they should be shaded very carefully. A protracted exposure to bright sunlight causes the foliage to turn brown and even to fall. I had several species in my garden at Gotha. Those in shade grew well, but the ones in full sunlight, though they were large and old plants, finally died. All were perfectly hardy and flowered abundantly during February and March, perfuming the air all around them with a most delicious fragrance.

[*Brunfelsia pauciflora* var. *calycina*] has beautiful large, shining green, lanceolate leaves, and is one of the largest flowering species. It is of free growth and produces its very largest trusses of rich purplish-blue flowers throughout the year, but particularly during the winter months. Flowers are not fragrant. It is a fine plant for shady places in the garden and makes a most exquisite show plant for shady verandahs.

[*Brunfelsia pauciflora* var. *eximia*]: A beautiful plant and a dense grower, forming handsome bushes. It is extremely ornamental when it opens its rather large deep violet-blue flowers. These flowers are produced from the points of the shoots and are about two inches in diameter. My plants always began to flower in January and lasted to July. Like the former, it is a native of Brazil.

[*Brunfelsia pauciflora* 'Floribunda'], is a fine free-flowering and dense shrub, smaller than the two former. The rich dark livid-green leaves are elliptic and the beautiful violet-blue flowers have a small white eye. It is beautiful in flower in mid-winter and forms an exquisite ornament to any garden where rare and distinct plants are appreciated.

[*Brunfelsia pauciflora* var. *calycina* 'Macrantha'] is a large-leaved, strong growing Brazilian shrub I have had for years in my garden at Gotha, where it was perfectly hardy and never suffered from cold. The large leaves are rich dark green and often as much as 8 inches long and over 2 inches broad. The large lavender-blue flowers appear in dense axillary or terminal cymes in January and February. There is a small inconspicuous white eye in the center of the tube, and the flowers are not fragrant. I received my plant, as all the above named species, from the late John Saul of Washington, D.C., one of the most famous gardeners of the past generation. At that time such men, great enthusiasts and plant lovers, were called gardeners. At present, though, they mostly have a very inferior botanical and horticultural knowledge; they prefer to be called horticulturists.

Brunfelsia latifolia: Among all the Brunfelsias this and the following species are my particular favorites because their flowers exhale a most delicious and luring perfume. It is a very handsome and shapely shrub, 3 to 4 feet high, very dense, and produces its lavender-blue flowers in great abundance in mid-winter. Its leaves are broad elliptic and acute, from 4 to 6 inches long and about 2 inches broad, and of a beautiful deep green. The deliciously fragrant salver-shaped flowers are produced at the ends of the branches. Of a beautiful lavender-blue, when first opening, they become almost pure white in a day or two. It is a native of Brazil. I lost my plants here in Naples, the soil being evidently not suitable. In my garden at Gotha I had magnificent specimens. I recently received a small plant from the Brooklyn Botanical Garden, and it is now propagated in my collection at Sebring. We shall have, in the course of time, all the Brunfelsias available for distribution.

Brunfelsia uniflora: I had particular success with this species at Palm Cottage Gardens, but lost my largest and finest specimen by removing some large shrubs—*Michelia figo*—near it. The bright sun was too much for it. This also came originally from John Saul of Washington, D.C. It is a small flowering species, making, however, a great display in the winter months. The flowers are deliciously fragrant and of a very beautiful light violet-blue, changing to pure white within a few days. My plants were 3 and 4 feet high and densely branched. A rich light soil and shade are important to grow it well. The leaves are lanceolate-oblong, rather thin in texture, rich dark-green above and a little paler beneath. These two last named species are real gems among the Brunfelsias on account of their fragrance. A native of Rio de Janiero, Brazil.

Brunfelsia americana: This belongs in a different category. I have two fine specimens in my Naples Garden, having attained a height of 5 or 6 feet in the open. This species also should have half-shady spots to do its best. Superficially viewed, it is very different from all the rest, the flowers being upright trumpet-shaped, creamy-white with faint purplish streaks on the outside. They are produced for a few times during the warm months, and perfume the entire garden during the night. It is easily grown and ripens its berry-like brownish-green fruits in abundance. The leaves are of good size, ornate and of a yellowish-green color suffused with brown. A very desirable shrub from the West Indies.

Ixoras

Another feature in my Naples garden are the Ixoras, of which I had a goodly number of species and hybrids. The Ixoras are Oriental tropical shrubs of great beauty, and delight in our south Florida climate. A little shade is necessary and a rich moist soil. They form immense bushes, and are always covered with large heads of exquisitely brilliant flowers. I have had about ten different kinds in my Naples garden. The *Ixora coccinea* (and some of its varieties) from India has grown 12 feet tall and was almost as broad, being continually in flower, but blooms most abundantly during the summer months. There is a yellow variety of it that originated in Ceylon and is known as [*Ixora coccinea* 'Lutea']. Among the hybrids I have had *Ixora* XDixiana, *I.* XWilliamsii and *I.* XWestii. March to August they always were a sheet of brilliant red color. These varieties do not grow as tall as the first-named species.

There is no shrub that in brilliancy and profusion of flowers can excel the old *Ixora coccinea*—the "Flame of the Woods" and the "Fire-bush" of our south Florida gardens. The great flat heads of flowers often completely cover the specimen, and the bush grows as freely as a Lilac, much more dense and symmetrical. I had a specimen in my Naples garden in rich, moist mucky soil, which attained in the course of about 3 years a height of 12 feet and was almost as broad. It flowered most profusely in summer, but was never out of its beautiful flower trusses, not even in winter. *Ixora javanica* and its variety *I. javanica* var. *flava* are of more slender growth, but soon make large bushes and are in flower all the time. *Ixora* XWilliamsii is a hybrid with vivid scarlet-orange flower-heads, which cover the entire shrub for a long time during our summer months. The Willow-leafed *Ixora* (*I. salicifolia*) forms a graceful drooping shrub and hangs heavy with flowers.

Of the white-flowered species, *Ixora cuneifolia* [?] is the most satisfactory. [*Ixora chinensis*], which has a far handsomer flower, is not a strong grower. It is, however, of sturdy growth, and soon makes a large bush, and, though not like others in perpetual bloom, flowers in abundance about every three months. The most fragrant of all—the red and yellow varieties being scentless—is *Ixora odorata*, which is of very large growth, and bears heavy drooping heads of long-tubed pinkish blossoms, which at night fill the air with fragrance. *Ixora* XWestii is one of the hybrids with flat heads of rosy flowers. When in bloom, the whole bush is a dense mass of color. There are a few other hybrids of beautiful salmon-red flowers, which make a brilliant show when in bloom.

Ixora duffii, named in honor of the late Mr. Duff, at one time director of the Botanical Gardens at Sydney, New South Wales, is the most vigorous grower of all, soon forming a small tree. The leaves are immense and I have had heads of the vivid red flowers as big as one's straw hat. This last species was known as *I. macrothyrsa*. I have also had the following: *Ixora* [cultivars] ['Chelsonii'], flowers brilliant salmon-orange; *I.* ['Fraseri'], flowers scarlet in the tube, brilliant salmon above [and many more].

All the Ixoras grow exceedingly well in the open in rich, moist, mucky well-drained soil. All my specimens grow best in soil rather acid. They will not thrive well in dry land, unless it is filled with muck or kept well watered. They are so extremely beautiful—all of them—that no trouble should be too great to grow them well. They only thrive in the open in extreme south Florida. I have found them just as hardy as the Crotons. My plants, all under lath-covers, in my Naples garden, did not suffer during our cold spell in January, 1926, and again in 1927 when Mango trees, *Terminalia catappa, Dombeya wallichii* and others were cut down to the ground.

The Camellia

One of the glories of our southern gardens is undoubtedly *Camellia japonica*. It grows well from South Carolina to at least Bartow, Florida, and it flowers in winter. Not enough of these plants can be used in our gardens. All of them are most exquisitely beautiful, particularly the semi-double kinds. A real acid soil is needed free from lime.

I would like to call the attention of Prof. Harold Hume of the Glen St. Mary Nursery, who makes the growing of these and other Chinese and Japanese plants his specialty.

Camellia reticulata: This is the most beautiful of all Camellias in foliage, growth and flowers. This lovely species flowers in February, just at the height of the tourist season. The flowers are the largest of any Camellias, and are semi-double. This is, in the opinion of many, the most beautiful member of the genus. The flowers are of a lovely shade of glowing pink, and have golden stamens. The individual blossom measures from 5 to 7 inches across, and lasts fresh for some considerable time. The habit of the plant is more graceful and slender than that of most other Camellias and instead of the glossy foliage of most of the species the leaves are of a duller and rougher appearance, and are more pointed.

I introduced it directly from Japan in 1897, and it grew well in my garden at Gotha, near the lake's edge. Unfortunately the plants—two of them—were killed when the lake began to rise in 1905. Both had flowered, and the blooms were extremely gorgeous and well formed. There is no stiffness in the flowers as in those of *Camellia japonica,* the petals being undulated and loosely and irregularly arranged. The flowers are 6 inches or more in diameter and of the brightest rosy-red, and they are also quite fragrant. The specific name refers to the reticulations of the leaf, which is not glossy as in the *C. japonica,* but of a rather dull green. This species is much more tender than the common Camellia, being found most commonly in southern China and particularly in Hong Kong. I have had several specimens since, imported from Europe. They had been grafted on the common species and did not thrive here. I think *Camellia reticulata* will do well in south Florida, where the common kind does not do well at all. Grows 12 feet high.

Camellia sasanqua 'Alba fl. Plens': This wonderful fragrant pure white intensely double Camellia I also imported (with the single form) in 1897 from Japan. It grows well in the dry ground at Palm Cottage Gardens and is always a sheet of pure white blossoms at Christmas time. For this reason it has been called in my household the "Christmas Camellia." It required little attention and never suffers from diseases; not even from long protracted droughts. It should be in all good gardens of Florida, because it is a floral gem of the first water. [See also companion volume.]

Variegated and Colorful Leaves

Crotons in Florida [= *Codiaeum,* not to be confused with the genus *Croton*]: The "Crotons" form the glory of our south Florida gardens—a permanent glory. They are always beautiful, always brilliant. No other class of fine-foliaged shrubs is so rich and varied in color as Crotons when grown under favorable conditions. But unless they get the necessary attention, and genial atmosphere, they are far from being attractive. South Florida only, in this country, offers them all they need in climate and soil. It is the only region where they can be grown in the open all the year round.

Though being very beautiful as single specimens I like them best in masses and in large beds. The gardens at Fort Myers not only show fine, tall, dense specimens, but we can also enjoy them in large beds and in borders and hedges. There are also fine specimens at Punta Gorda and Fort Pierce, but these points can be put down as their northern limit in outside gardening. Palm Beach and Miami, Coconut Grove and Coral Gables and many other points are made beautiful by this beautiful show plant.

Large specimens, when kept clean and healthy, are extremely impressive, though it is as young plants that I think their full beauty is seen. They may be grown from 2 to 3 feet in one season, and with well-colored cuttings to start with they will have highly colored foliage down to the base. Cuttings may be taken at any time during the spring months, and the stronger the cuttings the better. Where good propagating accommodations are not at hand, the tops may be rooted before taking them from the plants. A few leaves should be removed, and the stem cut about half through and the knife run up so as to split the stem about half an inch or rather less, a small wedge being inserted to keep the cut open, and then some peat and sphagnum and bound around. If this is kept moist, but not too wet, roots will soon make their appearance in the moss. If carefully taken off and potted, they will only require to be kept close for a few days.

Very effective specimens can be grown in 4 or 5 inch pots, but for larger specimens pots should be used according to convenience. Such plants form wonderful objects for dinner table decoration. Crotons are not so particular as many other plants with regard to soil. I have seen them grown successfully in various composts. A good sandy loam, leaf-mould and in addition a little bone meal is a suitable mixture for pot plants. Of course if we plant them out in our south Florida gardens, any good rich soil, well drained and never too wet, will do. The Crotons are sun-lovers. They will never show their glorious brilliancy in wet shaded spots.

Although Crotons require a high temperature and plenty of moisture while growing, if carefully hardened off they will last wonderfully well in the often quite low temperature of our winter months in south Florida. In January, 1927, and again in January, 1928, the temperature in my Naples garden went down to 25°F, but not one of my Crotons was injured in the least. Neither have I seen any damage done to them at Estero or Fort Myers, where Crotons belong to the most beautiful and effective garden decorations.

My old friend, Mr. J. E. Hendry, Jr., has made the Croton his specialty for many years, and they are now growing in his fine nursery—the Everglades Nursery of Fort Myers—by the thousands. They are also grown at Estero in large numbers for sale. It is my intention to call to the attention of all real plant lovers and of tropical beauty these gems of the plant world—plants that came originally to us from the South Sea Islands. The art of the hybridizer has given us the large number of most exquisite sorts, and new ones are continually appearing.

Yes, my friends, I have many of the most exquisite tropical plants which will interest you. So let us take a walk around the garden and admire them. First we will go to the lath house, west of the Cypress hammock. Two wonderfully large and broad Cuban Laurels [*Ficus microcarpa*] obliterate the view, and just when we enter this lath house two fine Royal Palms stand sentinel. The walk in the middle of the seven long Caladium beds is lined on either side with Crotons. These are the most brilliantly showy shrubs for a tropical garden, and I have had close to one hundred varieties of them, with great diversity of color and form of leaf.

When I just had started to form my collection I intended to have a specimen of every known Croton, but, finding that the numerous introductions were in no way superior to the older varieties and often very weak growers, I gave up adding to my collection. As grown in greenhouses some varieties have foliage wonderfully bright, and with good reason they hold high rank among gorgeous colored foliage plants, but to know them in all their brilliancy of coloring one must see foliage produced under a tropical sun upon plants which have had every opportunity for vigorous development. One must come to south Florida, where in places like Fort Myers, Palm Beach, Miami, Coconut Grove, etc., he will have a chance to go into raptures about what he sees. Which is the most brilliant variety it would be hard to say, for the diversity is so great that comparison is difficult, just as it is in the case of Fancy-leafed Caladiums, for more than a quarter of a century my most cherished specialties.

Our eyes first fall upon a dense tall specimen of *Codiaeum* 'Mooreanum', with long, heavy drooping yellow and green leaves, which is one of the best of its class. 'Autumn Beauty' shows a mass of deep brilliant red large leaves, reminding strongly of some of the colors of our northern woods in Indian summer. 'Sunset' is well named, its rich colors reminding me always of the enchanting colors when the sun sets over the blue waters of the nearby gulf in the western sky. 'Macleanum' has very large green leaves, irregularly marked with large blotches of yellow, and a very good companion is 'Grande', with dark red purplish foliage. Both of them are tall growers, soon forming large bushes. 'Maximum' and 'Mortii' are also tall yellow-leafed kinds with massive foliage.

Codiaeum 'Queen Victoria' and 'Williamsii' are fine red-leafed hybrids of the red-leafed class. Years ago I was spellbound when I came across a specimen of the first named, in the late Henry Flagler's garden, at Palm Beach. It was about 15 feet tall and almost as broad and very dense. 'Nigrum' has a deep crimson, almost black color, and 'Mangoldii' is almost yellow and one of the most distinct in the entire collection. Perhaps if we had to choose only a single variety of Croton we should take 'Stuartii', which though not particularly handsome in the glasshouse, is wonderfully brilliant under the south Florida sun.

Of the oak-leafed varieties the two best Crotons are 'Disraelii' and 'Lord Derby', with red and yellow markings respectively. 'Rodeckianum' has elegantly marked, long, drooping foliage and is a gem of its class. The old 'Cornutum', the midrib of the leaf of which terminating in a lighter brown just below the apex, makes a very symmetrical bush.

In the class with twisted leaves 'Tortile' and 'Spirale' are most desirable. 'Volutum' often has its beautifully disposed whorls of foliage of a rich yellow, and in its class 'Appendiculatum variegatum' is without a rival. 'Prince of Wales' is one of the choicest hybrids, but I have found it very difficult to propagate from cuttings.

Sanchezia nobilis: Several weeks ago I received a single leaf of the named plant for identification from a reader of the *American Eagle*, who had picked it up at Palm Beach. It belongs to the Acanthads, a family of plants which I would like to see as popular ornaments in our gardens. They should be largely grown, and many of them are fine winter flowering ornaments— mostly of a tropical nature. I intend from time to time to call attention to some of the best with the hope of bringing them to the front. It is astonishing what a bright display these plants make, and some of them may be had in bloom at all seasons, while not a few serve to brighten up the garden during our winter months.

Sanchezia nobilis is one of the most gorgeous of the family. It and a variegated form named *S. nobilis variegata,* of which I received the above mentioned leaf, were introduced from Ecuador. Both the species and variety are identical, save that the typical plant has rich green leaves, while those of the variety have a deep green ground, the midrib and all the primary nerves being broadly marked with bright, rich yellow and the margins are also of the same color. The shoots all produce terminal spikes of flowers which are very ornamental in the species, backed by the green leaves, but in the variety the effect is very striking. The panicles are terminal and lateral also, and are each about 2 inches long, and rich deep yellow in color, the lobes of the mouth being reflexed and the stamens exserted. [*S. nobilis* differs from *S. speciosa* chiefly in having leaves broadest near the apex, and staminodes only 3/16 of an inch long; material grown as *S. nobilis* is *S. speciosa.*]

I have had quite a number of fine specimens in my Naples garden, though the floods in 1926 destroyed quite a few. The plant is quite bushy, attaining a height of about 3 to 4 feet, and is always most conspicuous. I have grown them together with Crotons and Dracaenas and the arrangement was a benefit to all of them and formed lovely garden pictures.

Some Delightful Curiosities

[*Acalypha hispida*]: This is one of the most distinct and ornamental of the now very numerous new plants introduced by Messers. F. Sander and Co., St. Albans (England). It was discovered growing near the sea in the Bismarck Archipelago, by Mr. Micholitz when collecting in that region. He described it as a vigorous shrub 12 to 18 feet high, with large leaves and long tail-like flower-spikes colored bright red. It first flowered in the St. Albans Nurseries in the autumn of 1896, when Mr. N. E. Brown of Kew named and described it in the *Gardener's Chronicle,* calling it a very beautiful species, quite distinct from any other species in cultivation.

Most of the Acalyphas are grown for the brilliancy—mostly red—of their foliage, but the charm of this species is in its drooping female flower-spikes, which are dense and bushy, like a squirrel's tail on a small scale, and of a beautiful bright rose-madder color, effectively contrasting with the rich green of the leaves. Mr. Micholitz states that it is a sun-loving shrub of strong growth, very free-flowering, and that the beautiful flower spikes last a long time in perfection. Under cultivation the plant has exceeded the expectations formed from the collector's descriptions, the specimens shown by Mr. Sander at the Ghent Quinquennial and at the Temple show this year being really wonderful, whether viewed as examples of cultural skill or as decorative plants. I have seen the plant under cultivation ever since its introduction, and from its behavior I should call it a gardener's plant par excellence, as it grows freely and is practically always in flower. The tails attain a length of 21 inches and the thickness of a man's thumb, while in color they are of a vivid crimson, and in consistency they resemble the plush-like fabric known as chenille.

The genus *Acalypha* is well represented in our Florida gardens, particularly at Palm Beach and those southward to Miami. They evidently grow much better in the rocky limestone soil along the lower East Coast than they do in the more sour soils on the West Coast, though there are fine specimens at Fort Myers. They are all tropical or subtropical herbs, shrubs or trees, with small flowers in axillary or terminal racemes, and in many species the sexes are on different plants, while in others they are on the same plant, but in separate racemes. So far, quite a number of hybrids have been raised from [*Acalypha hispida*], but I have seen none finer than the true species. The only species known to have any horticultural value besides [*A. hispida*] are the ornamental-leaved, [*A. wilkesiana* 'Macrophylla'], 'Obovata,' 'Macfeeana,' and others, including the new 'Godseffiana.' In tropical gardens these plants play as important a part as the Crotons and Pandanuses. They are of the easiest cultivation, and when well grown they are most effective show-plants. They are particularly effective when bedded out on large beds in the full sun.

The cultural requirements of the Acalyphas are briefly stated—a tropical temperature, plenty of moisture and as much sunlight as possible. A rich loamy soil, liberal root space, frequently spraying overhead with water in dry weather to keep down red spider. I have had plants in flower from early

March throughout the summer, and their long tail-like vivid flowers have always attracted much attention, but, so far, the plant is not often seen in our gardens. Although new to European and American gardens and totally unlike all cultivated species of *Acalypha,* this plant has, as a matter of fact, been known as a garden plant in some countries of the East for 125 years at least. There is an excellent colored drawing of it in the Kew herbarium, dated 1812, and named *Caturus speciflorus,* which is a synonym of *Acalypha hispida,* and this is the correct name of the plant called here *A. sanderiana.* Sir Joseph Hooker says of *A. hispida* that it is only a garden plant in India, although it is included in Burmann's *Flora Indica,* and Roxburgh's *Flora Indica,* while Rumphius described it as *Caudafelis* (Cat's-tail). It is strange that a plant which has evidently been known and cultivated in Java, India, etc., for so long should have failed to attract the native collectors until Mr. Micholitz met with it. (Adapted from an article by W. W. in the *Garden,* 1898, pp. 62, 63.)

Hakea laurina: Where the conditions of soil and climate are favorable *Hakea laurina* is a gorgeous shrub when in flower. With me, at Palm Cottage Gardens, it was a winter-bloomer, flowering at the same time *Grevillea robusta, G. banksii* and other fine Australian shrubs are in full bloom. It forms a very fine, distinct shrub, 10 feet high, covered with balls of flowers, 2½ inches in diameter, their color being a brilliant scarlet, bristling with golden styles. Like most of the Australian Proteads (Grevilleas, Banksias, etc.,) it grows well in rather dry, sandy soil in central and south Florida. Mucky, moist soils are not adapted for these plants. There are about a hundred species of Hakeas, but this is said to be the most showy of them.

Banksia collina: Seldom are the members of this interesting genus, which belongs to the Proteaceae and is closely allied to our *Grevillea* or Silk Oak, found outside of our botanic gardens, and this is the more to be deplored considering the beauty of the foliage, and the remarkable character of their inflorescence. A plant of the above-named species I have had at Palm Cottage Gardens in flower late in November, the Bottle-Brush-like heads of blossoms springing from the forking of the branches being particularly striking. These are of yellowish color, with the pistil standing out, and the stigma turned back, in the shape of a hook. The leaves are about 3 inches in length, of a dark-green color above, while the underside is covered with silvery hairs. It is a native of Australia, where there are quite a number of distinct species of Banksias, all very beautiful. I have also had in bloom several of the allied Hakeas, but though very beautiful in foliage, their flowers cannot compare with those of the Banksias.

Protea cynaroides: Like *Banksia,* this is a Proteaceous plant, and it comes from South Africa. In spite of their noble foliage and gorgeous flowers, these plants find little favor with gardeners of the present day. Even in our botanical gardens they are poorly represented. This arises probably, in most cases, from insufficient space and from the inordinate demand for cut flowers and plants for decorative purposes. These latter are, no doubt, very beautiful, but they are monotonous and relatively devoid of a deeper interest. Some time ago I received a photograph from Natal, South Africa, showing a plant of *Protea cynaroides* in full bloom. It is, however, not necessary to go to South Africa to see it flower, as it will grow well in our Florida high pineland soil, and in full sun. I have grown it repeatedly from seed and the bushes flowered when about three years old. It does not grow in moist land. The flowers are disposed in heads of the size of the Sunflower, but the bracts are of a lovely shade of rosy pink, and the foliage itself is highly effective. These plants grow well with ordinary care, and dislike applications of commercial fertilizer—the Banksias, Hoveas, and small Grevilleas as well as this *Protea.* A mulch of a little old cow manure is quite sufficient for their well being.

Grevillea banksii: This beautiful [shrub or small tree] I introduced about six years ago from Melbourne, Australia [in 1918]. The director of the botanical gardens there sent me some seeds. They germinated at once and the fine tree in my garden here at Naples, about 10 feet high, has flowered every year since it was only a foot high. It is always in flower, but blooms most profusely during the summer. Being an extremely handsome plant, both in flower and foliage, and one of the best of the strong-growing Grevilleas, it is perfectly at home in our gardens from Orange County southward. Like most of the species, it can be grown without difficulty in our sandy soil, and probably there is no other more easily grown than this.

In my garden it is an elegant tree. The young stems are covered with a brownish woolly felt. The leaves are from 10 inches to a foot long, pinnately divided into about five pairs of narrowly lanceolate divisions, above deep green, and below beautifully silvery-white. The flowers are produced in dense terminal racemes, or in case of stronger branches, several of these racemes gather in a panicle, each raceme in either case being 4 to 5 inches long. The cylindrical calyx is not quite ¾ of an inch long, but with the long red style the flower attains nearly 2 inches in length. The outside of the calyx is covered with white hairs, the effect of which is to tone the most exquisite purplish-red of the rest of the flowers.

Grevillea banksii is grown perfectly successfully in my garden at Naples. My small tree is about 15 feet high, covered with leaves reminding one strongly of those of *Grevillea robusta*—the Silk-Oak, but they are deeper green. The flowers appear continuously throughout the year, but they are most conspicuous in February, March and April. They stand upright and are of a very rich deep rosy-red mixed with scarlet. There are always one or more flower trusses appearing just below the flower-stem just blooming, and for this reason it is not advisable to cut the flowers for decoration. Like all other Grevilleas this species comes from Australia. I think it may be perfectly hardy all over the Orange belt. It grows better in rather dry sandy soil.

The flowers produce a quantity of nectar, which must provide a plenteous food for certain birds and insects in their native land. In my garden I have never seen any insects, not even bees, search for this nectar. This is also the case with the most abundantly flowering orange-red *Grevillea robusta*, our common Australian Silk-Oak. There must be a biological cause for it, which needs further investigation. The fruits of our *Grevillea banksii* are compressed, ovate and turned to one side, still bearing the style, which always persists as a hook. These fruits are covered with white hairs, which cause slight viscidity. Unfortunately the seed-pods burst open as soon as ripe, or when still quite green, and the seeds drop to the ground. There is hardly ever a good seed found on the plants, and it is necessary, therefore, to bag each cluster of seed-pods in order to have the seeds for planting. This species grows well on our poorest and driest soils, and when in bloom always attracts the attention of all visitors, who are always struck with the rich soft beauty of the flowers. It is one of our noblest and most distinguished flowering small trees and should be found in the garden of every flower lover in Florida. As seeds from my flowering specimens have been largely distributed all over south and central Florida, there may be a chance to see it in bloom in many gardens in the near future.

Grevillea thelemanniana: Another beautiful species that does well, it is not quite as showy, but equally interesting. It is of neat and graceful habit, producing its racemes of flowers with such freedom that it compares most favorably with any occupant of the garden. Moreover it flowers over a very long period and is rarely out of bloom. The flowers are borne in terminal racemes abut 4 inches long, their color being a pale satiny pink tipped with green, and are rendered additionally attractive by the long protruding style. The pinnate leaves are very decorative, 1 to 2 inches long and slightly ribbed. This species, like all the others, is easily raised from seed. I received a small package of these seeds in 1918 from the Melbourne Botanical Garden. Unfortunately all my plants were destroyed by freeze in 1926.

This species was first discovered by Preiss near Perth, in western Australia, and is also known, for this reason, as *Grevillea preissii*. Mr. Jones, near Mountain Lake, had a large seed pan full of small plants several years ago, some of them flowering when only 6 inches high. It will grow with the same freedom where *G. banksii* is a success. As a winter-flowering shrub it will prove invaluable in our south Florida gardens. It will not do well in moist mucky ground.

Rhododendrons and Andromedas: Early in 1907 I introduced from England a splendid collection of Himalayan plants, among them such glorious species as *Rhododendron arboreum, R. barbatum, R. argenteum, R. grande, R. hodgsonii, R. falconeri, R. nuttallii, R. hookeri, R. dalhansiae, R. campanulatina, Andromeda aucklandii* and a few others. These are often tree-like in form and expand brilliantly large flower trusses.

All of them require cool, acid soil and a moist, shady position. They began to grow finely in my lath house, but were killed outright when the lake began to flood all the land a hundred feet from its natural borders. Hundreds of other plants,—even many Magnolias, Azaleas, Bamboos, etc.,—were destroyed at this time also. The old settlers say that these floods appear in cycles—once in about 20 to 25 years—and it requires several years before the waters recede again. In 1926 the waters again began gradually to rise, destroying thousands of plants, and they just now (March, 1929), began to fall slowly. The horticulturist making his garden on the low ground around his lake must keep this natural rising and falling of the waters constantly in mind, when he plants his garden.

I have not yet been very successful with the members of the Ericaceae or Heather family here in my Palm Cottage Gardens, though quite a number of the fine hybrids of *Azalea indica*—particularly the single-flowered ones—have done very well. A few of the native Azaleas also do well, and the beautiful *A. viscosa* is found all over our somewhat moist woodlands. This should be more extensively planted. Some of the Andromedas [= *Pieris*], so conspicuous around our low moist hammocks, are also available.

Among the exotic Andromedas I have found *Andromeda (Pieris) formosa* well suited to our soil and climate. I received a few small specimens from England at the same time when I obtained the above named Rhododendrons. It needs a cool, shady spot during the summer, and revels in our sour soils if they are well drained. It is a rare species.

The genus *Pieris* is represented in our gardens by some half-dozen species, the best known of which are *Pieris floribunda* from our southern states and *P. japonica* from Japan. Both these are well known in gardens under the name of *Andromeda*. The most beautiful seems to be *Pieris formosa,* a dense evergreen shrub from the mountains of Northern India, where it is found at an altitude of 7,000 to 10,000 feet, and from China. There it attains a height of about 12 feet and is a wide-spreading bush or even a small tree. In England it is hardy in the southwestern counties, where so many tender trees and shrubs grow in the open. In regard to hardiness *Pieris formosa* stands on the same footing as the tender species of the Himalayan Rhododendrons, except that it has the faculty of sending up new growths when killed down to the ground.

The leaves are 3 to 5 inches long and about 1½ inches broad, tapering to both ends, of a dark lustrous green, perfectly smooth with margins minutely toothed. I have had it in flower from February to March, the waxy-white, bell-shaped blossoms appearing in great numbers on a compound panicle 6 inches or more long. A large, dense, spreading specimen is a glorious sight when in full bloom.

Tecomas and Bignonias

The differences by which the very closely related Tecomas and Bignonias are distinguished are so slight that they would not be noticed by anyone except an expert botanist. Our native variety, *Tecoma radicans* [= *Campsis radicans*] is usually catalogued as *Bignonia radicans*. [*Campsis grandiflora*] is also listed as a *Bignonia* or *Tecoma*.

All the Tecomas, the climbing species as well as those growing in bush form, are very successfully cultivated in Florida, being well adapted to soil and climate, but most of them, to do their best, need to be planted from the start in rich soil, and in addition they should be well fertilized at least once a year. The bushy kinds can be grown in groups or as single specimens on the lawn, while the rampant climbing species such as *C. radicans* and *C. grandiflora,* should be grown on posts and tall stumps.

Tecoma capensis: A half climbing species, it is effectively used as a decoration on the verandah, its glowing scarlet flowers contrasting well with the exquisite blossoms and the tropical foliage of the Allamandas, Thunbergias and [*Clerodendron thomsoniae*], which all flower at the same time. *Tecoma stans* and [*Campsis grandiflora*] are the two showiest species of the genus, the latter one being a climber, flowering abundantly in May and June, while the first one is a large growing species opening its immense corymbs of vivid yellow flowers the latter part of November and early in December.

Tecoma stans: The "Palo de Areo" of Mexico, or the "Yellow Elder," as it is usually called, grows exceedingly well on high pineland, and is perfectly at home in Florida, attaining an immense size if well fertilized and mulched, dense masses eighteen to twenty feet high and as much through being not at all rare. This *Tecoma* is really the glory of the south Florida gardens in Autumn, as is the beautiful *Bauhinia purpurea* in April, never failing to call forth enthusiastic admiration.

I do not know a quicker growing, more decidedly beautiful and better adapted shrub for the new settlers in the sandy pineland gardens. The flowers, which harmonize admirably with the abundant light green foliage, are large, tube- or thimble-shaped, bright yellow, lined in the throat with a brownish tint, and are fragrant. They are borne in huge panicles at the ends of the branches and are produced so abundantly that they completely cover the plant, often weighing down to the ground the lower branches and younger shoots. At this time of the year insect life is very abundant among these immense flower clusters. The dainty little warblers just coming from the North on the way to their winter homes, as well as the lively blue-gray gnat-catchers and the humming birds, find an abundance of insect food; indeed, in large gardens these flowering masses of Tecomas are fairly swarming with different small birds.

Owing to the rapid growth and dense foliage from the ground, the "Yellow Elder" is highly valued as a screen for unsightly fences and buildings. I must say that no pen can adequately describe nor imagination truthfully picture the wonderful beauty of large specimens of this Tecoma in full flower. It cannot stand heavy frosts and may be injured even to the ground, but it will come up again with wondrous rapidity, flowering abundantly the same season. In fact, the writer has made the observation that plants which have been cut down by a sharp frost grow denser and bloom more abundantly the succeeding fall. Nature's pruning thus seems to be not without benefit to this plant. This Tecoma ripens its seed so abundantly that hundreds of seedlings come up around the old plant. The value of this shrub blooming so late in autumn cannot be overestimated.

Tecoma [*stans* var.] *velutina*: Also doing well in the writer's garden, this native of Guatemala is much less hardy than the former. It readily sprouts, however, from the thick rootstock if frozen down. Though being often described as a variety of *T. stans*, the writer thinks it is a very good and distinct species. The growth is more upright and stiff, the leaves are much larger, more serrate and much darker green, and the flowers, which are borne in terminal panicles, are scarcely half as large and without fragrance, than *T. stans*. Although beautiful, it does not show the gracefulness, nobility and charm of its congener. The foliage looks crimped and often blackish, being attacked by a kind of an aphid and by several fungi.

[*Tecoma* XAlata]: This is a hybrid raised near Melbourne, Australia, between *T. stans* var. *velutina* and *T. capensis*, by Mr. Edwin Smith, from whom the writer received seeds several years ago. The plant comes true from seed, and clusters of yellow and reddish trumpets in April and continuing with short intervals until cut down by frost in December. This hybrid is a rather dense growing shrub with an abundance of bright green foliage. The flowers are produced in large terminal panicles, often fifty or sixty of them being crowded together on a single shoot. They are bright orange yellow, streaked on the upper part of the outside with a dull orange or orange brown or peculiar orange scarlet, the lower part being clear bright yellow. If well fertilized and mulched it grows rapidly and repays for all the trouble by its profusion of flowers.

Tecoma capensis: The Cape Honeysuckle, is another species growing most luxuriantly in the Florida gardens and in those all along the Gulf coast, the writer having seen it about twenty years ago for the first time in New Orleans, where it was used in connection with Gloire de Dijon, Lamarque, Marechal, Neil and Cloth of Gold Roses on the broad and airy verandahs so common in the South and which impart to the southern homes that cozy, pleasant and homelike appearance nowhere else found in this country. It is usually grown on trellises, on verandahs and piazzas, with a southern exposure. The leaves, which are pinnate, as in all Tecomas, are of a beautiful dark green color, and all the numerous shoots terminate in dense upright corymbs of tubular orange-scarlet, somewhat honeysuckle-like flowers.

The dense flower clusters actually seem to glow among the abundant dark green lustrous foliage. If furnished with a support like a wire trellis, it climbs freely. If the long shoots are cut back severely it can easily be trained into a shrub form. These long shoots, usually lying flat on the ground, readily strike roots and form an excellent material for propagation. In Florida the "Cape Honeysuckle" is in flower almost throughout the year, though blooming most abundantly in the fall and early winter months. A little cottonseed meal and a mulch of stable manure will induce the plant to make a rapid and vigorous growth.

Posoqueria [longiflora]: This is, perhaps, identical with *Posoqueria latifolia.* I have the two plants side by side, and I cannot see any difference. I received the seed under the first name from British Guiana and under the second name from Prof. G. C. Higgins, of the Panama Canal Zone. These plants are seldom seen. This is to be regretted, for when in bloom the *Posoqueria* is a handsome plant with its fine trusses of long, pure white tubular flowers, the perfume of which fills the entire garden. Some of the trusses bear as many as thirty individual flowers. One of my plants, only 3 feet high and as much through, produced as many as fifty trusses. Unfortunately, when many of these are cut they last but a short time, but the individual flowers I have had in water quite fresh for ten days. This is the best way of utilizing these charmingly sweet-scented flowers.

Those specimens I raised from seed that came from Panama, have not yet flowered. There appears no difference in foliage and growth and I expect the larger ones to come into bloom at any time during the next few months. My specimens flowered from February to March, and there are some trusses opening just now (April 1). These plants belong to the family Rubiaceae. There are about a dozen species. *Posoqueria latifolia,* of Panama, may turn out to be different, as Dr. Paul Standley describes it as a tree attaining 30 feet in height. They all require rich, moist soil, and the drainage must be perfect. These Posoquerias are quite tender, and will not thrive in the open north of Punta Gorda. My specimens at Naples never suffered from the ordinary cold, though their flowering was retarded considerably.

Burchellia bubalina: This is another, very beautiful South African evergreen shrub. Though it is rare and little known, it grows well and flowers profusely in south Florida. Its ornamental qualities are of such a high order that one is apt to feel surprised that it is not cultivated more extensively. It forms a freely branched shrub, 5 to 6 feet high, clothed with ovate, oppositely arranged leaves, about 4 inches long, and of a rich green tint. The flowers, which are borne in clusters on the points of last year's shoots, are tubular in shape, a little over an inch long, and of a deep orange-scarlet color, which shows up very effectively from the rich green foliage-background. It belongs to the Rubiaceae, hence is a near relative to the Ixoras, Bouvardias, Gardenias, etc. It begins to flower in March and April and lasts about six weeks. A good, rich, well-drained soil is all it demands. From the hardness of the wood this *Burchellia* is known in the Cape Colony as the Buffalo Horn.

Sparmannia africana: This beautiful shrub was introduced from South Africa almost 150 years ago. It is extremely useful when a supply of flowers for decoration has to be maintained. It blooms almost all the year round, but most profusely in winter, and specimens 5 to 6 feet high are very showy when in full bloom. The flowers appear in terminal cymes. They are of a peculiar shape and are very showy, pure white, with a mass of brush-like protruding stamens of a bright orange-red color. Those flower lovers who are looking for a fine rare winter-flowering plant should not overlook the *Sparmannia*. It grows well in any rich soil not too dry. My plants came from the New York Botanical Garden.

Bixa orellana, the Annatto Tree: A few days ago I received a fine seed pod from a reader of my articles in Fort Myers. She had received it from a friend of hers in Fort Pierce, and asks why this fine plant is not found in other regions on the lower West Coast.

I have had the Annatto plant for years in my collection at Naples, and a small specimen I gave to Mr. C. W. Codwise of Bonita Springs—one of the most successful and enthusiastic plant lovers I ever met—is now full of its bunches of large crimson-brown seed pods. It also attracted the attention of all plant lovers when it was in full bloom in August, but at present not even the careless observer can pass it without being delighted. The flower trusses grow on upright shoots and the individual flowers are white with a pink suffusion. They are very pretty, but as they never open in large numbers at the same time, they are less attractive than the seed pods.

Last fall I passed a large shrub of the Annatto in a garden at Florence Villa, near Winter Haven, It made a most lovely show, but it was killed to the ground early last January. At present it is a dense mass of new shoots, but it did not flower. Mr. Codwise's plant, only about 6 feet high and quite dense, is so conspicuous and so extremely handsome that no real flower lover who has an opportunity to see it should pass it without closer inspection.

The Annatto is a most valuable economic plant. Dr. O. W. Barrett in his new book, *Tropical Crops,* gives the following description:

Annatto, *Bixa orellana,* is a small tree of the Bixaceae, native of some parts of tropical America. The Caribs called it *roucou* and one branch used to keep their bodies painted with the seed paste, whereupon they become known at the Roucou Tribe. The Arawak name was *Bixa.* It was long ago taken to India and Ceylon, and it became naturalized in parts of West Africa. Brazil, India, and the Antilles, particularly Porto Rico, supply the market which absorbs hundreds of tons a year.

The beautiful large lilac flowers are followed by spiny, dry, capsules, 1 to 1½ inches long, and these open like small brown clamshells exposing the mass of scarlet seeds about the size of small tomato seed. The powdered aril of the seed comes off at a touch and may be made into a paste by putting dry seeds into hot water and skimming off the waxy dust which rises.

Annatto is nearly tasteless coloring matter which has been used in Europe and America for a century or so to color cheese, butter and other foodstuffs, and even for dyeing fabrics. A good part of the rice served twice a day on tropical American tables is colored red with this *achiote,* as Latin-Americans call it.

Dr. Paul Standley, in his *Flora of the Panama Canal Zone,* has the following to say:

The family consists of a single genus and species, *Bixa orellana.* The specific name was given in honor of Francis Orellana, discoverer of the Amazon. The plant is a shrub or small tree, 2 to 9 meters high, widely distributed in tropical America, and common in this region (Canal Zone), both wild and planted. It has long-stalked alternate entire, broadly ovate leaves, minutely scaly beneath, and terminal panicles of white or pink flowers, with 5 petals 1.5 to 2.5 cm. long. The fruit is a globose or ovoid capsule, usually covered with spine-like bristles, but sometimes unarmed. Within are numerous round seeds surrounded by orange-red pulp.

In Panama the shrub is called "achote." This and the form "*achiote*" are the names used more commonly in Central America, the name being of Aztec origin.

The Annatto is a very ornamental and beautiful shrub, densely foliaged, flowers most profusely and shows its very ornamental, conspicuously colored large seed pods just at a time when it attracts most attention from Thanksgiving to Christmas. When in full bloom or in fruit it is a delightful sight. It grows easily from seed, and flowers the second year. Though a strictly tropical plant, my specimens were never hurt in my Naples garden. Rich light soil, rather moist, is preferred by it, though I have seen fine specimens on higher ground. When cut down by frost it invariably sprouts vigorously from the rootstock. It was introduced many years ago by Reasoner Brothers.

The Musk rose: Although no other garden flower has such an extensive literature as the Rose, it is surprising that the artistic side of rose growing has had so little attention. Nearly all that has been done is subservient to conventional methods, whose chief fault is that they represent to me but one aspect of the flower, and that the least beautiful from an artistic point of view. The consequence is that the roses that nearly everyone knows and grows are those which produce fine double flowers. May they long continue in popularity, but those who want their gardens sweet and gay should not rest content with these alone. Happily, there seems a growing desire to plant the single types of the noble family.

It is difficult to find in gardens such rose pictures as may be seen by the roadside in June, when Dog-Roses and Sweet Brier hang in wreaths from the hedges in Europe, or when our Cherokee and McCartney Roses form sheets of color in our southern woodland borders, where they have run wild. Yet we may have them, and even lovelier ones, too, if we look around us and study the lists of single roses. Take for instance the single Musk Rose. It is only one of the many single roses, but, so far as I can judge, it is the very best and gloriously adapted to Florida soil and climatic conditions. No words can possibly exaggerate its beauty. I have a finely colored plate before me, made from a water color painting by a real artist. It shows its fine form, size and delicate color, but the picture that this rose makes in the garden is truly wonderful. Although an old rose, it is evidently scarcely known in gardens, but it deserves to be brought from comparative obscurity.

W. Paul says in his book, *The Rose Garden,* that the Musk Rose is supposed to have been introduced into England over 300 years ago, and that the scent of the flowers was thought to resemble somewhat that of musk. The plant is described as being of rambling habit, producing its flowers in large clusters late in summer. Under this, as being the [*Rosa*] type, are enumerated several varieties, one of them being named *R. moschata* var. *nivea* and thus described: "Flowers white, shaded with rose, large and single form cupped, growth robust." This is quite in accordance with the character of the Rose as figured in the *Garden* (vol. 50, Plate p. 62), and as the plants come to us under the name of *R. moschata nivea*, this no doubt is the correct name, but as to its origin and history I can only say that it comes from southern Asia. The important point of all, however, is its value as a garden rose, and there will be few to compare with or equal it for covering a fence, making a hedge, or to ramble in perfect liberty over some low-growing tree.

In Florida and all over the South Atlantic and Gulf States it is perfectly hardy. It flowers usually in June and July and lasts for about six weeks. The trusses of bloom are enormous, many of them having 30 to 40 buds and flowers in a cluster, and every one comes to perfection, while from 6 to 10 flowers may often be seen fully open in one truss. The buds are of a lovely pink color, and there are exquisite shadings of pink in the flower when first exposed, with a cushion of the richest yellow anthers in the center, much brighter and more beautiful than we can imagine. The foliage is glaucous gray-green, and abundant, making a soft and pretty foil to the flowers, which have a powerful and delicious fragrance.

This rose is also known by Lindley's name *Rosa brunonii* [a distinct species]. Researches have revealed the fact that it is a native of South Asia and Abyssinia. In 1817 John Champney of Charleston, S.C., raised by hybridization from *Rosa moschata* and *R. chinensis* the class of roses now known as Noisette roses, among which the wonderfully beautiful and fragrant climber 'Lamarque' is an example.

Hedges, Privets and Berry Bearing Plants

[*Syzygium paniculatum*]: The Australian Myrtle is a fine evergreen shrub from Australia doing well in Florida, from the orange belt southward. It is very useful for decoration during the winter when it is covered with the showy, deep red, oval berries. Early in autumn it is covered with an abundance of white Myrtle-like flowers. I had a specimen at Palm Cottage Gardens, which was 8 feet high and very dense. Unfortunately the big freeze in

1917 killed it to the ground, and it never sprouted from the rootstalk. I see that the Royal Palm Nursery, Oneco, Florida, offers this fine plant in its collection.

Beautiful berry-bearing shrubs during the winter time are a most important feature in our Florida gardens. These plants are not common, but there are many spread over the tropics that should be introduced. Among native species we have two very fine Hollies (*Ilex opaca* and [*I. cassine*]), and there is also a deciduous species in our swamp. Dr. J. K. Small discovered another fine evergreen species a few years ago on the shores of Lake Mancesowee (Lake Jackson).

The common *Ardisia crenata,* probably a native of Southern China and India, is grown in large numbers in greenhouses for its bright and very abundant masses of berries, which are in great demand for Christmas decoration in dwelling houses. They are easily grown in pots, a fine specimen in a 5- or 6-inch pot, covered with its brilliant berries, each as large as a pea, being a most striking feature wherever seen. I have grown this plant from seed, and have planted them out in my lath house at Palm Cottage; but for some reason they did not thrive as well as those in pots. Mr. H. L. Beeman has many specimens on the verandah of his beautiful home at Orlando, where they always formed a beautiful sight among palms, Dracaenas, Crotons and other members of the plant nobility. This *Ardisia* should [not] be found in every garden and on every verandah in Florida. It stands, however, only slight frosts. [*Ardisia crenata* is a significant pest in places and is listed by the Florida Exotic Pest Plant Council as a category I species—invasive species disrupting native plant communities.]

When Mr. Chas. Ford was director of the Hong Kong Botanical Gardens he sent me many seeds of plants that he thought would thrive in Florida. I have now in my collection beautiful specimens of *Raphiolepis indica, Radermachera sinica, Aleurites cordata* and *A. fordii.* This was in the years 1906 and 1907. In this collection of seeds I found the dry berries of a most beautiful *Ardisia*—*A. mamillata* [?], a native of Hong Kong and described first by Hance. From 1907 to 1917 I had quite a number of dense compact specimens 2 to 3 feet high, and as interesting and conspicuous as *A. crenata,* though very different from it in various respects. I lost all my plants in the disastrous freeze of February, 1917. While exploring the southern part of the state for a new and frostless place, I neglected to take care of the many seedlings that came up from the fallen berries of the destroyed old plants. I found it, however, almost as hardy as *A. crenulata*. The leaves may be described as oblong-elliptic, 4 inches or more long and about 2 inches broad across the center. The leaf-stalks are short, and the margins are slightly crenate. The dark shining green of the upper surface is thickly studded with small raised dots or mamillae, which suggested its specific name given by Hance. On the under surface, which is pale green in color, there are small hollows, corresponding to the mamillae on the upper side. Each of the mamillae carries a single white bristly hair at its top. The hairs are also present on the under side of the leaf, and indeed, on every part of the plant, the flowers and berries excepted. When seen between the light they impart to the leaves a silvery aspect. The flowers, about a dozen in an umbel, are borne on axillary clusters about 2 inches long. They are star-shaped and white, tinged with rose. The berries, which are about as large as a pea, are of a brilliant rosy-red, presenting a striking contrast to the dark-green foliage. The plants, even when not in flower or fruit, are of a decidedly ornamental character. This fact, coupled with the ease with which it is grown under ordinary treatment, will no doubt lead to its becoming a favorite among lovers of rare and choice plants.

Several years ago I received from our Bureau of Plant Industry another *Ardisia* sp.—*A. procephala* [?], a native of India. My large plant is now about 7 or 8 feet high and very beautiful. It grows in rich mucky soil. From Thanksgiving Day to New Year's Day it is a sheet of the most exquisite light rosy-red color, which is caused by the masses of flower trusses which are entirely of that color, while the flowers themselves are pure white. These flowers form a beautiful decoration in vases, and I have often delighted my friends and callers with big bunches of them. The berries are provided in the greatest abundance in April and May. They are as large as a very small cherry and are of a glossy black color. I have distributed these berries among many of my friends, and my young friend, Mr. Harry Smith, of the Winter Garden Ornamental Nursery, has quite a lot of fine young plants, raised from these seeds. My plant at Naples never suffered from cold. [Another species, *A. solanacea*, no doubt introduced by Nehrling has displayed invasive characteristics at the "Caribbean Gardens," Nehrling's old "Garden of Solitude" in Naples.]

Our native Marlberry, common on shell mounds and in well drained hammocks, and which was known for many years under the name of *Ardisia pickeringia*, I must now get accustomed to its new name, *Icacorea paniculata*

[= *Ardisia escallonioides*]. It is just at present in full fruit in my garden, and in great abundance in Mr. J. Hackmeister's fine hammock nearby. It is a beautiful native evergreen shrub, with dull-green leaves and abundant panicles of whitish flowers, which exhale a delicious fragrance. I have raised it from seeds.

Among the Rubiaceae there are many glorious flowering shrubs, like the Ixoras, Gardenias and many others, and there are some with fine conspicuous berries. Our "Wild coffee shrub," [*Psychotria nervosa*] ripens its deep red fruits late in fall, just when the migrating birds are on their way to the tropics. The leaves of this plant are deep green and very undulated. These alone make it valuable for ornament. A closely related species, *Psychotria cyanococca* [?], is a most interesting ornamental plant, when in full berry. These berries are of the deepest purple-blue, about the size of a small pea, and produced in dense drooping clusters which are in fine contrast to the deep green leaves. It was introduced from Nicaragua in 1870, and belongs to a genus that comprises about 500 species, for the most part unattractive. It was introduced with, or about the same time as, *Psychotria chontalensis* [?], which is quite as ornamental as the species under consideration. It requires the same culture as the Ixoras. I have raised it from seed at various times, and had it in full berry, when the freeze of early February, 1917, killed it outright. I have not experimented with it in my Naples garden, where [*P. nervosa*] grows vigorously. All these rare and beautiful plants which I am calling attention to in my articles are not found in the trade. It costs much time and money and requires much patience to obtain seeds from their native habitat. One has to wait often a long time until he succeeds. I waited 27 years until I could get seeds from various *Ficus* species in Mexico. Many futile attempts were made until I found a new friend, the famous botanist, Dr. C. A. Purpus, in the state of Vera Cruz.

I enjoyed the beauty of the dense clusters of bright indigo or purple-blue berries for several years. The shrubs flowered and fruited when only 18 inches to 2 feet high. As these berries ripen in winter—they were with me at their best in February—and as the appearance of the plant when in full fruit, is strikingly beautiful, this plant should be grown by all who love rare and characteristic flower gems. It is a rather soft growing shrub, with light-green leaves, each about 4 to 5 inches long, and crisped at the edges. The flowers are small and inconspicuous, but this is atoned for by the beauty of the berries, which retain their freshness for a considerable time. Plants may be easily raised from seeds, or cuttings strike easily enough. *Psychotria chontalensis* is similar, but more robust. Its berries, purple-blue, are its chief feature. Another species, *Psychotria jasminiflora*, is a most beautiful flowering shrub. It blooms at different times, but more particularly during the winter months. It forms a dense fine shrub, the pure white blossoms, appearing in clusters.

Privets or Ligustrums: Many years ago a friend of mine in Florida wrote me: "I fully agree with you that our Florida gardens should be full of evergreens—the noble evergreen trees and shrubs from China and Japan—but I am not 'sweet on Privets.'" Neither am I, but there are Privets and Privets. While enjoying the sight of the most beautiful gardens at Winter Park during the sessions of the Federation of Florida Garden Clubs we had the pleasure to see a number of fine large-leaved species of *Ligustrum*, which vie in beauty with any other broad-leaved evergreens. There were *Ligustrum ibota*, [*L. indicum*] and others. All these are excellent for foundation plantings, for lawns, for shruberies, etc. Quite a large number, recently discovered by Mr. E. H. Wilson (usually known as Chinese Wilson on account of his work as a plant explorer in Southwestern China) by Rock, Forest and other plant collectors. Many of these have been distributed by our Bureau of Plant Industry, and I have now about a dozen of these new Privets in my collection at Naples. All of them seem to be small-leaved, but their growth is exceedingly dense and large and at certain times of the year they are covered with masses of white flowers of the size and shape of the Lilac.

One of them sails under the name of *Ligustrum quihouii*. I find a most beautiful and impressive illustration of it in the *Gardener's Chronicle* (vol. 70, 1921). The entire tall and dense plant, covered with branches from the ground up, is ornate with immense panicles of pure white flowers. Even without its flowers the fact of its being such a fine evergreen [*Hortus Third* (1976) indicates "deciduous"] should win it a prominent position. But its main value lies in its flowers. In some of the Privets the somewhat overpowering odor of the flowers is objectionable to a few plant lovers, but it does not appear to be any account in this species. In fact, added to the merit of its natural beauty, these long and freely borne panicles of white flower trusses will average about a foot long and 9 inches across. It usually flowers late in August and during September. The fruits are bluish or purplish-lilac in color.

It is interesting to note that Mr. E. H. Wilson—at present acting Director of the Arnold Arboretum, Jamaica Plain, Mass., the most beautiful garden in America—during his journeyings in China found *L. quihouii* in various parts of Western Hopah and Western Szechuan in 1907 and 1908, and he records several times that it was found on the side of streams as though it needed much moisture. Cultivated specimens show that it will finally grow to the size of a small tree.

Not far from my old home, Palm Cottage Gardens, we find in the beautiful and richly embellished garden of my friend, Mr. Louis Bosanquet, at Fruitland Park, another fine Privet—[*L. indicum*]. Its beauty was so striking, its dense and tall growth so impressive that the picture of my first glimpse of it shall never fade from memory.

Silver Shrubs or Oleasters

I cannot recommend too highly the various species of the genus *Elaeagnus*—the Silver Shrubs or Oleasters. All the best species are natives of China and Japan, having been cultivated there since times immemorial. The dense evergreen species, though very rampant growers, must be placed in the list of the finest subtropical ornamental plants we have. They are hardy all over the orange belt, and can likewise be grown everywhere in the south Atlantic and Gulf region. The late Mr. P. J. Berckmans, who imported so many of the beautiful evergreens from China and Japan, has distributed them largely all over the lower South. Many years ago I received about a dozen different species and varieties from him. Two of these Oleasters are renowned for their excellent cherry-like fruits,—*E. umbellata* and [*E. multiflora*], the *Gournie* of the Japanese. Both grow finely in Palm Cottage Gardens and fruit abundantly. The one ripens its almost cherry-like drupes in May, the latter in June and July. They are quite ornamental.

The subject of this sketch is the Large-leaved Oleaster (*E. macrophylla*), a most beautiful and very dense evergreen, half-climbing shrub. The leaves are deep glossy green above, broad-ovate or broad-elliptic, wavy, on rather long petioles. They are scaly above, silvery-white beneath. The flowers are produced in axillary clusters, white with silvery and brownish scales outside the tube. They appear in November and exhale a very pleasant odor. A little after New Year's Day the fruits ripen in great abundance, being oblong and very juicy and of fine flavor. These fruits are very similar to those of [*E. pungens* 'Reflexa'].

Elaeagnus [*pungens* 'Reflexa'] is a dense spreading shrub similar to the above, but not much grown. Its variegated forms, which originated mainly in Japan and are passionately loved by the Japanese, have been widely distributed over the South. I have the following varieties: *E. pungens* 'Frederici.' The leaves have a yellow center and green margin. *E. pungens* 'Maculata' with leaves having large yellow blotches. *E. pungens* 'Simoni' with leaves variegated with yellowish and pinkish white. *E. pungens* 'Variegata' with leaves margined yellowish-white. All of these variegated forms are of importance, excellent for smaller city gardens. They usually form dense bushes 5 to 6 feet high. All grow to perfection on high sandy pineland.

I have about a dozen rampant specimens at Palm Cottage Gardens. All grow without care on high sandy pineland, and all were planted, when quite small, near rather large Willow-Oaks. They first formed dense bushes about 5 or 6 feet high, and as much through, and then made strong, brown, upright leafless shoots, provided with reclining hooks. These switch-like shoots made a growth of about 10 feet or more in one year and did not stop until they had reached one of the lower branches of the oak, to which the shoot attached itself by one or more of the reclining hooks. During the following year these tall shoots cover themselves densely with foliage and side branches, climbing all the time higher and higher. Within a few years they entirely cover the tree, often 30 to 40 feet tall, with their dense masses of twigs and foliage.

From the top of the supporting tree large numbers of new shoots strive upwards, but finding their endeavor futile, they droop downwards to all sides, finally forming garlands of densely foliaged reclining branches. I have found it advisable to plant these Oleasters near medium-sized Live Oaks, Catalpas or even Long-leaved Pines, because the Willow Oak is a short-lived tree and the heavy burden of a large Elaeagnus hastens its end. Still there are fine healthy Willow Oaks at Gotha that have been adorned with this Japanese evergreen for more than twenty-five years. Quite a number, however, succumbed after they had carried the dense, heavy masses of growth for about fifteen years. When the supporting tree finally falls it carries the entire tangled evergreen canopy with it to the ground. This accident is no obstacle in its way for progress, no hindrance to growing as vigorously as before. It goes on as usual, forming extremely dense and intricate thickets, 6 to 10 feet high, and quite often 20 to 35 feet long.

The leaves of [*E. pungens* 'Reflexa'] are deep glossy green, covered with thin light-colored scales, and showing a beautiful silvery-white underside with numerous minute brown dots. They strongly resemble those of *E. macrophylla,* but are somewhat smaller. The young leaves, appearing early in March, and also the young succulent branches, are silvery-white. Later in the season the new branches show a cinnamon-brown color. During November the entire place, consisting of over ten acres, is pervaded with the wonderfully delicious perfume of the flowers, which strongly reminds one of the odor of the carnation. Many of the people passing along on the highway are charmed by this intensely pleasant perfume and many are the callers who are anxious to find the source of this odor. The flowers that exhale this sweet fragrance are small and inconspicuous, clove-like in form, and appear in small axillary clusters in great abundance. Their color is of a peculiar grayish-white on the outside of the narrow tube and white within. The fruits are small, berry-like, oblong or cylindrical, rounded on both sides, covered with a dull red skin and very juicy, having a fine acidulous flavor and can be used for making a very delicious jelly. They ripen in great profusion during January and are much relished by the many winter birds sojourning in the large garden.

A few of these beautiful evergreen shrubs should be found in every garden in the orange belt and other regions where noble plants are appreciated. The species in question is an extremely charming evergreen, very dense, requiring no care and opening its delicious fragrant flowers in one great abundance during January. It can be pruned and grown as a large evergreen shrub, but it forms a much more conspicuous object when grown on a large tree or over pergolas.

Vines and Sweet Scented Plants

Thunbergias, though strictly tropical plants—mostly rampant climbers—belong to the most valuable climbers of our Florida gardens. The dainty and lovely Black-eyed Susan (*Thunbergia alata*) has run wild in my garden at Naples, as well as at Palm Cottage, and the same can be said of the pure white *Thunbergia fragrans*. These plants belong to the family Acanthaceae, and were named in honor of Karl Peter Thunberg, professor of botany in the University of Uppsala in Sweden.

Thunbergia grandiflora is a very lovely tropical climber with light-blue flowers, showing a white tube. It must be described as unique, especially so when we can enjoy its flowers in the winter months. In the color of the flowers alone there is a delicate charm that almost defies description. At any rate it is this exceeding delicacy that attracts, and the more closely the flowers are viewed, the more beautiful they appear to become. In our south Florida gardens, where sufficient warmth is forthcoming during the winter months, the long trailing shoots of this plant are rendered most effective by the beautiful light-blue blossoms dangling here and there, this beautiful shade of color being intensified, as it were, by the nearly pure white throat. The flowers, like a huge *Gloxinia* of the half-drooping type, appear rather freely on plants that are not trimmed back, but are allowed to grow freely and naturally. Thus grown, it is surprising the number of flowers a large plant will produce in a single season. The leaves are broadly ovate, angularly cordate and lobed.

Thunbergia laurifolia, with deeper blue flowers which have a yellowish throat, is much more abundant in our gardens than the former, and it seems to be preferred by many garden lovers. Before the big hurricane, in September, 1926, I was often delighted to view the beauty of large flowering specimens along the street at Four Way Lodge, Coconut Grove. They rambled up tall Casuarinas (Australian Pines) fully 50 and 60 feet high, and festooned their branches with masses of dangled growth in full bloom. All Thunbergias are beautiful ornaments for verandahs, pergolas and lath houses.

Solandra is a small genus of tropical [sprawling] shrubs related to *Datura*—the Angels Trumpet. It commemorates the name of Dr. Solander, fellow traveler of Captain Cook and Sir Joseph Banks. A native of Jamaica, whence it was introduced in 1781, *Solandra grandiflora* produces great masses of bloom in January, in south Florida.

The late Mr. Henry Pfister, for more than 30 years the ideal and efficient gardener of the White House in Washington, D.C., showed me in late November (1890) fine dense specimens in magnificent bloom. There were hundreds of its large flowers open at one time. He sent me cuttings in 1891, and I succeeded in growing fine specimens which always flowered profusely during winter. I did not succeed well with it at Palm Cottage, as the cold November nights destroyed its flowering capacity, but in my Naples garden, 200 miles south and near the Gulf, it grew and flowered splendidly. It is evidently a dry land plant, because it never succeeded in shady, moist spots. Full sun, and a rather dry spot, are what it demands.

My friend, Mr. C. Wittgeustain Codwise, and his wife are passionate flower lovers and expert horticulturists. They have built their home south of the Imperial River, near Bonita Springs. Though I introduced *Solandra grandiflora* into Florida many years ago, I have never seen it so wonderfully in bloom as with the Codwises. The flowers are very large and conspicuous, trumpet shaped, yellowish-white and marked with very fine deep purplish-red bands inside of the tube. This plant is a most valuable winter bloomer, and therefore of great importance in extreme south Florida.

The Solandras are rampant climbers with fine, large, succulent leaves. I have seen plants 25 to 30 feet high on walls and trees. At Fort Myers I admired specimens 5 to 6 feet high and very dense. They were kept purposely in this bushy form, and flowered beautifully all winter long. When thus grown, the treatment should be one of starvation as regards root room and soil, with exposure to bright sunlight all summer and absolute drought from November to March. This renders a short growth and the production of flowers in winter, when they are particularly welcome. The flowers vary in size and color. According to the *Botanical Magazine* (Plate 1874), they are pale flesh-colored in Jamaica, and are known as peach-colored Trumpet

Flowers. In other gardens they are said to have been white and purple. I have had blossoms 8 inches long and 5 inches wide. I have also had ripe fruits, which were heart-shaped, about 4 inches long and of green color. I have grown the following species:

Solandra grandiflora is the most common species. Flowers white, or often yellowish-white, with deep purple splotches in the inside. A beautiful sight when in full bloom in winter.

Solandra guttata is a Mexican species, very similar to *S. grandiflora*, differing chiefly in having hairy leaves and a narrow-tubed corolla, colored ochrous-yellow, streaked with purple. I received cuttings from my friend, Dr. C. A. Purpus, of Vera Cruz, Mexico. It flowers easily and abundantly.

[*Campsis grandiflora*], Chinese Trumpet Creeper, is the most floriferous and gorgeous of all the climbing species. In the writer's garden a large pine stump about sixteen feet high in May and June is completely covered with masses of brilliant fiery orange-scarlet flowers which can be seen at a distance of half a mile. The flowers are much larger and more brilliant and much more abundantly produced than those of our native [*Campsis radicans*]. Indeed the plant flowers so abundantly that scarcely a trace of the stump is visible. It would be difficult to imagine a grander and more unique picture than that represented by a large, well-grown and well-flowered specimen of this plant, its brilliant red trumpet-shaped flowers, clustered together in large loose panicles, each flower lasting in perfection several days and opening in quick succession, having a most attractive appearance even among the brightest of spring and summer flowers, such as *Hibiscus rosa-sinensis, Lagerstroemia indica, Punica granatum, Bauhinia purpurea,* etc. The light green foliage is abundantly produced, but while all of the other Tecomas are almost free from the attacks of insects, this one is infested by a voracious caterpillar, that devours the leaves greedily. The lubber grasshopper also attacks the lower foliage. *Tecoma grandiflora* grows well in poor sandy soil, perfecting luxuriant shoots twenty-five or thirty feet long in one season, if well fertilized. The stump in the writer's garden covered with this magnificent climber, full of gorgeous blossoms, has a singularly beautiful landscape effect. Like our native species, this one is deciduous. The large flowers are of a most vivid orange color, lined darker in the tube; the outside a salmon yellow. This species is most effectively used on old pine stumps.

[*Campsis radicans*], our native Trumpet Creeper, is very common in our southern woodlands and fields. It is a plant of great beauty when used in the right way. In the writer's garden it is planted along fences and among small oaks which it adorns with its handsome and abundantly produced dull orange or orange-scarlet trumpets, beginning to bloom early in May. There is a great variety in the brilliancy of the blossoms, some plants bearing much more brightly colored flowers than others. This is an excellent species for covering the bare trunks of palmettos. I have seen along the St. Johns and other water courses many of these grand native palms covered completely with the Trumpet Creeper, which adorned the crown with a wealth of bright flowers in May and June, and stray blossoms were even seen as late as November.

Trachelospermum jasminoides, the pure white Star Jasmine or Malayan Jasmine is as hardy and as desirable as the Carolina Jessamine, being an ideal plant to cover verandahs, pergolas and tree trunks. In March and April—farther south even in February—it forms a sheet of small crimped pure white and deliciously fragrant flowers. Both of these climbers are gems and are easily grown. They should never be missed in our gardens, and they are particularly valuable because they are winter bloomers. The Flame Vine [*Pyrostegia venusta*] is more tropical and quite tender, being often killed back by frost in the central parts of the state, where it opens its gorgeous flame-colored flowers usually at Christmas time. It can be trained on a large shade tree or pine, which it often covers to the very top with its orange-yellow flower masses.

Antigonon leptopus, Love's-Chain, a strictly summer flowering vine is of particular value on account of its immense masses of deep rosy-red flowers—a color so delightful and so captivating that no one can pass by it without exclamations of joy and pleasure. Its festoons of pink and rose-colored flowers adorn many a garden in central and even northern Florida. Years ago at Orlando I often enjoyed the glorious sight of a large specimen of the Antigonon being trained on a wire from one side of the street to the other. The flower masses, 6 to 8 feet wide, festooned the entire street with indescribable beauty. This plant was trained from the Rosalind Club House to the opposite side of the street, and it is still impressed on the minds of many of the flower lovers having seen it at that time. The tourist rarely ever has a chance to see this beauty in full bloom. Its roots are tuberous, and this plant needs cultivation and fertilizer to do its best. Belt says that it is called *la vegissima,* "the beautiful," by the natives of Nicaragua, its home, where he found it growing wild near Matagalpa and Segovia, where it was one of the greatest favorites of the flower-loving Indians. In order to see this glorious vine at its best, it must be cut down early in March to induce the forming of new flowering shoots. An old unpruned plant is valueless, because it grows scraggy and scarcely ever flowers satisfactorily.

Petrea volubilis, among blue-flowering climbers—also called "Rough Leaf" and Bluebird Vine—is of particular value. It was introduced into Florida many years ago by Mr. E. N. Reasoner. The color of the flower masses varies a good deal. Some are more or less lilac-blue, while others show a real blue-bird blue. Coming from the American tropics, it is quite a tender vine, but I have had it for many years in flower at Palm Cottage Gardens in the orange belt and also in my garden at Naples. It is no exaggeration to say that the bushes are literally laden with flowers from top to bottom. My plants usually begin to flower early in March. The plant can either be grown as a climber or in bush form.

Stigmaphyllon periplocaefolium, the most brilliantly showy of all the vines in my garden in March and April is the Golden Creeper. I never have seen it outside of my garden. It was introduced by the Bureau of Plant Industry about ten years ago. My plant grows with extreme vigor in wet mucky soil, where it has attained a height of about 15 feet, climbing over a dense *Lawsonia inermis* (Mignonette shrub) on one side, and over a Cabbage Palm on the other. A large part of the roof of the lath house is also covered with it. The evergreen leaves are hard, long and narrow and deep green in color. When in full bloom no pen and pencil can depict the glorious brilliancy of the flower masses. Though the individual flowers are not large, they are borne in very dense corymbs all over the plant from top to bottom. No green leaf is visible; all is a flowering mass. The flowers are yellow, but such a yellow as I never have seen before. It is a brilliant glowing yellow, or rather a glossy yellow. My plant was covered from March to May with a complete yellow veil 8 to 10 feet long and 5 to 6 feet wide. In spite of the mosquitoes I daily enjoyed this feast for the eyes. Dr. and Mrs. Fairchild saw this Golden Creeper in bloom in April, 1928. Though the flowering season was almost over they were thrilled by the beauty that came before their eyes. I shall never forget the enthusiasm Dr. Fairchild expressed about this brilliant new woody climber, the stems twining each other, one as thick as a thumb and the smaller ones as thick as pencils.

This plant is so rare and so extraordinarily beautiful, of such easy growth and so gorgeous when in flower that it should find a place in every good garden. It is excellent for verandahs, pergolas and trellises and is particularly adapted to grow on the trunks of Cabbage Palms. I do not believe that it will be successful in poor dry soil. My plant never suffered from frost during the past exceptionally cold winters. No finer, no more floriferous, no more brilliant plant can be imagined than this *Stigmaphyllon* when in full flower, covering a medium sized Cabbage Palm. All the members of the genus belong to the American Tropics, being members of the family Malpighiaceae.

There is another species in cultivation, much more common, but much less showy. This is *Stigmaphyllon ciliatum.* I have had it in my collection at Gotha for many years. It proved quite hardy and flowered profusely, but never in such masses as the former. The flowers are of a light yellow, with a slight touch of green, and they are produced in corymbs of 4 to 5 on a strong stalk, all summer long. Each flower reminds of certain orchids (Oncidiums). The leaves are very handsome, soft and beautifully fringed, with rich crimson colored berries. This species also requires rich, moist soil, but it is easily grown. Self sown seeds come up in abundance near my large plant. It is rarely seen in our gardens, but it is cherished in the rich collection of rare tropical plants of Dr. John Seeds at Miami.

Solanum wendlandii, Wendland's Blue Climber, is one of our most beautiful summer climbers, opening its masses of bright pale lilac-blue flowers in enormous heads, almost a foot in diameter. It grows exceedingly well all over Florida in rich, rather dry well drained soil. It will not thrive in mucky wet places. I do not know for a certainty, but I believe this fine Solanum was discovered by Herman Wendland, the late great Palm authority and director of the famous Botanic Gardens at Herrenhausen, Hanover, Germany, who sent it in 1882 to Kew with the information that it came from the colder regions in Costa Rica, where it climbs upon trees. It has thick, succulent stems, covered with prickles, slightly hooked when young, but becoming blunt and corky with age.

The leaves vary in size and shape, those near the ends of the branches being oblong, acuminate, and about 4 inches long, while those lower down are more or less pinnatifid and 10 inches long. The flowers are in compact cymose heads on the ends of the growing branches, which, when allowed to hang downwards have an elegant effect. Each flower is from 2½ to 3 inches across, pale lilac-blue, shaded and lined with purple; a little pyramidal cluster of stamens standing erect in the middle, being yellow, adds to the attraction of the flowers. The plant grows with real luxuriance in most of our Florida gardens, trailing over lath houses, verandahs, pergolas and trellises.

I have had this plant for many years at Palm Cottage, where it formed a wonderful ornament from May to August, when in full bloom. The single stems or shoots—and there are many—grow from 15 to 20 feet in one season. In winter the leaves fall off, the plant remaining at rest till February or March. As a tropical plant it cannot stand severe freezes, though my plants were scarcely injured by 26°F. A freeze of 20°F kills it to the ground, but it usually sprouts again from the rootstalk. I have grown it very successfully in my glasshouse at Milwaukee. Cuttings root easily in sand, and it also grows well from layers. Several years ago I saw at Maitland, Fla., a large lath house covered with it and the entire roof was a sheet of lilac-blue color.

We have two other climbing Solanums in our Florida gardens, *Solanum jasminoides* with pure white flower clusters, and *Solanum seaforthianum,* a native of Trinidad, with large drooping clusters of fragrant lilac-blue flowers and later with dense branches of vivid red berries which form a great relish to the mocking-bird and thrushes.

The fine climbing Solanums should be found in all our gardens, as they are not only very easily grown, but of distinct beauty and of quite unique appearance. In the *Garden* (Vol. 37) there is a beautiful colored plate of *Solanum wendlandii,* and an excellent account of it and other species.

Beaumontia grandiflora, the Nepal Climber is one of the most conspicuous plant aristocrats imaginable—a glory in every Florida garden where it is cultivated. It came from Syulhet, in Northwestern India, about a hundred years ago, and was introduced into Florida by the late E. N. Reasoner, in the early nineties of the last century, if my memory serves me right. Belonging to one of the largest and finest tropical plant families, the Apocynaceae (Dogbane family)—a family, containing such members as the Allamandas, Dipladenias, etc., as close relations, this *Beaumontia* is an outstanding beauty in every garden where it flowers and perfumes the air.

Not long ago I received a parcel by mail from the lower East Coast, containing a large cluster of pure white lily-like flowers of this plant. When opening the package the entire house was perfumed by the strong and delicious odor. The fragrance was so strong during the night that the flower cluster had to be removed from the house. It came under the name of "Easter Lily Shrub," and I was asked for the correct name. I was informed that the plant was growing in bush form in a large tub and in good rich soil. More than half a hundred of the flowers were open when the cluster was cut from it.

Beaumontia grandiflora is a bold growing climber with large opposite, oblong-ovate leaves, which are about 8 inches long and upward of 3 inches broad, deep shining green on the upper side and paler beneath, the principal ribs of the lower side being clothed with a ferruginous tomentum. The flowers are bell-shaped, some 4 to 5 inches long, thick in texture and pure white, borne in terminal and axillary corymbs.

Unfortunately this grand plant is rarely found in our gardens. In the rear of Mr. J. E. Hendry's garden, at Fort Myers, there grew for years a very fine and healthy plant which flowered each summer regularly. Mr. Hendry is not only a successful nurseryman, but he is pre-eminently a passionate flower and plant lover and a plant student. He cultivated everything rare and beautiful; everything that appeals to him, first in his beautiful home garden, and later tries to propagate from his specimens. He found the *Beaumontia grandiflora* was very difficult to propagate, particularly without bottom-heat. This may account for its rarity. [Bottom-heat applies to providing a heat source to the rooting medium.]

It is really surprising that such a magnificent plant is so rarely seen in our Florida gardens, where it grows so well and so easily if cared for in an ordinary manner. Well drained good rich soil is essential under cultivation. It does not grow in wet and mucky soils. It is a profuse bloomer, increasing in beauty year by year. To repeat: It is a plant easily cultivated, and as it is a native of northern India, will be found to thrive well with a little protection as far north as Orange County. It flowers best in bright sunshine and grows best in a soil composed of loam, peat or mulch, and sand, but it requires good drainage at all times. It flowers upon the previous year's growth, and therefore when the blossoms have fallen the whole plant should be cut back, or pruned, in order to induce a greater quantity of lateral shoots for next season's bloom. Plants have been grown with 450 flowers open at one time, and the fragrance of the mass of pure white blossoms was almost overpowering.

What a wonderful climate are we enjoying in Florida! And what an immense number of glorious tropical plants we are able to grow with all the climbers mentioned in some of my late papers, with all the palms, bamboos, Pandanus, Crotons, Fig Trees and thousands of similar plants we can create garden paradises as found nowhere else. The main interest in Florida, the main beauty of the state rests in that wonderful plant growth.

Ipomoea horsfalliae 'Briggsii,' Lady Briggs Climber. A few weeks ago I was struck with the gorgeous beauty of this tropical climber. It was seen in Dr. J. Petersen's place at Homestead, Fla., and as everything the doctor grows this was not only a mass of brilliant rosy-purple, but it was above all a dense, fine and healthy specimen. I have had this beautiful plant in my collection at Palm Cottage Gardens, having received it from the late Henry Pfister, for over thirty years the able head gardener of the White House conservatories, which he had built up. My plant grew and flowered, but it was far behind what I saw in Dr. Petersen's place. I have seen a fine specimen of it, years ago, in the old and now extinct Heitman place at Fort Myers. It was trained along the front fence and displayed its fine flowers during the early spring months.

Lady Briggs variety is quite distinct from that typical species, *Ipomoea horsfalliae,* which was introduced in 1835 and figured in the *Botanical Magazine* (T. 3315). A description cannot give the reader a true impression; you have to see both before you. For garden purposes only, 'Briggsii,' as I prefer to call it, is by far the most beautiful and the most brilliantly floriferous. When well grown it is a gem and, I think, the most beautiful of all the Ipomoeas. It usually starts into bloom in December, and I have seen it in full flower as late as early August. It has tuberous roots and thrives best in a rich well-drained soil, not too wet and not too dry.

With reference to the home of *I. horsfalliae* and the other plants of the section viz: *Ipomoea ternata, I. macrorhiza* and *I.* 'Briggsii,' sent to Kew by Sir Graham Briggs, it is now settled beyond doubt that they are natives of Jamaica and a few other West Indian Islands. Dr. Masters, with the assistance of the late Mr. Hart, who was then in Jamaica, obtained specimens of all of these and published an account of them in 1885. All these Ipomoeas, the finest of all being *I.* 'Briggsii,' form great ornaments on verandahs, pergolas and even on not too densely branched trees. All are perfectly hardy from central Florida southward. A heavy freeze may cut them to the ground, but they usually start again vigorously from the root stalk.

Porana paniculata, the Snow Creeper, which means traveler—is, as its name implies, a climber of riotous growth. Left to itself the quick-growing shoots drop upon the ground and root so that it takes possession of a large area of the garden if not looked after. It climbs to the tops of the highest trees. Its chief use in the garden is to cover walls and fences, and we like to have it within reasonable height. By affinity it is a *Convolvulus,* but Lilac in what it looks like. It should be found in all good gardens in Florida.

This fine climber, which was introduced into Florida by the late E. N. Reasoner many years ago, is seldom heard of and seldom cultivated, though it is a most beautiful and an ideal plant for dry soils. It does not do well in moist ground, though a certain amount of humidity in the soil is important. I had a fine strong plant for years at Palm Cottage Gardens but I have only seen it once in full flower,—in 1916 late in November. It is very tender, and a slight cold even kills it to the ground, though it always sprouts again vigorously in spring. I quote here from an article by the late Dr. E. Bonavia, who was for many years an army physician in the Indian army. He writes:

> *Porana paniculata* is now—November—in full bloom here—Etawak, India—and a most charming thing it is. It is a twining plant of the family Convolvulaceae—Morning Glory family. Besides the tiny branches, it gives off, on the level of the ground, long straight shoots which have a tendency to twine, but root readily in favorable places. This is a common feature in various perennial Convolvulaceae. The largest leaves of this Porana are about 5 inches across and have a rather rough surface. The stems and small leaves are covered with a grayish down. Single panicles are often a foot long and 4 inches across, but often terminal compound panicles are 3 to 4 feet long. The flowers are of the purest white, a quarter of an inch across and bell-shaped, with a yellowish tube, and sweet-scented. The flowers open at once, from tip to base, so that the climber is covered with pure white minute bells in cloud-like masses, with here and there gracefully drooping panicles. This beautiful tropical climber, I think, would do extremely well in the dry, rocky soil of the Redlands and Homestead region of south Florida where even slight frosts rarely occur.

[*Pandorea pandorana*] (Wonga-Wonga Vine) is rather difficult to grow on high pineland, as it needs a soil rich in humus. In rich soil, however, and liberally fertilized, it is a very strong and rampant grower with beautiful dark green glossy foliage. The abundant and dark green leaves are so lustrous and handsome that for this reason alone it is worthy of cultivation. In the writer's garden the plants grow on arbors and sheds, in the center of which are high posts, or in the tops of old pine trees, partly still provided with their limbs protruding high above the top of the structure. [*Pandorea pandorana*] soon reaches the top, mingling its foliage and blossoms with those of *Bignonia capreolata,* [*Macfadyena unguis-cati*], *Passiflora caerulea* and *Ipomoea* 'Briggsii.' In some years it flowers very profusely, the blossoms being borne in loose panicles at the ends of the shoots, about ten to twelve in a truss. Though the flowers are quite handsome and interesting, they are not showy, being comparatively small, yellowish, with a brown throat. The plant is hardier than either [*Pandorea jasminoides*] or [*Podranea ricasoliana*], and if frozen down it readily sprouts from the very strong and vigorous root-stalk. It is a gross feeder and must be well taken care of and well watered during the dry spring months or it will dwindle away in a very short time.

[*Pandorea jasminoides*], "Bower Plant" of Australia, is a species very beautiful in foliage and flowers and a fine object for verandahs, sheds, arbors and small trees. It is a tall, rampant, glabrous climber, reveling in the bright Florida sunshine and in the mild and balmy air, but it needs a very rich soil and during dry weather an abundance of water. A heavy mulching also proves very beneficial. If not well cared for the plant remains small and unsightly. The pinnate, dark green, smooth and lustrous leaves are abundantly produced, and the flowers appear in large compact panicles. They are large, Gloxinia-like, pure white, with a deep purple throat. The writer had plants only two feet high which flowered profusely. It is easily affected by frost and often killed down to the ground, but it pushes up an abundance of new shoots when the weather gets warm. In good soil it grows in one season twenty to thirty feet high, clambering from tree to tree.

[*Podranea ricasoliana*] from Natal and Kaffraria, has foliage somewhat similar to the Wonga-Wonga Vine, but neither so large and dark green, nor so leathery and glossy. It is a rampant grower, demanding a very rich soil and a heavy mulch of stable manure. Its leaves easily drop from the woody branches after a cold night, and six or seven degrees of frost kill the plant down to the ground. Plants raised from seed under the name of *Tecoma ricasoliana* [= *Podranea ricasoliana*] from Italy are much hardier and more floriferous than those obtained from seed imported from South Africa, but the flowers of both are exactly alike. It is one of the most beautiful of all climbers when in full flower. The trumpet-shaped blossoms appear in large racemes. They are large, with a few darker lines and with a blotch of yellow in the tube.

In order to flower profusely this [*Podranea*] must be planted in the full sun. It usually takes a few years before it starts into a vigorous growth and it rarely flowers before its fifth year or before it has attained considerable size. In the writer's greenhouses at Milwaukee a specimen planted out in rather heavy soil, in company with [*Pandorea pandorana*] and [*Macfadyena unguis-cati*], has made a very luxuriant growth, flowering abundantly if the glass is not shaded. In large greenhouses this magnificent climber would make a fine object and should be made use of more frequently, as its bright rosy flower trusses, appearing on the end of every shoot, are worth all the trouble and care bestowed upon it. [*Pandorea pandorana*] is worthy to be grown in large greenhouses for its beautiful glossy foliage. In Florida [*Podranea ricasoliana*] should be planted on tall stumps, or on arbors and sheds by itself, never mingled with other species.

Fragrant Flowers

The sense of smell is generally considered to be one of minor importance; that the idea of comparing it in any way with those appertaining to the eyes and ears would seem at first sight preposterous. Yet this sense is, as regards one's aspect at least, more highly strung than either of the two. Now and again I have been arrested by a wandering breath of perfume that momentarily stirred some chord of memory, yet with such a down-soft touch that, even if we are aware of the vibration, it had ceased. The scent is still in the air, but its illusive message has fled, and in vain we search for the clue. We only know that at some period of our lives a like fragrance has held a meaning for us.

Several correspondents requested me to give them the title of a good book on fragrant flowers. The subject may be of interest to many others of my readers, and so I shall give a short review of one of the books, which appeared under the title *Sweet Scented Flowers and Fragrant Leaves*. It was written by Donald McDonald, with an introduction by W. Robinson and published by Sampson, Low, Marston and Co., London, England.

The object which this little volume so well fulfills is to give concisely, in the most convenient form for reference, what was greatly needed, namely, all necessary practical information about the sweet-smelling flowers, shrubs and plants which are found in our gardens, field and hedgerows, not excluding those which come to us from other countries and climes—from our own country, America, the East, Australasia, and which are not hardy like the *Olearia*, *Eucalyptus* and many others.

In the historical sketch which precedes the main alphabetical list of sweet-smelling plants, which is the main purpose the book, there is a great deal of interesting matter concerning the use of sweet-smelling flowers and herbs in the distillation and manufacture of perfumes from the earliest recorded times, and also the association of aromatic plants with the religious and social observances of the most ancient peoples. "Thus in the East scented flowers and the shade of perfumed trees were considered one of the most indispensable enjoyments of the higher classes of society," as they are now in fact; and again, "The luxurious and refined habits of the Assyrians involved the use of perfumed plants to an excess," and we read of one potentate who, driven to extremities by continuous defeat, "caused a pile of fragrant herbs to be lighted, and, placing himself with his wives and treasures upon it, all were swiftly suffocated, with aromatic smoke."

The Egyptians also made the most luxurious use of fragrant incense, and the Greeks ascribed a divine origin to perfumes. Sweet-smelling flowers— the Rose particularly—play a prominent part in eastern fables. Later and in our own country the poets are seldom happier than when telling of our native flowers. It is, perhaps, not generally known that the one much used, but now rather out of date,—Sweet Patchouli,—comes from an Indian herb of that name; and from a tree found on the islands of the Indian Archipelago comes the perfume known as Ylang-Ylang. It is more costly than even the attar of roses, and the odor of the flower is so powerful that it scents the air for miles around. The writer has seen beautiful large trees of the Ylang-Ylang at Palm Beach as well as at Miami, where the air was wonderfully heavy with the perfume of the flowers."

The following excellent article, "Jessamines or Jasmines," was written Dec. 2, 1887, by the late Pliny W. Reasoner, shortly before his untimely death. P. W. Reasoner is a shining star—one of the really great men who made Florida their home. He is the real pioneer of ornamental horticulture in Florida.

A Jessamine may be almost any flower in existence, especially as applied by some people, if it be sweet-scented. In literature it has become almost as popular and as general as Myrtle and Ivy. Nobody knows what a literary Ivy may be, whether a [Parthenocissus], a *Hedera* or a *Linaria*. It is supposed to combine all such desirable qualities as constancy, beauty, grace and delicate tenderness, and in the meantime to keep up a vigorous clinging to the sturdy oak. The literary term Myrtle may apply to a variety of plants equally at home in a cemetery or on the poet's brow, and it has come to be that whenever there is a cottage containing a pretty girl, there a Jessamine is placed.

Even the florists' catalogues, which should be public instructors, in many cases hopelessly muddle Jessamines, Gardenias, Cestrums and other plants. First there are the Gardenias, popularly known as Cape Jessamine [now better known as Cape Jasmine], though the name is a misnomer, the common species, [*Gardenia jasminoides*], having been introduced, it is said, from China in 1754, and named in honor of Dr. Alexander Garden, of Charleston, S.C. This species is well known everywhere. In the South it has been popular for years, as it is perfectly hardy throughout the lower southern states. In the North, though long cultivated, it has suddenly become popular on account of the whims of metropolitan florists. Its popularity, however, is for once well deserved. Other species of Gardenias are not so well known, though *Gardenia radicans* [= *G. jasminoides*] is sometimes seen. Other fine species and varieties are: *G. thunbergii, G. lucida, G. citriodora* [= *Mitriostigma axillare*] etc. *Randia floribunda* is a closely related Indian plant, which is said to be well worthy of cultivation. It succeeds well in the open ground in south Florida.

The Cestrums are also often confounded with the Jessamines. *Cestrum nocturnum* is the most common sort, and is usually known as the Nightblooming Jessamine. It is a coarse, quick growing shrub, but when in bloom it exhales a most delightful fragrance in the night. The flowers are produced in the greatest profusion, and the shrub quickly attains a height of 15 and more feet in the open ground in Florida or the West Indies. *Cestrum parquii* is also quite well known.

Gelsemium sempervirens, the so-called Carolina Yellow Jessamine, is a plant worthy of special attention. It is found in every hammock and on every rail fence from the Carolinas to south Florida, and a more beautiful and delicate climber does not exist. Evergreen, with glossy dark green foliage, and in February and March covering every branch of *Myrica* and *Persea* and *Gordonia,* and clumps of Palmettos, with sprays and wreaths of the sweetest golden yellow bells, often breaking into perfect sheaths of color. *Gelsemium* should be seen in its native hammocks to be appreciated. I have no doubt, however, that it could be forced under glass at almost any time. A double-flowered variety, first introduced by P. J. Berckmans, is worthy a place in any collection of plants.

The Carolina or Yellow Jessamine, *Gelsemium sempervirens,* our most beautiful native climber and one of the most exquisite plants in existence, is a real aristocrat among our woodland plants. It has only good qualities—a noble, dense, but not an aggressive growth, masses of deliciously fragrant, yellow flower trumpets and dainty, rather small, but finely formed leaves. It should be in every Florida garden. As it flowers in winter, February and March, it is of particular value. When I first came to Orlando there was a nice little garden-house on one of the Englishmen's grounds. It was covered with the Yellow Jessamine; the sight when in bloom—a sheet of color—was one never to be forgotten. I have also grown the double flowering variety. It is most beautiful, but the plant itself is a rather weak grower and needs some attention. I sent several specimens to the editor of the ornamental plant department of the *Florida Agriculturist,*—the late W. R. Steele, an excellent plant expert and enthusiast,—and he raved over the beauty of the double flowers when it first began to bloom with him. I have found that the Carolina Jessamine is a most important plant to grow on medium-sized Cabbage palms, which it covers completely with its sheets of yellow flower-trumpets when in full bloom. The growth of the plant is not dense enough to injure the palm. It never should be planted on small palms.

The Cestrums are all very interesting and dense plants and very floriferous. Orlando gardens were replete with the Night-blooming Jasmine, *Cestrum nocturnum,* when I first saw the place in 1886. At that time it was a home town. The many Englishmen living there had all planted fine gardens full of rare plants. During many a night, summer or winter, the soft balmy air was heavy with the strong delicious perfume of the night-blooming Jasmine. The flowers are light green, and are produced 4 or 5 times during the year. This is a valuable species for tropical gardens. It seems to be hardy all over the state, and though often frozen to the ground it soon sprouts again from the rootstalk.

Cestrum latifolium is an excellent plant, but I prefer *Cestrum diurnum,* the Day-blooming Jasmine. Its flowers are white, in small bunches and are quite fragrant,—easily grown and an excellent winter bloomer. I have had at Palm Cottage Gardens seven additional Cestrums, all very tender, and all producing big pendant clusters of yellow, orange, white and light rosy red flowers, followed by large bunches of black berries, which were much sought by many birds. One of the species with large bunches of yellowish flowers and large crops of black berries escaped from the garden and is now found in many parts of the grounds. All the Cestrums are tropical American.

The real Gardenia or Cape Jasmine is now called *Gardenia jasminoides,* though the old name *Gardenia florida* is still much in use. I have grown

Gardenia thunbergia and *G. citriodora*. The latter is found under the name of *Mitriostigma axillare* in Bailey's great work, *Standard Cyclopedia of Horticulture*—the most important and dependable reference work on ornamental plants in existence [now replaced in importance by *Hortus Third* (1976)]. I have also had [*Rothmannia longiflora*] at Gotha as well as at Naples. It is a tropical species from West Africa and very tender, but perfectly hardy at Naples.

Triphasia trifoliata (the Lime Berry) is also a very handsome shrub with white fragrant flowers and small, dull red berry-like fruits. These fruits are filled with a slightly aromatic pulp and are sometimes used in tropical countries for making marmalade. It forms a beautiful ornamental shrub for lawns, but it is easily injured by severe frosts. As it is able to grow in soils too salty for citrus fruits it has been recommended as a stock for use on such soils. Its native country is unknown [probably Malay Peninsula].

I have known, in Tampa and elsewhere, the unique little plant *Triphasia trifoliata* (allied to the citrus) to be called "Orange Jasmine," and in Key West the great bare-stemmed, bouquet-laden Frangipani (*Plumeria*) are called Coffee Jessamine, for no better reason that I can see than that they do not in the least resemble either Coffee plants or Jasminums. They will probably be known, however, under that name until [*Parthenocissus quinquefolia*] shall be no longer known as an Ivy in parts of the United States, or until some of our leading florists quit selling that weak-kneed little [*Cymbalaria muralis*] under that misnomer of Kenilworth Ivy. [Reasoner.]

Orange Jessamine, known as *Murraya* [*paniculata*] (or *Chalcas exotica*), did not occur in catalogues of 1887, and it seems to have come to Florida several years later. It has no trifoliate, but pinnate leaves, and is not provided with spines. The large solitary or terminal clusters of pure white, very fragrant flowers, are abundantly produced in south Florida where the Orange Jessamine is often seen in gardens. It is not hardy in central Florida. The flowers and the mature red fruits are often seen together which makes a striking contrast with the panicles of white flowers and delicate foliage. This fine tall shrub should be found in every good garden in south Florida.

Many sorts of the true Jessamines (*Jasminum*) are universal favorites. Perhaps the most common is *Jasminum grandiflorum*, known as Catalonian Jasmine or Star Jasmine (though the stars, in the Jasmine family are as plentiful as the "Johns" in the Smith household). The plant is half shrubby, half climbing, and is almost always covered with its pinkish-white fragrant flowers.

But there are said to be 60 or more species of the genus *Jasminum*, and some are hardy even in the northern states. The flowers are usually white and yellow, and I can only mention the names of other better known species, such as *Jasminum officinale, J. odoratissimum, J. paniculatum, J. angustifolium, J. nervosum, J. humile, J. fruticans, J. nudiflorum, J. revolutum*. Many of these are highly prized and largely grown for their perfume along the Mediterranean. [Reasoner.]

The true Jessamines of the genus *Jasminum* are not as often seen in our Florida gardens as their beauty, fragrance and fine dense growth entitles them to be. They are all first-class flowering plants and their delicious fragrance has been praised in the songs of many of the oldest poets. This is a large genus of plants. According to Bailey's *Standard Cyclopedia of Horticulture*, probably upward of 200 species are widely distributed in the warm parts of Europe, Asia, Africa and the Pacific region; nearly absent from America. The genus is closely allied to *Ligustrum*. They belong to the Oleaceae or Olive family.

Though mostly tropical plants, Jasminums are a diverse horticultural group, some of them being hardy in the middle and southern states, whereas others are winter flowering plants in glasshouses, or in Florida in the open air. They are easily propagated by cuttings of nearly mature wood or by layers. Some of them are tall climbers, while most of them are only half-climbing and some are shrubs. [Reasoner.]

The following should be grown more extensively in our Florida gardens: *Jasminum officinale* is the Jasmine of plenty, a native of Persia and now widely distributed. The glossy foliage, the white, fragrant, single summer blooming flowers render the plant very attractive in the south where it is hardy.

Another favorite is the Arabian Jessamine, (*Jasminum sambac*). This is a climbing species with simple leaves. (The leaves of the Catalonia and most other species are compact, and single, semi-double, or double white flowers, very fragrant, as are those of all the species of the genus). This species and the preceding will stand but a very light frost, unharmed. The variety 'Grand Duke of Tuscany' seems to belong, botanically, to this species of the genus *Jasminum*. It is, however, not a climber, but of low shrubby growth, and produces many double flowers, often to the extent of deformity, which are perhaps more fragrant than those of any other of the species or variety. They are larger, too, than those of the common varieties of the Arabian Jessamine. [Reasoner.]

Jasminum sambac, Arabian Jasmine, is a climbing native of India much cultivated in Florida. Branches are angular. Flowers white, turning to a purple color before they fade and very fragrant! One form of it is grown under the name of 'Grand Duke of Tuscany.' There is also a double form. In frostless regions *J. sambac* is a perpetual bloomer.

Jasminum grandiflorum, Catalonian, Italian, Royal or Spanish Jasmine (also of India), is said to be naturalized in Florida. A perpetual bloomer in warm countries, it is much used in perfumery and stands 10 to 12°F of frost.

Jasminum multiflorum has formally been pronounced by a leading Florida nurseryman the "finest flowering plant of south Florida," and it is a beautiful plant, but hardly equal, I think, to the newer *Jasminum gracillimum,* which, when well grown in the open ground in Florida in late summer and fall, is a sight never to be forgotten. The great sprays of white flowers and delicate green leaves are only fit for bridal wreaths, which indeed they are. [Reasoner.]

~ 10 ~

Annual, Perennial, and Bulbous Plants, Etc.

Malopes; Fine Winter-flowering Annuals: The beauty of the large beds of petunias and *Phlox drummondii* at Winter Park during the sessions of the Federation of Florida Garden Clubs (March 27–28) attracted much attention. But there are many more of such annuals that can be used advantageously. The importance of annual flowers in adding beauty to gardens is well known, but perhaps a special reminder of the nature of the Malopes may be of use here. Strong growing and very showy when well grown, the Malopes have an advantage over some other annuals in that they have very attractive leaves and the flowering period continues until the plants are finally crippled by the hot weather. Another great point in their favor is that Malopes do not get "played out" so quickly as do less vigorous annuals before our winter garden flowering season is over. They should be sown directly in the open ground in October, as seedlings do not transplant very readily. Being of robust habit, the rather large seeds should be sown thickly, the resulting plants being again thinned, so that each may have reasonable development. The varieties [*Malope trifida*] 'Rosea' and [*M. trifida*] 'Alba,' mixed in a long border, are very effective. While beds, or long lengths of borders of these flowers, give the most brilliant results, odd groupings among tall herbarium subjects and in front of shrubs, etc., are always admired.

Whitfieldia lateritia: Our Florida spring and summer gardens show a lack of gorgeous perennials. They cannot compare in this respect with our northern gardens. The tropics are full of such plants—plants that would render our ornamental grounds tremendously effective. Specialists should make a special study of them in Florida. *Whitfieldia* belongs into this category. It is the only plant of this small genus of two species which has been introduced. As it flowers in December it requires only to be better known to become more popular. It is a native of the interior of Sierra Leone, from where it was brought by the late T. Whitfield in 1841. It bears flowers as late as March. This is accounted for by its racemes of flowers opening in succession from the base, which are of a bright red color, and produced from the apex of the growth. The leaves are of a pleasing green and produce in abundance, forming a pretty contrast to the drooping inflorescence. It requires loam and leaf soil and full sun. Cuttings start easily in spring in sand. In winter, during our cold spells, it needs some protection. I have found Spanish-Moss or dense Cedar branches mostly sufficient during our ordinary frosty nights. A real freeze, such as we had early in February, 1917, kills the plants outright. Perhaps a covering with dry sand would be all that is necessary to save them.

[*Dietes vegeta*] and Allied Forms: The beautiful German Iris, often called the orchid of the poor man, does not succeed in Florida. But we have a few fine native species of Iris and the closely allied [*Dietes vegeta*], introduced by Reasoner Bros. many years ago from South Africa. It grows well in our Florida gardens and flowers profusely. I have had large beds of it at Palm Cottage Gardens in bygone days.

The beautiful [*Dietes vegeta*] 'Johnsonii' is the finest of all [*Dietes*]. All these plants have suffered neglect by gardeners in Florida from the fact that their blossoms, lovely as they are, are remarkably fugitive, scarcely surviving more than the morning hours. But [*Dietes vegeta*] 'Johnsonii,' imported from the mountains of Ceylon by Mrs. Johnson, behaves in the most satisfactory way. Its blossoms are not only double the size and far more brilliantly colored than others of the type, but they persist for about four days in half-shade, a little less in full sunshine, the substance of the petals being much thicker than that of the rest of the genus. The flowers are beautifully creamy-white, blotched with yellow, with the three central "standards" of a rich shade of violet and feathered at the base with crimson-brown markings. The flower is of singular beauty and the various hues are most harmonious. The plants soon form large clumps. As there is no indigenous [*Dietes*] in Ceylon, it is believed that plants of the original form have escaped from cultivation and that the new form is the result of the warm climate and rich soil of their new home. Said to be easily raised from seed. As far as I know, it is not yet introduced into our Florida gardens, but it is hoped that we soon may see it in our gardens.

Flowering Bulbs

[*Eucharis grandiflora*]: The Amazon Lily is at present a very popular bulbous plant in Florida, being usually grown in large masses in tubs and plant boxes. As they are vigorous growers with pure white blossoms, and as they flower profusely during winter, they are much cherished by all amateur gardeners. I saw the first flowering masses in large tubs in the grounds of the Arcadia House, at Arcadia, where the proprietor, Mr. Roe, an ardent plant lover, was very successful in their culture. I have seen 65 flowering spikes, overtopping the fine dark green leaves, all open at one time, and they were a sight to see.

[*Crinum jagus*]: From Old Calebar in West Tropical Africa, this is even more stunning when opening its large, pure white, fragrant bell-shaped blossoms. I introduced this plant in 1904 from Horticultural Hall, Philadelphia, whence it had been brought by a missionary from Old Calebar. It is easily grown in rich moist soil, but requires a half-shady position. Big clumps are soon formed, and these flower five or six times during the year, being particularly acceptable during the winter and at Christmas time. These masses of pure white blossoms always overtop the fine large, dark evergreen leaves. I regard this as the most beautiful of all Crinums. It is excellent for hybridizing. I have crossed it with *C. moorei,* with *C. scabrum,* with [*C. bulbispermum*] and with *C. americanum,* but only a few of the hybrids, so far, have flowered. The fleshy, variously formed seeds ripen in abundance, and large patches of the seedlings appear under and near my old plants. [Perhaps *Crinum* 'St. Christofer' is one of the progeny.]

With the exception of the Easter Lily we are not able to enjoy masses of the true lilies in our gardens, as is the case up north. Here in Florida the fine Crinums take their place, and though not generally as regal and distinguished, they form wonderful substitutes. It is always a revelation to the tourist to see the large pure white clusters of *Crinum americanum* lifting their heads on strong stems above the water along the Tamiami Trail during winter. This species can be made to form dense beds in low mucky spots of our gardens. All the Crinums are tropical or subtropical plants, many of them evergreen, and all are hardy in Florida.

Hymenocallis species: The Spider-Lilies, are, strictly speaking, all natives of the American tropics, though one of them occurs in West Africa (*H. senegambica*) [a name based on a mixture of *H. littoralis* and *H. pedalis*].

The common Spider Lily of our Florida gardens is *Hymenocallis caribaea*. It grows in large clumps and flowers in dense masses in February and March. The flowers are pure white and fragrant. There are two smaller species along our lower West Coast, but they are not yet well understood.

I received years ago from the late Mr. James Douglas in England, *Hymenocallis macrostephana,* perhaps the most floriferous and distinct of the entire genus. The flowers are exceedingly beautiful, and can be used in the most distinct cut-flower arrangements. Such beauties as these flowers undoubtedly need no other embellishments than that of foliage to display them to advantage. Like the Amazon Lily, this last named species should be grown in pots or tubs. The larger the clumps eventually grow, the more flower-spikes will be produced. The best place to grow them is on our verandahs, or the pots or tubs can be given a half shady, moist place in the lath house. They require careful watering. If neglected in this way the leaves will suffer or die down and the entire plant suffers in such a way that it may lose its roots. Drainage is a most essential point. Drainage should consist of equal parts of well-decomposed leaf-mould, good loam, and a little old cow manure and muck, and it should be quite sandy.

[*Lapeirousia laxa*] or *Anomatheca cruenta*: This beautiful bulbous plant is a most important winter-bloomer in our Florida gardens,—a native of Transvaal, South Africa. My first bulbs came, many years ago, from the director of the Missouri Botanical Garden. They were a perfect success in my lath house, at Palm Cottage, where they came up in masses every year from self-sown seeds, and I have them now in abundance also in my Naples garden. It is a rare and a very beautiful plant, when in flower. The bulbs are a good deal like those of *Freesia,* but smaller, while the sword-shaped leaves are disposed in two rows. The flowers, which are produced on scapes from 8 to 12 inches high, are nearly an inch across, and of a bright carmine red, the lower segments being blotched with rich, dark, velvety crimson. When masses of these flowers are seen, the effect is most brilliant, and they always attract the attention of every flower lover. I have a large clump of *Crinum pedunculatum* which is surrounded by a dense carpet of this *Lapeirousia.* The effect of pure white flowers of *Crinum,* and all around it the brilliant sheet of "Anomathecas," is a very charming one. This little bulbous plant is a great favorite of mine, needing no attention at all, because it comes up every year from self-sown seed. The little bulbs can be grown in beds with perfect success, and all they need is weeding and a little old cow manure now and then.

Blood Lilies,—*Haemanthus:* A few weeks ago a mass of *Haemanthus katharinae* was in gorgeous bloom in my garden at Naples. The flowers appear in round ball-like umbels and are of a most brilliant red color. In habit it is one of the most luxuriant of all the 20 or 30 species of *Haemanthus* now known from the Cape of Good Hope and elsewhere on the Continent of Africa. Even if it never flowered this species, as well as *H. lindenii* [?], *H.* XKonig Albert, etc., would be worth a place in our gardens for its foliage alone. Its leaves are strap-shaped, much undulated, each about 3 ft. long and of a bright apple-green color, and the venation is more strongly marked than is usual in *H. multiflorus, H. cinnabarinum,* and other allied kinds. One of my specimens bore a number of fine spikes, each flower-ball being about 8 inches in diameter, and of a glowing orange-scarlet or flame-color, with its anthers tipped with gold, as is usual in the genus. *Haemanthus* is a genus belonging to the Amaryllis family. When well grown and in full flower it is not at all easy to convey an adequate idea of the stately beauty of this species. My plants grow in rather rich moist soil. They die down in December and begin to grow again in March, the young leaves appearing at the same time the flower scape makes its growth. I received my plants years ago with the hybrid *H.* XKonig Albert, from the Botanical Garden at Leipzig, Germany.

Quite a number of years ago I saw a fine clump of Golden Amaryllis, *Lycoris* [*africana*], beautifully in flower in a garden at Sanford. I never was able to obtain this species, but in 1888 Mrs. Thompson of Spartanburg, S.C., an ardent flower lover, sent me about 50 fine bulbs of another species, *Lycoris radiata,* and last summer Judge E. G. Wilkinson of Naples brought me a few of the hardy *Lycoris squamigera* (*Amaryllis hallii*).

Lycoris [*africana*]: This plant has been in cultivation more than a century, having been introduced by Dr. Fothergill in 1777, when it was called *Amaryllis aurea.* This is generally described as a greenhouse bulb. In July, 1894, Kew Gardens received from Hong Kong, which has a decidedly tropical climate, a box of bulbs of this species. Along with them came the following significant note.

> I send you a box of *Lycoris aurea* [*africana*], and I hope it will reach you all right. Is it not somewhat remarkable that these bulbs should remain dormant in the ground all summer in such a climate as this, with a tem-

perature of 85°F in the shade, and a rainfall of 100 inches in a year,—heat and moisture sufficient, one would think, to start into feverish growth the most hide-bound of bulbs? The Lycoris, however, sleeps through it all pushing up its tall scapes of yellow flowers at the end of our summer. Here it is one of the most popular of garden plants, ranking with Crinums, Pancratiums, Eucharis and *Lilium longiflorum*.

The bulbs sent flowered at Kew, and they are now in full leaf (January) in an intermediate house, a few of them having been placed in a hot stove as a test. The bulb is like that of a Daffodil. The leaves, which are numerous and start into growth along with the flower-scapes, are like those of *Nerine sarniensis*, and the scape is 18 inches high, with an umbel of deep yellow flowers, like my huge Nerines, strong bulbs producing twelve flowers in an umbel. There is a most exquisite colored plate in the *Garden* (London), Vol. 47, p. 42 (1895) of *Lycoris aurea*. This brilliant species will undoubtedly do well in Florida in rich, moist, well drained soil. It would not grow in poor sandy ground. It is a common garden plant not only at Hong Kong, but also in Canton and other parts of southern China, and importations from these two points should be made into Florida. The beauty of the gorgeous flowers merits all the trouble that can be bestowed on their introduction.

Lycoris squamigera (Amaryllis hallii): This is a good species and bears umbels of brilliant reddish flowers. It was introduced many years ago into our country by the late Dr. Hall, and was grown by the now obsolete firm of Mr. Howey of Boston, Mass., who named it *Amaryllis hallii*. It is perfectly hardy, perhaps, all over our country, as I have grown and flowered it very successfully in my garden at Milwaukee, Wis., where it usually opened its blossoms in September. In Mrs. E. G. Wilkinson's beautiful garden at Norwalk, Conn., there are large fine clumps of this Lycoris which make an indescribably beautiful show in the early fall months. My bulbs here at Naples did not succeed, though Judge Wilkinson has quite a number in his beach garden here where they apparently establish themselves. The flower scapes are about 2 feet high and carry an umbel of about 5 flowers, which are large and very conspicuous. The color of the flowers is lilac-pink, with a flash of blue down the center of each petal. Clumps should not be disturbed for years.

The foregoing notes are founded on an article on *Lycoris* by the late W. Watson, Curator at Kew, one of the most brilliant and scholarly gardeners that ever lived.

Owing to the difficulty that has been experienced in the past in flowering the very beautiful *Lycoris* [*africana*], the following note from a correspondent in China may be of interest:

> The temperature this *Lycoris* grows in varies from 95°F in the height of summer, when the bulbs are resting, to 55–60°F in winter, when they are growing. Sometimes for a few days in January the thermometer falls to 40° or lower, but that is for but a short time. When the plants make their leaves there is absolutely no rainfall, or next to none. When they rest it is our wet season. It is a most lovely thing; I think it is the most beautiful bulbous plant I ever have seen.

Ginger-Wort and Allied Plants

Many of the Ginger-Worts, all of a tropical nature, do exceedingly well in our Florida gardens. I call particular attention to the rather common Butterfly-Lily (*Hedychium coronarium*), which grows most luxuriantly in rich, moist soil and whose pure white and intensely fragrant flowers can be seen in the greatest abundance during the summer months. The Curcumas, known also as Queen Lilies, also flower beautifully and are very showy. The real Ginger-Worts, *Zingiber zerumbet,* and the beautifully variegated green and white *Zingiber* [probably cultivar 'Darceyi'] are splendid ornaments of our gardens in leaf and flower.

The most ornamental of all, the Alpinias, soon form immense clumps, attaining a height of from 5 to 10 feet and flower during summer. The blossoms appear in large trusses and are very showy, orchid-like and last for a considerable time. The large tropical foliage masses and dense sturdy growth adapts them well for foundation planting. Among their class they are the most sturdy and dense growers, being evergreen, and the foliage emitting a strong aromatic odor when crushed. This is particularly the case in *Alpinia auriculata* and *Alpinia mutica,* while *Alpinia* [*zerumbet*] grows tallest. My plants never attained more than 5 feet in height, but it is reported that it often assumes a height of from 10 to 12 feet. They all have done well at Palm Cottage Gardens where they not only grew well in rich moist soil, but made an almost equally large and dense growth on high pineland soil near the house. When cut down by a heavy freeze they always recuperated as soon as warm weather set in. At Naples, Fla., all grew finely and soon formed dense clumps. All belong to our very best tropical foliage and flowering plants.

Alpinia mutica [Small Shell-Ginger]: One of the finest tropical foliage and flowering plants for Florida, being at home everywhere in good rich, moist soil. It reminds one of [*A. zerumbet*], but the growth is stronger, denser and the leaves are thicker, deeper green and of greater substance. It is an excellent subject for foundation planting. It reminds one also of some of the Hedychiums, but it is an evergreen and much more elegant and vigorous, and grows about 5 to 6 feet high. The chief charm is the flowers, which are carried on erect or half drooping spikes and display rich and unusual colors. They are white, with the base crimson in the bud, but when fully open the calyx is pure white, and the lip of the corolla that likens the flowers to those of an Orchid is deep orange, brilliantly striped with crimson and finely crimped at the edge—a beautiful contrast of intense colors. It was introduced from Penang and Malaya in 1882, and does not as yet appear to be much known in Florida. My plant came from England, a single root, in 1894. If frozen down, it loses its leaf-stems, but pushes up new as soon as warm weather sets in. It is a beautiful counterpart to [*Alpinia zerumbet*], which it very much resembles.

The Amomums are closely allied to the Alpinias, but they are much more difficult to grow. They are best grown in lath houses in very rich, moist soil. [*Nicolaia elatior*, Torch Ginger], from Tropical Africa, attains a height of from 10 to 12 feet and forms large clumps. The very numerous flowers appear in a gaudy bracted head, being large vivid red.

The species of the genus *Costus* are quite different in growth as well as in blooming. I have only two species but both are always very beautiful and fine in flower. *Costus speciosus* forms a mass of fleshy roots from which are pushed up stout bamboo-like shoots, but they are succulent ovate, smooth above and silky beneath, being arranged in a spiral manner. The largest leaves are 9 to 10 inches in length, 4 to 5 inches wide, on the stems. Each stem is terminated by a cone-like flower truss, deep red in color. The individual flowers are white, thin and of short duration. The plant requires moist, rich ground. A native of India, and very conspicuous in any collection. *Costus igneus* is a Brazilian species. Its flowers are clustered and of an orange red color. The bracts are not conspicuous. It grows 3 to 4 feet high. The genus consists of about 30 species, but few of them are in cultivation in this country. They are best planted out in moist, mucky soil, though they also do quite well under pot-culture.

"Asparagus-Ferns": Last summer I received some sprays of a fine foliaged plant under the name of *Smilax* with an inquiry whether or not this can be grown commercially in Florida in a like way as *Asparagus plumosus.*

The specimens sent by W. T. L. belong to [*Asparagus asparagoides*], a native of South Africa. It has been known in Europe for over 200 years, but it was only found in a few gardens till about 40 years ago, when the young slender sprays became very popular for table decoration. The idea of employing the plant in this way was, however, first in vogue in our country, where it was largely grown under the name of Smilax. This is a misnomer, as it is really quite distinct from Smilax, being in fact a near ally of *Asparagus,* and indeed, it is by some botanists included in that genus.

The treatment required is simple. Being a native of the Cape of Good Hope, the protection of a lath house—just as for [*Asparagus setaceus*]—is necessary to its well being. It forms a mass of small tuber-like roots from whence the slender shoots are pushed up. They are at first so delicate that slugs soon make havoc among them. When required to be used in a cut state each shoot should be trained separately to a piece of thin twine, as when wanted the entire shoot can be taken without trouble, whereas if allowed to become entangled with each other it is a difficult matter to separate them. This *Myrsiphyllum* [= *Asparagus*], too, makes a very pretty climbing plant on the posts of the lath house and even on the roof, and in this way the bright green foliage is very attractive, added to which the small greenish-white blossoms which are borne in February and March impart an additional feature. These flowers are supported on rather long, slender stalks, and a very elegant appearance they present in quantity. They also emit a very pleasing perfume.

The plants may be grown either in pots, where they make a very elegant appearance on verandahs, or they can be planted out in a bed of a half-shady lath house in well prepared soil, rich, moist, and well-drained. A suitable compost is two-thirds of loam, one-third of cow manure and sand. In whatever position it is grown, although drainage is essential to its well-doing, it needs a liberal amount of water, but at the same time is very impatient to stagnant moisture. I have treated it just like I treated [*Asparagus setaceus*] and with the same results, having also used the same commercial fertilizer. I have grown it on Bamboo shoots with the branches left on, and it soon formed on them a dense canopy of fine foliage. But it is when growing freely as a climber, and the shoots allowed to dispose themselves in a natural manner, that this "*Myrsiphyllum*" is seen at its best. It is very useful, too, for draping the front stage of greenhouses, thus helping to take off the hard formal appearance.

Propagation is effected by division which is readily carried out early in the year before growth commences, while in the case of established plants seeds are often produced, and plants obtained in this way are by many preferred to divided specimens. Seeds of it can, as a rule, be obtained from most dealers of repute. They should be sown as soon as possible after receipt, using rather a lighter compost than recommended for established plants. As a rule I have found the sowing, the growing of seedlings and their treatment, etc., just as easy as in the case of the well known and much grown *Asparagus* [*setaceus*]. Very likely the spray can be transmitted in the same way to Northern wholesalers, as those of the Asparagus. In Bailey's *Cyclopedia of Horticulture* the name of *Asparagus medeoloidea* is used. The names Fern for *Asparagus* [*setaceus*] and Smilax for the species in question are idiotic.

Mackaya bella: Many years ago the late Mr. E. N. Reasoner introduced this fine plant from Natal, South Africa, its native home. I received it from him and had it in full bloom every year early in winter, or from December to February. It grows easily in rich, good, rather moist soil. The flowers appear in terminal sprays, and are campanulate in form. Their color is a delicate shade of pale lavender. These elegant sprays are well set off by the dark shining foliage. My plants were never taller than about 3 feet, quite dense and bushy, and flowered in a small state. It is easily raised from cuttings during our rainy season. I lost all my plants in the February freeze of 1917, and I do not know whether the Royal Palm Nursery still lists it in their catalogue. The reader may perhaps find it is under the [old] name *Asystasia bella*.

Selected References

Andrews, Allen H. *A Yank Pioneer in Florida; Recounting the Adventures of a City Chap Who Came to the Wilds of South Florida in the 1890's and Remained to Grow Up with the Country.* Jacksonville, Fla.: Douglas Printing, 1950.

Baensch, Ulrich, and Ursula Baensch. *Blooming Bromeliads.* Bramsche, Germany: Rasch Druck und Verlag, 1994.

Benson, Lyman David. *The Cacti of the United States and Canada.* Stanford, Calif.: Stanford University Press, 1977.

Broschat, Timothy K., and Alan W. Meerow. *Betrock's Reference Guide to Florida Landscape Plants.* 4th printing. Cooper City: Institute of Food and Agricultural Sciences, University of Florida and Betrock Information Systems, 1996.

Burch, Derek, Daniel B. Ward, and David W. Hall. *Checklist of the Woody Cultivated Plants of Florida.* SP-33. Gainesville: Florida Cooperative Extension Service, Institute of Food and Agricultural Sciences, University of Florida, 1988.

Dransfield, John, and Henk Beentje. *The Palms of Madagascar.* Kew [Surrey: UK]: Royal Botanic Garden and the International Palm Society, 1995.

Godfrey, Robert K. *Trees, Shrubs, and Woody Vines of Northern Florida and Adjacent Georgia and Alabama.* Athens: University of Georgia Press, 1988.

Graf, Alfred Byrd. *Exotica.* 7th ed. E. Rutherford, N.J.: Roehrs Company, 1974.

Hawkes, Alex D. *Encyclopedia of Cultivated Orchids.* London: Faber and Faber, 1965.

Hitchcock, Albert Spear. *Manual of the Grasses of the United States.* 2nd ed. Washington, D.C.: United States Government Printing Office, 1950.

Hortus Third: A Concise Dictionary of Plants Cultivated in the United States and Canada. Ed. L. H. Bailey and E. Z. Bailey. Revised and expanded by Liberty Hyde Bailey Hortorium staff. New York: Macmillan, 1976.

Jones, David L. *Cycads of the World.* Washington, D.C.: Smithsonian Institution Press, 1993.

———. *Palms throughout the World.* Washington, D.C.: Smithsonian Institution Press, 1995.

Lellinger, David B. *A Field Manual of the Ferns and Fern-Alies of the United States and Canada.* Washington, D.C.: Smithsonian Institution Press, 1985.

Long, Robert W., and Olga Lakela. *A Flora of Tropical Florida: A Manual of the Seed Plants and Ferns of Southern Peninsular Florida.* Coral Gables, Fla.: University of Miami Press, 1971.

Luer, Carlyle A. *The Native Orchids of Florida.* New York: New York Botanical Garden, 1972.

McClintock, Elizabeth May, and Andrew T. Leiser, *An Annotated Checklist of Woody Ornamental Plants of California, Oregon and Washington.* No. 4091. Berkeley: Division of Agricultural Sciences, University of California, 1979.

Meerow, Alan W. *Betrock's Guide to Landscape Palms.* Cooper City, Fla.: Betrock Information Systems, 1992.

Moore, Harold E., Jr. "An Annotated Checklist of Cultivated Palms." *Principes* (Journal of the Palm Society) 7, no. 4 (October 1963): 119–84.

Morton, Julia Frances. *Some Useful and Ornamental Plants of the Caribbean Gardens.* Naples, Fla.: Caribbean Gardens, 1955.

Neal, Marie C. *In Gardens of Hawaii.* Honolulu: Bishop Museum Press, 1965.

Nehrling, H. *The Plant World in Florida.* Ed. A. and E. Kay. New York: Macmillan, 1933.

———. *My Garden in Florida and Miscellaneous Horticultural Notes / From the Manuscripts of Dr. Henry Nehrling.* Ed. A. H. Andrews. 2 vols. Estero, Fla.: Koreshan Unity Press, 1944–46.

Nicholson, George, ed. *The Illustrated Dictionary of Gardening, a Practical and Scientific Encyclopaedia of Horticulture for Gardeners and Botanists.* 8 vols. London: L. U. Gill; New York: J. Penman, 1887–89.

Nicolson, Dan H., with Robert A. DeFilipps, Alice C. Nicolson, and others. *Flora of Dominica. Part 2, Dicotyledoneae.* Smithsonian Contributions to Botany, no. 77. Washington, D.C.: Smithsonian Institution Press, 1991.

Small, John Kunkel. *Manual of the Southeastern Flora: Being Descriptions of the Seed Plants Growing Naturally in Florida, Alabama, Mississippi, Eastern Louisiana, Tennessee, North Carolina, South Carolina, and Georgia.* Chapel Hill: University of North Carolina Press, 1933.

Smith, L. B., and R. J. Downs. *Flora Neotropica.* Monograph no. 14, pt. 2 (Tillandsioideae). New York: Hafner Press, 1977.

Wunderlin, Richard P. *Guide to the Vascular Plants of Central Florida.* 3rd printing. Tampa: University Presses of Florida, 1992.

Index

Names preceding (=) are used by Nehrling; modern equivalents follow.